Friends on Listening Spirituality, Volume I

As a writer, Patricia Loring h[...] complex subject and making [...], and inviting. Listening Spirituality [Vol. I] *is ... a rich and wonderful resource for individual Friends, for spiritual support or study groups, for meetings, and for the Society of Friends in general.*

> William J. Kreidler, Beacon Hill Meeting,
> New England Yearly Meeting

• Patricia Loring makes something happen between her and the reader; it is more than just words on the paper;

• sometimes the way Pat uses words is wonderously provocative; they set you to thinking deeply, to going deeper and deeper inside yourself;

• you can't just read this book and talk about it, you need to do it—to pray, journal, practice the exercises she suggests; you need to take time each day; it is a workbook in spiritual practice;

• the book is so poetic; Pat Loring is a mystic who makes it more accessible to us than do some better-known writers.

> Comments from Cleveland Friends Meeting
> Monday night study group,
> Lake Erie Yearly Meeting

Listening Spirituality [Vol. I] ... *a wonderful resource for the Baltimore Yearly Meeting Spiritual Formation Program. At last we have a book that speaks directly to many of the program participants.*

> Betsy Meyer, Clerk of Committee for the
> Nurture and Recognition of Ministry,
> Baltimore Yearly Meeting

... the book is worth using for anyone knowing a hungering for God.

> Patty Levering, Davidson (NC) Worship Group,
> North Carolina YM (FUM)
> and Piedmont Friends Fellowship

Listening Spirituality

Volume II

Corporate Spiritual Practice Among Friends

Patricia Loring

Openings Press
P.O. Box 547, Washington Grove, Maryland 20880

For permission to copy, please contact Bethesda Friends Meeting,
P.O. Box 30152, Bethesda, Maryland 20824, phone 301/986-8681
for Patricia Loring's current address.

Loring, Patricia.
Listening Spirituality:
Volume II, Corporate Spiritual Practice Among Friends

ISBN 0-9657599-1-1
The Religious Society of Friends: Appropriate Corporate Structures; Community; Corporate Discernment; Corporate Practice; Corporate Business Meetings; Fellowship; Mutual Service; Spiritual Formation; Study; Worship.

Book design and illustration by design: Robert W. Schmitt
855 Ford Center, 420 North Street, Minneapolis, Minnesota 55401-1348
612/333-1881

Printed in the United States of America

This book may be ordered from:

Friends General Conference Bookstore (Philadelphia, PA)
phone: 800/966-4556
e-mail: bookstore@fgc.quaker.org
fax: 215/561-0759

Pendle Hill Bookstore (Wallingford, PA)
phone: 800/742-3150, request bookstore extension
fax: 610/566-3679

The Quaker Book Shop (London, England)
phone: 0171-387-3601
fax: 0171-388-1977

AFSC Book Store (Pasadena, CA)
phone: 818/791-1978
e-mail: afscpasa@igc.apc.org (bookstore)
fax: 818/791-2205

or directly from Openings Press
PO Box 547, Washington Grove, MD 20880

I am the vine;
>   you are the branches.
Those who live in me and I in them
>   will bear abundant fruit,
>   for apart from me you can do nothing.

John 15:5
the inclusive new testament

Stay close to the root.

Old Quaker Advice

All Friends everywhere, meet together and in the Measure of God's Spirit wait. That with it all your minds may be guided up to God, to receive Wisdom from God, that you may come to know how you may walk up to him in his wisdom, that it may be justified of you ... and be glorified. And Friends, meet together and know one another in that which is Eternal, which was before the world was. ...

... with the Light, in which is Unity ... in the Light wait and walk, that you may have fellowship one with another. ... Dwelling in Love, you dwell in God and from the Life the eternal Love does flow, which Life comes from the Father of Life, whose Love does not change. And so with the Light. ... you will come to witness the Faith unfeigned and the Faith which works by Love [and] purifies the heart. ...

George Fox, Epistle #149
The Power of the Lord Is Over All
T. Canby Jones, ed.

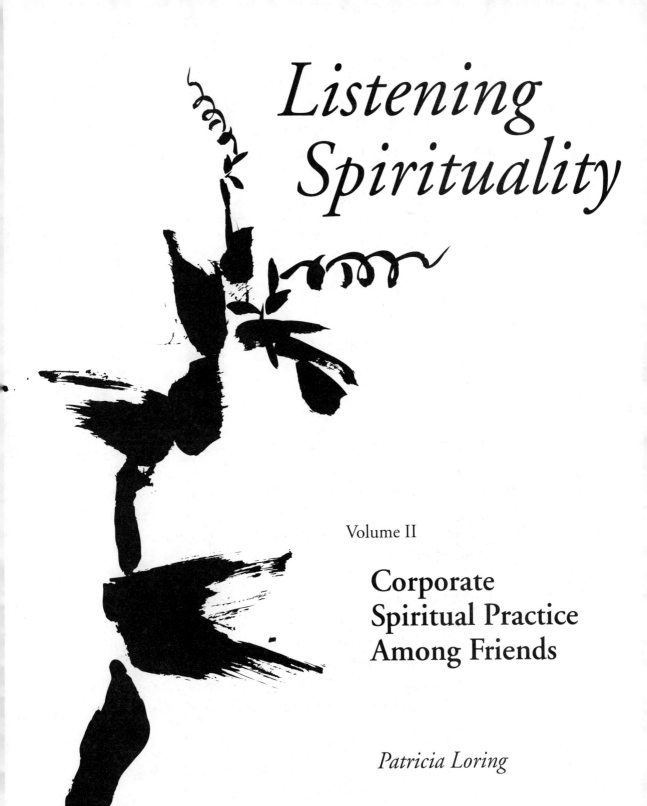

Listening Spirituality

Volume II

Corporate Spiritual Practice Among Friends

Patricia Loring

This book is dedicated to the members and attenders of the diverse meetings in which I have sojourned and held membership over the years since I came to Friends, who have taught me by experience, example and vision wherein Quaker practice and spirituality consist; and to the wonderfully gifted teachers and spiritual guides who were on staff in the years I was at Pendle Hill.

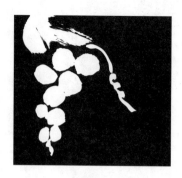

Table of Contents

Celebrations

As in Volume I of this book, I want this volume to have pages of *Celebrations*, rather than acknowledgments. That means a certain amount of repetition of some celebrations from Volume I; but the celebration is an ongoing fiesta of things God has drawn forth from us in response to the gifts and leadings each has been given. I'm celebrating the unique, God-given creativities of many people; and I'm celebrating the generous gifts they have made of their abilities, time and energy to one dimension or another of my leading to produce this book. I'm truly grateful so many people thought it worthwhile, and sometimes even exciting, to give themselves to the project. Especially I celebrate that some have felt for the first time how their particular giftedness could be put to service of the spiritual life.

This book is also a celebration of our traditional Quaker knowledge that we are all one in the loving Spirit of God, with unique parts to play as we work together, not only in particular projects but in continuing co-creation with God's work in the world—whether to bring us together with the Divine, with one another, or with the creation, which all turn out to be facets of the same reconciliation.

It's daunting even to begin a list of the people who have contributed their unique gifts to this book, because my memory is so poor and I'm certain to leave out precious souls whose work was more hidden than that of others. Using the expression of John Woolman, I celebrate all the unnamed who contributed—as "those who have labored out of sight for our good."

I celebrate the gifted and generous teachers who were on staff at Pendle Hill, the Quaker Center for Study and Contemplation, in Wallingford, Pennsylvania when I was in residence. Sandra Cronk, Parker Palmer, Bill Taber and Sally Palmer especially have been variously teachers, spiritual guides, mentors, friends and colleagues over the years. Sandra Cronk and Parker Palmer guided me into understanding different dimensions of the communal aspect of Quaker life. Bill Taber and Sally Palmer, in their very different ways, guided me into fuller sensitivity to inward motions and attentiveness to guidance that comes outwardly.

I celebrate the members of Bethesda (MD) Friends Meeting who have released me annually since 1991 for "A Ministry in Nurture of the Spiritual Life", to follow my leading into the adult religious education and retreat work that laid the foundation for this book as a still wider outreach; who, for nine years, have supported me in what feels like the work for which I was made, to which God has led me; who have given me a rare opportunity to gather up the gifts and experiences of a lifetime and offer them to God and my community in the Religious Society of Friends; who have now gone through a painfully searching process that has led them to reduce their support for my work, ending it in late 1998. I trust that if writing the third volume is truly led of God, Way will open to support both the writing and the publication.

In the meantime, I'm listening to the drawings in my own body and mind to spend at least part of the year in an as-yet-undetermined part of the dry West, where my body seems to function better and I find new Life, if not livelihood. I'm also listening to the tender bonds of F/friendships formed up and down the East Coast for the past twenty-five years. I ask God whether I'm really being told, like Abram, to get up and leave my home and my people and go into a new place that I'll be shown. I try not to laugh, like Sara, that I'm too old for a new life. I wait on Way to open or close, to shift course or hold steady.

I celebrate the Religious Education Committee of FGC, which minuted its support for the undertaking early on, waited patiently through my time of illness, then—together with FGC's Publication and Distribution Committee—gave considerable practical advice and support for the publication and marketing of Volume I, and now for Volume II.

... Marty Grundy of Cleveland (OH) Meeting, who continues to be a tireless, cheerful and encouraging liaison between me and not only FGC, but Friends in many parts of the country. As we've come to the final phase of this book, she's invited me into her home for a rich collaboration on the final editing and proofing of this volume. I celebrate the hospitality, patience and generosity of Marty and her husband, Ken.

... Baltimore Yearly Meeting's Committee for Nurture and Recognition of Ministry, which first invited me to give retreats in its "Spiritual Formation Program"; which not only minuted its support of my work but participated in the Committee for Oversight and Support in the early years; especially Paris Kern of Baltimore, Stony Run Meeting, who, after the committee minuted its support for my teaching ministry, said, "Let's not just hang her out to dry. Let's see that she has real Oversight and Support." Members of the Oversight and Support Committee from BaYM's Committee for the Nurture and Recognition of Ministry, in its early years, included Ellen Cronin, Virginia Schurman, Kathy Orchen and Marshall Sutton.

I celebrate the shifting, but faithful and loving, endlessly supportive and hard-working Bethesda membership of the Committee for Oversight and Support of Pat Loring's Leading, co-clerked for years by Esther Delaplaine and by Criss O'Neill, who regarded it as her leading to see that my leading was supported. The first member of the committee to volunteer from Bethesda was Jane Nutter of Overseers, then Edith Couturier of Worship and Ministry, and Susan Kanaan of Advancement and Outreach. Over the years, the committee has also included Peter Nielsen-Jones, Edward Hawkins, David Zarembka, Joann Hunt, Ellen Pletsch, Katrina Mason, Stephanie Koenig and Aline Autenreith.

... My clearness committee: Frank Massey and Trudy Rogers of Sandy Spring (MD) Meeting, and Benj Thomas and Katrina Mason of Bethesda (MD) Friends Meeting: eight sensitive ears and four discerning hearts.

Most especially I celebrate the eagle eyes and meticulous work of the editorial readers: Sandra Cronk, of Middletown (PA) Meeting, sojourning at Stoney Creek Meeting in Princeton, NJ and of the School of the Spirit; ... Marty Grundy, of Cleveland (OH) Meeting and FGC's Religious Education Committee; ... Jeff Fishel and Susan Kanaan, both of Bethesda (MD) Friends Meeting—both with considerable editorial experience. Susan also set the course for the design and printing of Volume I so that her precedents could be followed by the Working Group for Volume II.

... Kathy Soltis of Cleveland (OH) Friends Meeting who volunteered her professional skills to guide me through the final edit for this volume. Unfortunately our schedules meshed for only part of the process.

... Trudy Rogers and Marty Grundy for contributing excellent bibliographies on the conduct of business. ... Amy Nabut of the Pendle Hill Book Store, Judy Van Hoy of Philadelphia Yearly Meeting's Library, and Carole Treadway of Guilford College's Quaker Collection, who helped with the last, few recalcitrant entries in the bibliography.

Thanks to Anthony Stern of Hasting-on-Hudson, New York, for identifying the source of the Hasidic story freely used in my own, more elaborate version in Volume I. It comes from Martin Buber, *Tales of the Hasidim: The Early Masters* (NY: Schocken, 1947), p. 65.

I celebrate the members of the Working Group, all from Bethesda Friends Meeting: Evamaria Hawkins, for coordinating the business management and marketing, without easy precedents to follow; ... Bob Nutter, for undertaking the accounting; ... Katrina Mason who has written grant proposals, liased with Baltimore Yearly Meeting and worn many hats; ... Catherine McHugh, for contributing business advice and for storing what amounts to a pick-up truck full of books—as well as my belongings—in her lovely home; ... the "Moving Group" of Bethesda Friends who packed up my belongings and moved them into Catherine's home one hot day in June; ... Aline Autenreith, who—in addition to organizing the Moving Group—with exuberance created a variety of flyers and handbills to announce the book to Quaker meetings and gatherings; ... David Zarembka has filled the orders of the book stores listed on the first page of this volume with dispatch and efficiency. He receives individual orders or peddles books on appropriate occasions.

... Janice Domanik, the present clerk of Friends General Conference; Tilden Edwards, the Executive Director of the Shalem Institute for Spiritual Formation; and Carole Treadway of Guilford College Library's Quaker Collection, all of whom read the manuscript in order to write comments for the cover, for your guidance as to this volume's contents.

... Bob Schmitt of Twin Cities (MN) Friends and of "design: Robert W. Schmitt", who went beyond the work of a graphic designer in seeking a form that would gather up all the diverse materials to visibly express and enhance the spiritual meaning and invitation of the book—then contributed his *sumi-e* art work as a gift.

I didn't always take the excellent advice of all these generous people. But they invariably brought me to consider my experience and understanding more deeply, and to seek greater verbal and organizational clarity.

I celebrate my beloved uncle, John Pike Grady, who assisted my attendance at both Pendle Hill and the Shalem Institute for Spiritual Formation, as well as a number of other edifying places;

... the Lyman Fund, which also assisted my participation in programs of the Shalem Institute for Spiritual Formation.

... the Ethel Reynolds Fund of Baltimore Yearly Meeting, which granted funds for book and cover design;

... the Bogert Fund for contributing funds to the preparation of the camera-ready copy for Volume I;

... Cleveland Friends Meeting that lent funds to cover printing;

... Philadelphia Yearly Meeting's Bequests Fund for contributing funds for publication.

I celebrate Janet Boys and Don McGuire, now of Chestnut Hill Meeting in Philadelphia, who generously supplied up-to-the-minute computer hardware and software for the project.

... Benj Thomas of Bethesda (MD) Friends, who spent countless hours getting everything running—and teaching and re-teaching me to use the word processor, with the occasional assistance of Jubran and Usama Kanaan.

Finally, I celebrate the refuge I've been given from the storms of the Potomac Basin in the dry climates of the West while working on Volume II:

... First, by my Shalem friend, Sally Adlesh, who put me up in her new home in Clovis, California, for three months while I recuperated from the stresses of the past year and resumed work on this volume—and Fresno (CA) Friends who welcomed me there.

... Then, as the monsoon season subsided in the Southwest, by Sister Therese of Our Lady of Solitude Contemplative House of Prayer in Black Canyon City, Arizona, who gave me blessed solitude and silence, for three and a half months, to write and retreat in a hermitage named "Adsum" ("Here I am, Lord") on a desert mesa overlooking canyons, buttes, mesas, peaks, numerous cacti and infinitely varied sunrises and sunsets—and Phoenix (AZ) Friends who became a community for me during that time.

The editorial work was partly done on the road, seeking a new home. Some was completed in the apartment of my gentle and generous son, Rob Basine, in Reno, Nevada, where Reno Friends made me feel at home in the light and airy, new meeting house that they renovated with their own hands, to their own plans.

Other editing was completed at Quaker Center in Ben Lomond, California, with the gentle distance of joint directors, Traci and Walter Sullivan and the powerful presence of the Center's mountain redwood forest. Some waited on my return to Catherine McHugh's home in Maryland and on my subsequent stay with the Grundys in Cleveland Heights, Ohio. Then the work was handed over to the designer Bob Schmitt of Twin Cities (MN) Friends, to Marty Grundy for final proof reading, to Whitehall Printers in Tallahassee, Florida, and from there to the Bethesda Working Group.

Above all, I celebrate the gift of God in filling my life with so many wonderful F/friends who have mediated Divine Love, encouragement and generous support for this leading and for me in my needs. God's grace and love be with all of them and with you in your search.

Patricia Loring
Our Lady of Solitude
Black Canyon City, Arizona
First Month, 1998

Key to Abbreviations

[BaYM]	na. Baltimore Yearly Meeting. *Faith & Practice*. Religious Society of Friends.
[BrYM]	na. *Quaker faith and practice: The Book of Christian discipline of the Yearly Meeting of the Religious Society of Friends (Quakers) in Britain*. London: QHS, 1995, no pagination, excerpts are numbered and noted here by #.
[CD]	na. *Friends Consultation on Discernment*. Richmond, IN: Quaker Hill, 1985.
[CE]	na. *Friends Consultation on Eldering*. Richmond, IN: Quaker Hill, 1982.
[CG]	na. *Church Government*. London: London Yearly Meeting, [©1968], no pagination; excerpts are numbered and noted here by #. (Recently London Yearly Meeting changed its name to Britain Yearly Meeting.)
[CTQA]	na. *Friends Consultation on Testimonies, Queries and Advices*. Richmond, IN: Quaker Hill, 1988.
[DF]	Dean Freiday. *Barclay's Apology in Modern English*. [np], [©1967].
[DR]	Linda Hill Renfer, ed. *Daily Readings from Quaker Writings Both Ancient and Modern*. Oregon: Serenity Press, [©1988].
[FHSC]	Friends Home Service Committee of London/Britain Yearly Meeting.
[FJ]	*Friends Journal*, a monthly publication in the Friends General Conference tradition.
[FUM]	Friends United Meeting.
[FUP]	Friends United Press, publisher for FUM.
[FWCC]	Friends World Committee for Consultation, a catalyst for consultation and spiritual nurture for Friends around the world; sometime publisher of lectures, papers, etc.
[LYM]	na. *Christian faith and practice in the experience of the Society of Friends*. London: London Yearly Meeting, [©1960], no pagination; excerpts are numbered and noted here by #.
[int]	*the inclusive new testament*. Brentwood, MD: Priests for Equality, [©1994].
[KJV]	*King James Version* (of the Bible).
[NJB]	na. *New Jerusalem Bible*. Garden City, NJ: Doubleday, [©1985].
[NT]	*New Testament*.
[OT]	*Old Testament*.
[PH]	Pendle Hill. Publishers of Pendle Hill Pamphlets (numbered) and Quaker books.
[PHP]	Pendle Hill Pamphlet, numbered and noted herre by #.
[PYM]	Philadelphia Yearly Meeting; sometimes publishes for its constituency.
[QHS]	Quaker Home Services. A Publisher for LYM, now BrYM.
[QL]	*Quaker Life*, a monthly periodical of FUM.
[QR]	Jessamyn West, ed. *The Quaker Reader*. [©1962], reprinted, Wallingford, PA: PH, [1992].
[QRT]	*Quaker Religious Thought*, sponsored by the Quaker Theologicial Discussion Group.
[QS]	Chuck Fager, ed. & introduction. *Quaker Service at the Crossroads*. Kimo Press, [©1988].
[QW]	Frances B. Hall, ed. *Quaker Worship in North America*. FUP, nd.
[Tract Ass'n]	Philadelphia, PA: the Tract Association of Friends.

A Note on Notes and References

References are cited in the text by author's last name.
Titles and specific chapters or page numbers are included in the brief bibliographies at the ends of chapters
and sections. Complete publication data is included in
the Bibliography at the end of the volume. For abbreviations see the previous page. Titles without specific
citations are general resources on the topic of the section
they follow.

Introduction

Adapted from Volume I and extended to include the contents of this book

This volume, located within the context of Quaker spirituality, formation and transformation, is part of a longer work on Quaker spiritual formation. The first volume is addressed to personal spiritual practices compatible with inward Quaker listening for the presence and guidance of God, and to the Quaker sense of a lifelong transformation by the Spirit of God.

This second volume examines the ways in which our communal practice in meeting and other gatherings is a spiritually formative influence on us, both as individuals and as a corporate body. Our communal practice is also an expression of the transformed life we seek to lead together. The third volume, on Quaker ethics, will look at both the root of our ethic in spiritual experience and transformation and, reciprocally, the way the ethic forms us and opens us to spiritual transformation.

Although each of the three parts is being published separately as it is completed, an important part of the underlying vision is that personal practice, corporate practice and ethics are inseparable within Quaker formation and transformation. Neither the inner life, nor meeting life, nor an active relationship with the rest of the world is optional. Prayer that does not issue in a transformed life and deeds of love becomes a form of narcissism or an aesthetic exercise. Worship that does not open us to being gathered into unity and mutuality with others is a hollow exercise. It leaves us separate from the flow of Love, Life and Power in the world, rather than drawing us to participate with others in the mutual mediation of that flow of Love. Activity that does not take time to find its source and grounding in prayer, worship or divine leading becomes dry, exhausting, and exasperating—or an exercise in power.

Origins of the book in teaching and retreat ministry

This book has grown out of nine years of teaching and leading retreats and workshops under the oversight of Bethesda (MD) Friends Meeting. The basic curriculum as a whole was intended as a spiritual formation program for Friends. The constant interplay between the personal, corporate and ethical dimensions of our spiritual lives means that the placement of several chapters is somewhat arbitrary. Some aspects of our personal practice rest in part on corporate practice. Corporate practice rests on the personal. The ethical is grounded in both. Don't be deceived by the necessary structuring of the book into thinking that it reflects a tidy structure of spiritual reality. The pattern and the movement between its parts is much more fluid than the divisions of this book might lead you to believe.

Listening and gathering as they pattern Quaker spirituality

"Listening" is one of two major themes throughout all three volumes of this book. By listening I mean the widest prayerful, discerning attentiveness to the Source intimated within us, evidenced through others, and discernible through the experiences of life. This kind of listening is not only auditory. It may be visual, kinesthetic, intuitive or visceral as well, depending on the deepest attentiveness natural to the particular person. My thesis is that this kind of prayerful attentiveness is one of two major elements patterning Quakerism into what Lloyd Lee Wilson has called a "gestalt".

The word, taken from the German, means an organic whole that is somehow greater than the sum of its parts. As I use the term, I am not referring to the specific behaviors and institutions that compose the gestalt, but rather to their shared, underlying patterning by listening and gathering.

Gathering—or the felt union of the spiritual community in the Love, Life and Power of God—is the second element patterning the Quaker gestalt. It is experienced in "graced" or "favored" times of corporate worship. Gathering is second only in the sense that it is more apt to be a spiritual fruit, or a gift of spiritual maturation in listening. It is what we hear, recognize or experience when we listen at the most profound level. Both the longing for, and the actual experience of, being gathered and united in God's Love have shaped our sense of right relationship within the spiritual community of our meetings. Where the sense of being gathered and united in God's Love includes the rest of humanity and the whole of the creation, it has formed our sense of right ethical relationships in the wider world.

I think that Quaker practice is not only a spiritual gestalt of unique wholeness and coherence. It also has a hologramic aspect, in that listening and gathering are present in all its parts. When we are faithful, they form and inform all the dimensions of our personal and corporate practice. The patterning element of listening makes us attentive and responsive to manifestations of the Mystery that lies at the heart of the universe and of each of us, the Mystery that gathers us in the Love and Life that is a manifestation of its nature or being. The element of gathering both shapes and expresses our unity in the Love we experience when we listen, in our personal lives, in our corporate life and in ethical relationships with the world. It helps us transcend forms, and it helps us be self-transcendent in our sense of reality, and in our understanding of our place and work in it.

I believe we've never come close to realizing the possibilities inherent in the unique Quaker gestalt bequeathed by generations of faithful Friends.

Being formed and transformed within the Quaker gestalt

The term "formation", or "spiritual formation", as I use it, refers to this patterning of our practices and our lives: both our interior life and the outward life we share with other people. We are formed, shaped or patterned in the Quaker gestalt of practices that enhance and encourage prayerful listening for the divine—and in practices that express outwardly our union in divine love.

"Transformation" or "spiritual maturing", as I've used both terms, refer to the work of God within us when we open ourselves in this listening mode and are mysteriously, profoundly changed in ways we might not be capable of by ourselves. Older writings referred to this life-long process of interior change as "perfection". We are more comfortable with less traditional words, like "transformation" or "spiritual maturing", that emphasize the ongoing process rather than falsely implying, to the modern mind, the endpoint. In Quaker journals that speak of "how the Lord has dealt with" various individuals, preparing them for and leading them into activity in the world, we find numerous anecdotes of ongoing revelations, continuing changes of heart and lifestyle, and deepening understandings, right up to the final chapters of people's lives.

Our outward formation is for the sake of opening ourselves to the inward transformation of our hearts and minds. The inward transformation, in turn, is for the sake of the outward transformation of our lives in a service of Love and Truth that arises from the center of our being, from a transformed nature, rather than from duties or rules or legalisms.

A personal vision of Quakerism

Although I haven't attempted a scholarly study, I've tried to show as I go the points of connection I've found between my inward experience of Quaker practice and experiences expressed by Quakers who have come before me. I've also tried, in turn, to show earlier Quakers' discoveries of connections between their experience and expressions in the Bible—and, occasionally, the experience of other writers on spiritual matters. Regardless of the immediate sources, these practices are consonant with my own deepest sense of the underlying experiences and meanings embedded in Quaker practice and history, in relation to our present circumstances.

Because Quakerism is, probably, the most practical of the interpretations of the Christian message, gospel, evangel or good news, this book is meant to be primarily a practical book. It is the very practicality of Quakerism that makes me refer to "spirituality" rather than "theology". The word "spirituality" is often used quite vaguely. I use it here to refer to the shape and practice of our lived experience toward and with God.

Sometimes I've included my own connections with writers in other traditions. Where I've done so, it's been with a sense that a number of other Quakers also are discovering these connections at this point in our history. There is a sense in which the entire Christian tradition, and Quakerism within it, has always borrowed vocabulary, expressions and understandings from other religious traditions and philosophies to point to the ultimately inexpressible experiences of the heart. This is how the Gospel has been preached anew, how the astonishing news of the relationship between the Divine and humanity has been told to each generation in terms that it can understand, terms taken from prevailing systems of thought.

The effort becomes syncretistic only if the new terms, or the new preaching chosen, substantially alter the message about Spiritual Reality in ways that contradict or subvert what has gone before. That's happened often in the history of Christianity. A notable example is Constantine's adoption of the Sign of the Cross as an emblem of "God with us" in armed combat and military conquest, rather than as the sign of "God with us" in humility and in the midst of human suffering. Many popular modern preachers have updated their portrayals of Jesus in terms of contemporary cultural values of "winning" or "being a success"—turning Jesus' prophetic subversion of worldly values inside out.

Such substantial alterations of the Quaker or Biblical message over time are another reason for us to formulate the underlying pattern or gestalt of our practice, against which to test new or different expressions of our faith. We must first know the profound intention of the old, before we can test the new. There is, however, no point in insisting on a single old way of expressing our faith, if the terms no longer open up or evoke the same meanings they did for people in the Hellenistic, Medieval or Reformation periods. To insist on a single formulation opens it to the risk of idolatry: giving the formulation the veneration owed to the unknowable God alone (McFague).

The contents of Volume II, chapters 1-8

Many people, when they are newly aware of their spiritual lives, think of it as an utterly personal relationship with God, in which the primary areas are prayer and ministry or service. In an individualistic culture such as ours, it's easy to become focused on our personal relationship with God and our personal service. It's quite easy to lapse into thinking of oneself as God's only child.

If many of the practices in the first volume are not conducted in a rhythm that includes community as well as solitude, they might foster such a private, individualistic sense of self and of relationship with God. On the other hand, the corporate spiritual life can languish, become secularized and be reduced to empty forms when insufficient attention is given to personal spiritual life. Lloyd Lee Wilson reminds us that the quality of our silent worship together is dependent, in part, on the quality of the personal silences each individual present has cultivated and experienced during the week (Wilson).

Quakerism has placed as great an emphasis on corporate discipline as on personal spiritual experience. Quaker structures have been grounded in and shaped by what is experienced in favored times of corporate worship: mystical unity with one another in the Love of God; being drawn together around the burning bush; the melting of boundaries of ego; being gathered together in the Fisherman's net. Corporate practices that foster the experience of unity, and that refer and defer to it in the life together, have traditionally received greater emphasis than those that foster personal spiritual life.

This volume is devoted to major ways in which Friends have sought to enter as a body into the presence, guidance and service of God. It is also devoted to our unity, communion and community, which are grounded in that entering. The experience of listening, and of being gathered together in that which we hear, has shaped and ordered our nonhierarchical organizational forms, with the intention of giving the leadership of the corporate body to God—or, in certain limited instances, to those discerned to be authentically led by God.

There are significant differences between the practices explored in the previous volume and the practices described in this one. First, corporate or communal practices have been shaped to foster our listening for God together. But corporate practice also embodies, expresses and supports *what has been heard by earlier Friends* about the spiritual life together.

Second, it is not possible to suggest particular undertakings that correspond to the personal practices of the previous section so that you might discern those to which you are led. Instead, I present a vision of some of the spirituality underlying our corporate life. From that, you might discern how you are called to give yourself more fully to the corporate spiritual life and work, or which areas of relationship or behavior might be calling for more intentional opening on your part.

On one level, the practices in this volume are simply those of participation in the corporate life. Part of the discipline is to participate with people who might not have been on our personal list for our beloved community. We trust that God has brought together this disparate group of people for our own good and growth, as well as for that of others. It is important that we live in community and are spiritually formed by relationships with people whose contribution to our spiritual growth may be through pain or irritation, as well as with those who nurture us through enduring warmth. We do this in the confidence that we have been mysteriously drawn together in community with these people at this time, by God, for God's own work and purposes within each of us and among or through us all.

On another level, the discipline is to remember, to nurture, and to keep close to our deepest spiritual intentions for our life together—both as an organized body and as an intimate community of Friends of God, Friends of Truth, friends of one another. Participation in the corporate life, with spiritual commitment, is formative in itself.

Community is one of those spiritual realities which are both "already" eternally present and "not yet" fulfilled or perfect. On one level of our being, we live always united in and by God's Love. On another level of our being, we work and stretch all our lives toward the fullness and fulfillment of community, both personally and corporately. In the "already" of the spiritual life, communal practice embodies, and is expressive of, the mystery of our oneness in God. In the "not yet" of the spiritual life, corporate practice is supportive of our communal listening for God—both for guidance and for our oneness. At the same time, communal practice is also supportive of our struggles to live out that oneness and guidance in the company of others, as part of our ongoing, not-yet-perfect process of transformation. This intimate connection between our interior life and our communal practice is the root of our unique Quaker ethos and ethics.

Corporate practice and personal practice support one another, support us on our way to and with God. They are not sequential. Although these two volumes are designed to stand alone, the practices they speak of are mutually dependent on one another.

Volume II begins with the experience of being gathered together in and by God's Love. It spirals into the ways we live out the felt sense of oneness in personal relationships. The spiral swings through the expression of that gathering, union or oneness in behaviors of mutual love and in nonhierarchical forms of service to the community and the world. It moves through questions of the nature of appropriate structures by which to express our unity. Our corporate forms, in turn, further support seeking, finding and living out the oneness. The spiral continues with the ways in which we reinforce our fellowship in the kind of countercultural life required and shaped by our devotion to God. In the final chapters, the exploration moves into the realm of study that will support personal spiritual development through listening for the relationships between our personal spiritual experience and Quaker tradition.

Chapter 1 treats the qualitative difference that comes when we enter intentionally into worship together. We are no longer just seeking support for our personal spiritual lives. We have entered, become part of, helped to create a "we": a spiritual community in which we listen for the Spirit among us corporately as well as within us individually. To the degree that this intention is present and is realized, with grace, we may experience being gathered into unity with one another as well as with God.

Chapter 2 explores further how our personal conduct and attitudes affect our corporate life. It looks at the ways in which we are woven and weave ourselves together in mutual care and service. It touches on what it means to be under the care of the meeting. The fact that we need common intentionality, expectations and commitment if we are to carry on these activities together underlies a discussion of commitment, membership and pastoral care. Most especially, this chapter encourages us to move past the vision of sweetness and light in community into the ways God forms us and offers us self-transcendence in the midst of human difference, struggle and pain.

Chapter 3 goes to the heart of Listening Spirituality, that is, cultivating over a lifetime the fallible gift of discerning what is and is not of God. It also describes some of the meeting structures that support discernment in various dimensions of community life.

Chapter 4 focuses on both personal and corporate discernment. It focuses on distinguishing authentic spiritual concerns and leadings into service from principled action, from those that come from good ideas or from a mistaken sense of leading. This chapter speaks at length of some traditional kinds of gifts and service to the meeting community, such as vocal ministry, eldering and pastoral care.

Chapter 5 treats the effects that corporate, rather than private, listening has on the conduct of the business of our life together. It examines how listening affects our personal attitudes and conduct as we struggle to discern God's guidance for us through our inevitable differences of opinion in spiritual community. It examines how listening shapes the peculiar forms that support our communal life together, where spiritual authority in the meeting comes from, and how the experience of gathering and unity affects corporate decision making.

Chapter 6 turns to the problem of discerning and supporting appropriate structures for our corporate life of discernment of God's guidance. This issue is of particular importance in contemporary Quakerism. Often we are drawn into organizational structures assimilated to secular models in this era of corporate giantism, concentrations of power and emphasis on efficiency and efficacy. It takes discerning care to feel which structures are consonant with our gestalt and which ones undercut or destroy it.

Chapter 7 names some traditional ways that Friends have supported one another in their countercultural testimonies and lives together. It goes on to consider how we continue outwardly to uphold our community and testimonies, by fellowship and other means, as we continue to be called into a life counter to the culture in which we are embedded. George Fox has enjoined us to "meet together and know one another in that which is eternal." The rest of this volume is devoted to the intersection of the Eternal and our life together. This chapter talks of the simple, human ways in which Friends meet together to reinforce our communal bonds and strengthen ourselves for a life dependent on God rather than on the surrounding culture.

Chapter 8 speaks of ways to support the holy expectancy of a gathered meeting and the commitment to discernment as a way of personal and corporate life. Such support is needed in the process of educating and clearing people for membership. We need group settings for people to explore the tradition and to be supported in their inner search. Without such provisions, we are much more likely to fall into wrangles as people struggle over good projects rather than discern the authenticity of leadings, or to fall into the uses of hierarchical or coercive power rather than of mutual love.

This chapter describes and comments on adult religious education and spiritual formation programs developed and in use in Baltimore and Philadelphia Yearly Meetings, sometimes imported *in toto* or in part to other yearly meetings. It also offers some ways that have been devised to bring components of such programs into individual meetings, without an elaborate yearly meeting program, in places where that is not feasible. Implicitly, the emphases and uses of these *Listening Spirituality* volumes are part of the discussion.

Resources and References

Full publication information is in the Bibliography at the end of this book. For abbreviations, see p. xix.

Georgia Fuller.
"Johannine Lessons in
Community",
in Fager, ed. *The Bible, the
Church and the Future of Friends.*

Douglas Gwyn.
"John 15 and its
Community".
QRT, spring 1980.

T. Canby Jones, ed.
*The Power of the Lord Is
Over All: The Pastoral
Letters of George Fox.*
epistle #149, pp: 114-115.
Also quoted in BrYm, #2.35
and LYM, #237. Used here as
an epigraph for Volume II.

Sally McFague.
*Metaphorical Theology:
Models of God in Religious
Language.*

Lloyd Lee Wilson.
*Essays on the Quaker
Vision of Gospel Order.*
pp. 16, 36.

Chapter 1

Listening for–and Hearing–the Spirit among Us in the Meeting for Worship

Corporate listening as worship

Corporate worship is the foundational experience of our communal life. Our personal prayer life is as diverse as the listening, hearing and speaking that occur in conversation between two people and as varied from occasion to occasion. Consider, then, the multiplicity of possibilities in worship when even a few people come together. Much depends on having a common understanding of what we are there for, while we try to remain open to the surprises of the Spirit. Common understanding is complicated by the fact that we are a mixed gathering, people with disparate backgrounds and at many different places in our inward journeys. Still, Friends do not assume that everything that takes place in that silent time together is worship.

Some people who join us view the silence from the standpoint of what is *not* there: the absence of some objectionable element that forced them from another congregation. In the absence of liturgy, creed, preaching or instruction, many people come to their own understandings of the meeting for worship. These are often molded by their experiences in other settings that may look similar but, in fact, are grounded in totally different intentions or assumptions.

Some people see the meeting as a forum for an exchange of views. Others see its similarity to therapeutic or support groups in which they've felt encouraged to confide their personal lives or distresses. For others, it looks like a group of like-minded people who may be spurred to examine or share a political concern, or to get behind some good cause. Still others see it as a kind of undisciplined Zen meditation hall in which to practice personal meditation.

Each of these possibilities lifts up some dimension of the truth of the way we are together. But none of them touches the heart of worship as it has been experienced in the Quaker tradition. It's hard, then, to know how to convey what Friends, for three hundred and fifty years, have felt is present in the silence. How can we gather together these disparate notions and take them to the depths in authentic worship? This chapter explores the similarities and differences between Quaker worship, on the one hand, and other activities and forms of worship that resemble Quaker worship.

Origins in the English Reformation

The earliest generation of Friends was one of the last and most radical groups that emerged in the English Reformation. From one point of view, the Reformation was a progressive stripping away of certain outward aspects of worship and church government that had developed in the history of the Christian Church over 1500 years. Ordinary people, with access to vernacular Bibles for the first time, searched for a "true worship" which would most nearly resemble what they found for themselves in Biblical accounts of the primitive church. In those accounts, the most radical Puritans found a naked dependence on the Spirit of God which they sought to emulate.

In many ways, the Civil War and Commonwealth eras of the English Reformation resemble our own time. Old religious, social and political forms and hierarchical lines of authority were found unworkable and unsatisfying. They either disintegrated or were deliberately destroyed. Several political experiments were tried. At the same time, people moved from experiment to experiment, in search of satisfying worship.

In the North of England and the Midlands, at a relatively safe distance from central authority, the experiments were numerous. People moving from group to group seem to have cross-pollinated many theologies and practices. One group, centered on Preston-Patrick in Westmorland, had tried many forms of worship without finding a sense of authenticity. Eventually they settled on meeting together for communal Bible reading, prayer and waiting on Divine Guidance to bring them into a true form of worship.

George Fox was one of those who moved about England in search of outward spiritual guidance into true worship. His search and his disappointments were particularly intense, even for that religious era. Eventually, his unsuccessful outward investigations culminated in a profound, inward, revelatory experience. He experienced that authoritative guidance into true worship was available, but only inwardly, from Christ, who had "come to teach his people himself." Fox found much in scripture that assisted his articulation and integration of his experience and its implication. He also found support and vocabulary for expressing it in practice.

He relied particularly upon the "prologue" to the Gospel according to John (1:1-14), concerning the Word as the Light within people empowering them to become children of God. He drew also upon that Gospel's "farewell discourse" (13:31-17:26) promising Jesus' followers that the Spirit of Truth, the Holy Spirit, the *Paraclete* (variously translated as "Advocate", "Counselor", "Comforter") would come to teach and nurture them in Jesus' place (John 14:16-17, 25-26; 15:26; 16:7-8). Fox's initial revelatory experience was later supported by a series of "openings" that refined his sense of how a community that worshiped inwardly, in Spirit and Truth, might be ordered.

Like many of his contemporaries, Fox was intimately familiar with the Bible. As he reread scripture in light of his openings, he continued to find further support and articulation there for his understanding of worship and church. As he traveled in the North, Fox's invitation to inward worship was whole-heartedly received by the Preston-Patrick General Meeting and their informal leaders, later called the Westmorland Seekers. Together they and Fox, with other Seeker communities in the Midlands and elsewhere, grew into the Quaker movement and evolved the original Quaker form of worship.

For all its waiting in silence upon guidance from the Light Within, this worship was not as shapeless as it seemed. The Seekers' sense of the potentialities and realities of silent worship was grounded in a deep, experiential, religious search within the Christian tradition, as expressed in the Bible. Most of them were as familiar with the Bible as was Fox—and as eager to recover the "true religion" of the early church.

Most had had experience with other modes of worship. Many of them had been reared in the Anglican liturgical tradition. They had absorbed and been formed by its vocabulary and its outward and inward practices. Most of them had also experienced the Presbyterians' reformation of the national church, had heard of other new religious ideas afloat in their century, had experienced one or more of the religious experiments going on all around them—and had rejected them all as inadequate supports for authentic religious experience. This background came with them into the silent waiting. It inevitably shaped or interpreted their experience there.

Comparison and contrast with modern seekers

We have much in common with the Seekers who became the Quaker movement. Our differences, however, are significant and should at least be named and acknowledged. We, too, live in a time of transition, with a breakdown of confidence in old political, social and religious structures and no clear sense of where our transition is going. A great many of us, too, have gone through painful experimentation with one or more churches, after leaving the one in which we were raised. Rarely, however, has our religious seeking had the intensity experienced by those earliest Friends. In large part, the difference is due to modern social conditions, which delimit and diffuse our searches.

We are more mobile socially and geographically than that first generation. Increasingly, our economic and social circumstances squeeze our religious life into a single day, or a single hour a week. The possibilities for entertainment, engagement and fulfillment are more widely dispersed through different areas of our lives. It is difficult for us to imagine the pervasiveness of religion in daily life in seventeenth-century England, its close relationship to the major political and economic issues of the day, and the intensity of engagement and feeling it inspired.

The upheaval in the seventeenth century gathered up the time, attention, energy, enthusiasm and devoted partisanship that today go into sports, media, popular figures, popular social and psychological issues, politics and a wide variety of other diversions. We tend to bring all these interests into worship, often without a clear sense of what would make them a matter of spiritual concern rather than secular interest. Much of the time, we are pulled this way and that, torn and fragmented by these diverse forces. Most of us need periodically to touch again, intentionally and immediately, the experiences and assumptions that underlie our worship—as distinct from our meditative reflections on the superfluity of our daily experience.

Worship in the wider tradition

In every religious tradition, worship is mainly an offering to God. What is outwardly offered to God, how it is offered and the motivation for the offering vary from tradition to tradition and from person to person. Ultimately, however, what is offered is usually oneself, one's heart, one's life.

Luther, in his Reformation, defined the church by its preaching of scripture and rightly administered sacraments. Among present-day Protestants, some have preserved the sacramental strand of encounter; but Protestant churches in general are better known for their emphasis on the encounter with God primarily or exclusively through the words of the Bible. In that case, listening to the reading of the Bible and to the learned exposition of its meaning in sermons, by people specially given over to study of it, is the chief exercise of the worshipers. This listening does more than express reverence and literal obedience. It is both a symbolic and an actual offering of oneself to be shaped by the spiritual understandings conveyed by the Bible as the Word of God. The attention of the congregation is usually focused on the lectern and pulpit, from which the Word of God is received. Where emphasis on the sacramental strand has been preserved, the focus on "the table" as a place of offering is not unlike the focus on the altar in liturgical traditions.

In those traditions in which objects are offered ritually, they are usually in some way symbolic of the deeper offering of oneself and one's life. In this case, there is liturgy. The formulaic words and ritual actions that constitute liturgy are mostly drawn from parts of the tradition that are felt to express deeply and to evoke various dimensions of the offering. This helps people to focus on, and to offer themselves to, the work and experience of God, as it has been formulated in the tradition.

Many movements of the heart in religious experience are expressed and evoked in ritual liturgy. In the Roman Catholic and Episcopal traditions, the liturgy commonly begins with an invocation of God's mercy, grace, presence—which is implicitly an invitation to the worshiper to enter intentionally into a frame of mind and heart oriented toward God. Following on the invocation is usually a review of what hinders that orientation. The review is expressed as a confession of sins, flaws and failures, both in orientation of life and in following the guidance of God. With this confession can come contrition and a turning again to God, in awareness that God receives us regardless of what we deserve. At this point, the priest asks for and affirms God's forgiveness of the congregation. The congregation responds with a ritual expression of adoration and praise for God.

Other inward motions expressed in liturgy include:

> • ritual prayers of petition and intercession;
> • a consideration of stories that encapsulate or open some aspect of spiritual truth, read from the Bible and developed in a homily;
> • an expression of receiving one another in the forgiveness and peace of community by handshake or kiss;
> • a rededication and consecration of one's self and one's life;
> • an offering of bread and wine: both as a thankful returning of God's gifts which, given to us, sustain us and join us to one another in God; and as a reliving of Jesus' death and resurrection.

When the Presence of God is felt to be most focused or concentrated in the consecrated bread that God has been asked to bless with his Presence, the altar or table where the bread is present or the tabernacle where it is reserved is the focal point for the worshipers' attention.

Worship in the Quaker tradition

Early Friends were among those who rebelled against both the Protestant and the liturgical ways of worship, and who were led to search for yet another way.

Some of the reasons for the rebellion and search were more social and economic than religious. Priests who were the younger sons of landed families were handsomely provided for by compulsory tithes, often from several parishes. Many of them seldom ministered to their flocks, however, instead turning the work over to dependents. Their dependents were often poorly educated and ill-equipped to bring the deeper meanings of the faith into people's lives. The "leveling" tendencies of the period militated against the inequities of a tithe system that was designed to provide for the economic needs of the well-to-do at the expense of the spiritual needs of those less well-off. The spirit of rebellion—which characterized the century in which a king was beheaded and a commonwealth established—was at work against such hierarchical authority in both church and state.

Among the specifically religious reasons for the rebellion and search was the desire for worship close to that of the early church. It was also some people's experience that orderly, liturgical repetitions—no matter how profound the content—often became dry and mechanical exercises without reference to one's own heart or life or relationship with God, especially if they were read in Latin by someone with no spiritual vocation and little education. In fact, the spontaneous upwelling of the heart toward God might be stifled by such an order of worship.

The Westmorland Seekers' relinquishment of a sense of how to worship—in favor of reading the Bible together, praying and waiting on a prophetic word as to how to proceed—converged with Fox's opening that Christ's revelation and guidance were available inwardly. The convergence led to Quaker worship grounded in silent waiting on the Lord. Although it can be seen as a metaphor for the unknowable aspect of God, silence was not valued for its own sake. Rather, silence was a medium in which to be open and willing to being led in worship—in God's own will and not according to human plans, agenda and will. Robert Barclay says, "Our worship consists neither in words nor in silence as such, but in a holy dependence of the mind on God."

The interior practice of listening in meeting for worship

Translating and editing Barclay's *Apology* to make it more accessible to the modern reader, Dean Freiday entitled the Proposition on worship "Holy Expectancy". Note that it is expectancy, *not* expectation. The inner stillness is a mode of listening, of reverent anticipation that does not prescribe the way in which God may speak to us—nor even what is and what is not a distraction. As in contemplative prayer, we rest from our own work and wait on what will be given to or done in us. Sometimes it is a blessed stillness, a peace literally beyond understanding, a unification and gathering-up of the disparate parts of ourselves—which takes place beyond cognition.

Often we arrive at meeting driven by harassments prior to meeting, the unfinished business of the previous week, our obsessions, and our own willful agendas—and with our eagerness to control the events and outcomes of the coming week driving us onward. As we settle into the collected quiet, the knots may loosen, our obsessively tight focus may open and widen to admit space and light around our drivenness. The stillness may gently wash away what clings to us or what we are clinging to. We may not enter into peace beyond understanding; but we may be cleansed or healed of some of the low-grade craziness of our lives. We may, like the crazed, dirty, ragged person in Mark 5:1-20, who was possessed by an unclean spirit named Legion, receive the gift of being returned to ourselves, properly clothed and in our right minds.

We may find some of our bothers returned to us shorn of their compulsive force, stripped of trivia or pettiness, revealed in proportion to their true importance or illuminated at the level of their most profound meaning. Our healing liberates us to listen to them as they deserve, rather than to be overpowered by them. The grace to deal with our lives and our human condition as gifts and opportunities for spiritual growth—rather than to be possessed by them—is just one dimension of the work of God within us, to which we open when we listen, attend or wait on the movement of the Spirit in meeting.

Modern Friends are more sophisticated about human psychology than was the earliest generation of Friends. The modern acceptance of our intellect, the wholeness of ourselves as body/mind/spirit, makes our listening more complicated in some ways than it was for early Friends. Listening in the silence, we may hear precisely what is most painful for us. We become more aware of our wounds and brokenness, of our complicity or connivance with the very forces that have wounded us. We may come to know the destructiveness we have inflicted in the spasms—or avoidance—of our own agony or responsibility. Most painfully, we may come to know the ways we sow again the misery we have reaped, although we rarely sow the misery among those who sowed it in us.

Early Friends, too, knew that the first thing illuminated by the Light is our sin. We are more cautious in the expression of emotion today. We are more wary of the word "sin" because of the Calvinist notions of irrevocable human depravity that have accrued to it and because of psychiatric explorations of the effects of a sense of irrevocable depravity.

Challenging the very notion of irrevocable depravity was a major theme in early Friends' teaching, and something for which Fox and others were repeatedly jailed on blasphemy charges. Accepting Calvinist understandings of sin, rather than the experience of our own tradition, robs us of Fox's witness. It also robs us of the hope for— and confidence in—God's work to change our hearts and liberate us from the effects of brokenness, that was one of the gifts of Quakerism. If we trust that change can come only through therapeutic techniques, we exclude from our hearts and lives some of the most profoundly loving, healing and saving work of God as Friends have understood and experienced it.

What early Friends experienced, and what we sometimes lose sight of in our psychological sophistication, is that "The Light that shows you your sin will light your way out of it." They neither expected to proceed directly and painlessly to peace beyond understanding, nor expected to have to work it all out themselves. A part of what Barclay called "the holy dependence of the mind on God" was the confidence that God was at work in the heart and soul of the individual as surely as in the rest of the Creation.

George Fox's exhortations such as to "be still and cool in thy own mind" or to "stand still in that which is pure" were often the preface to assurances that this would be but the opening step. The posture of stillness and coolness or of standing in that which is pure could be the overture to receiving the strength and empowerment to overcome temptations, evil and emotional turmoil. It was the opening movement of being brought up into the new creation, the new person, the child of God in the image of God. It was not painless; but the inner work was God's.

One of the ways Friends interpreted this experience was through the imagery of baptism, of death and resurrection, of the cross. The reference to baptism may be startling to modern Friends because we do not practice water baptism. Yet earlier Friends' journals make frequent reference to baptism in the context of the meeting for worship. As with other dimensions of worship or sacramental life, Friends took baptism to its most profound level of interior spiritual experience. They took very seriously the New Testament references to a baptism of fire and the Spirit that was to surpass water baptism. Characteristically, they felt that such a gift of the Spirit was to be waited upon. It could not be evoked; neither did it need to be affirmed by an outward ritual.

Whether by water or by fire, Friends took the baptismal symbolism of death and resurrection very seriously. John Woolman was very much in this tradition when he interpreted the dream of his own death as the death of his will, and the life he lived subsequently as the life of Christ or the Spirit in him. For Woolman's dream experience, as for many "baptismal" experiences of others, the death of aspects of their willfulness and egocentricity was a repeated part of ongoing transformation. In this process, people gradually came to recognize, and to be able to give over—albeit with struggle and pain—areas of their lives in which they were clinging to control, or behaving willfully or in egocentric, unloving ways.

Another symbol for this death was the crucifixion of the will or "living under the cross" that crucified the will. Faith made possible cooperation with, and yieldedness to, the fiery, cauterizing deaths of the inward baptism of the Spirit, the watery inward baptismal deaths and washings, the crucifixions to human willfulness. Faith was, in fact, trust that what was dying or being removed from one's being was the very distortion of the image of God within that precluded abundance of Life in the Spirit. It was a trust in resurrection, in being reborn as a child of God, liberated from the deformities inflicted by sin both visited on oneself and visited by oneself on others.

Not everyone experienced such an affirmation of the thorough-going death of his or her will as did Woolman in the dream he had well on in a lifetime of yieldedness. Some Friends would record a series of baptismal experiences. Occasionally a minister would record in her journal that there had been many baptisms, perhaps attended by weeping or remorse, among those present at a given meeting for worship (Bacon). These baptisms through death of willfulness into the fullness of life, these crucifixions and resurrections, were experienced as the work of God in the meeting for worship over time.

Our response to God's work in worship

If worship is the dedication of ourselves to God, part of the listening exercise may be a simple, wordless turning of our being toward God, as in contemplative prayer. Open awareness, and the opportunity to remain in that stillness apart from discursive thought, may come as a gift. More often, it is given to us to attend prayerfully to what arises in our consciousness from our hearts and lives—always in relation to God, or to the fundamental orientation of our being in the direction of God (Volume I, pp. 48-51, "Intentionality").

Worship may be an occasion for self-knowledge, where we come to know what lies beneath the superficial movements of our consciousness. In the undefended quiet, we may become aware—with immediacy—of motives, implications and consequences of our actions, that have been concealed from us by the busyness of life, by the rationalizations of our conscious mind, by our efforts to maintain the face we present to the world. It may be a time to ask for, or to begin to permit, a purification of our motives; a time for recognizing and letting go of what stands in the way. We may see the implications of our insight for our relationships with others. We may feel the need to grant or seek forgiveness, to make amends, to change our attitudes toward or relationships with others.

It may be a time in which we become aware of the source and the implications of our deepest concerns and desires for ourselves and others. Holding them in the Light, we may see their purity, or see where they are clouded by self-centeredness or prevarication. We may be given strength and impetus to proceed; or we may experience that inner constraint Friends have referred to as "a stop in the mind".

It may be a time of sensitizing to movements of God in the heart, of becoming acquainted with the promptings of Love and Truth—which so much of our rationalist and psychological culture teaches us to discount. To sit in stillness, in openness, may carry us past not only the rationalism of discursive thought, but also past the scientific, psychological and material reductionism in which we have been schooled. When they fall away in the Light, we may more easily become sensitized to the intuitive and feel motions of the heart in which early Friends found the movements of the Spirit.

We may need to learn to be much less controlling of what arises, much less quick to label something a distraction. Instead, we may learn to draw it intentionally *into* the Light in order to see it whole and clearly, to feel whether it may be a nudge into prayer or change. This relinquishment of our own agenda and our own criteria for what is and is not a distraction can be the beginning of allowing the unexpected to arise. It may permit us to be guided in directions we had not planned for ourselves. It is a recognition and an acknowledgement that we may not know, to begin with, what is being called for in our lives at their deepest level. William Penn asks,

> When you come into your meetings, both preachers and people, what do you do? Do you gather bodily only and kindle a fire, compassing yourselves about with the sparks of your own kindling, and so please yourselves and walk in the light of your own fire and the sparks which you have kindled, as those did in the time of old whose portion was to lie down in sorrow?
>
> Or, rather, do you sit down in true silence, resting from your own will and workings, and waiting upon the Lord, with your minds fixed in that Light wherewith Christ has enlightened you, until the Lord breathes life in you, refresheth you and prepares you and your spirits and souls to make you fit for His service, that you may offer unto Him a pure and spiritual sacrifice.
>
> *William Penn. D.R.*

Notice the echo of the passage from Romans 12:1-2 that speaks of worship as offering oneself as a pure and spiritual sacrifice. Notice also the themes of "life" and "refreshment", which were experiential terms for what was felt in worship and, at the same time, some of the Biblical terms that Friends felt pointed to their own experience. Many Biblical words and phrases—such as "living water", "fountains of life", "heavenly dew", "heavenly rain", "manna", "leaven"—expressed the restful, yet enlivening and nurturing, quality that arose in Friends when they were liberated from ordinary thought and from words of their own making. This same vocabulary also expressed the sense of the Source beyond themselves for the Life-giving nourishment and refreshment. It could only be received when they had "rested from" their "own will and workings".

To remain "fixed in that Light", to maintain such an intentionality, such a directedness of being, requires a focusing and refocusing of attention and of the heart. It is not unlike a time of individual meditation in which, without fuss, we simply come back to the Center each time we find we have wandered. Some feel that the refocusing itself is of central importance in worship. The repeated inner choice to come back to God, the practice of returning again and again to the Center, the iterated affirmation of the desire to listen in faithfulness, can form a habit of the heart that we can carry out of the time of worship. It can bring worship into the dailiness of all life, erasing the distinction between the secular and the sacred.

The interior corporate experience of the meeting

All of the above might remain a purely private exercise, undistinguishable from a personal time of retirement. But one difference between private meditation and corporate worship is the directionality of our listening, the quality of our willingness and holy expectancy, *in the context of a corporate search*. To be truly together, we listen for what the Spirit is bringing forth from us as a body, for what new thing God is bringing forth within us corporately, for how our communal life may be of service to God. We also listen for the Spiritual State of the Meeting in its responsiveness to the work of the Divine within it. This is an expanded or multidimensional version of our private prayer experience of being joined with the living ongoing stream of prayer, with the ongoing work of the Spirit, with God's will flowing though us and the universe— or being joined with the pain of the world.

Together, we may come to a deeper sense of the gifts, trials and purposes of being drawn together in this particular meeting, at this time. Occasionally, one of us may be favored with vocal ministry to articulate a sense of God's work among us or to pray for a corporate willingness or capacity to respond.

Friends have also found that there is help in being with other people similarly directed to God. This help is not only a matter of mutually supporting one another by our intentional companionship. Over, above and through the presence of others, we often experience the presence of a Light, Life, Power and Guide at work, a Presence that is as personal as it is cosmic.

Friends have felt that "Presence in the Midst" to be a fulfillment of the Biblical promise that "Where two or more meet in my name, I am there among them." (Matthew 18:20, *NJB*) This understanding is expressed visually in the nineteenth century print, "The Presence in the Midst", which shows a translucent Jesus standing in the middle of a traditional meeting. This print was one of only two visual representations that might be found hung in almost any meeting house. It expresses the experience of Presence as the Spirit of Christ that filled and fulfilled the life, words and ministry of Jesus of Nazareth.

Such a corporate exercise differs from private prayer. Friends' worship may be seen as a kind of nonverbal liturgy—or "work of the people"—that is sometimes called "a service". One way in which coming together for worship may differ from a "time of retirement" is in special and intentional awareness of, attention to and care for the others with whom we worship—both individually and together. Sometimes it seems right to attend to each person in turn. At other times, as we wait, one face or another may draw us to feel a concern whether we do or don't know of any cause. Some people incorporate this prayer in a time of inward greeting of others as they arrive. For others, the greeting may follow a time of centering. Still others wait on a particular inner prompting. What matters here is the intentional embrace of our partners in worship, rather than the exclusion of them.

Another difference from private meditation and prayer is the concern for the quality of the communal worship. Some outward practices that support this concern have to do with arriving punctually and entering—without fuss, noise or conversation—into the creation of a climate of prayer and worship that will support those who will arrive later.

Some Friends feel a special leading to pray for the corporate spiritual life of the meeting. This may take the form of praying for its centering, or praying that all present may know the presence and guidance of the Spirit. Prayers may be offered that each person present may be fed according to her or his deepest need. It is helpful to pray that the meeting may receive the vocal ministry most needful for its nurture, and that those whose ministry is required will heed the prompting to speak, while those who may be moved to speak from some other urge will feel restrained. Finally, we can pray that the meeting may experience together the gift of "gathering", or "covering".

Those who experienced a special calling to, and gift of, prayer for the meeting were traditionally recognized as elders. Those of us who no longer recognize elders may feel moved, at least occasionally, to shoulder this particular care for the meeting. Some feel that we will surely languish as a meeting if no one undertakes this care. We will inevitably be richer as a worshiping community if we undertake this work together.

The heart should be as open to the unpredictable movements of the Spirit in worship as it is in times of private prayer. Part of the exercise is the attempt to attend to what is happening within and to discern what is of the Spirit, what is of something else—and how to bring that "something else" into the Light for illumination, transformation, or whatever God is calling for. Interestingly, the movements of the heart in worship may be quite similar to those that are ritualized in the liturgies or orders of worship in other churches. The difference is that the Quaker worshiper waits for confession, contrition, petition, intercession, praise, thanksgiving or other movements to be brought forth in herself by the Spirit.

There is no expectation that all of these movements will take place in a single period of worship. There may be only one. Where there is more than one, the sequence may differ from that of an order of worship. It should arise naturally from the deep interaction of the soul and God, rather than from an agenda. Where other churches attempt to express the major ways of relating to God and to help the worshiper to enter them, Friends leave that work to the Spirit in the heart.

Relying on the Spirit is both simpler and vastly more complicated, without the support of a creed or a verbal liturgy. It means we worshipers are responsible for directing ourselves Godward; for being sensitized and sensitive to the promptings of the Spirit in that direction; for being faithful to however the Spirit is moving us in the moment. The risk in liturgical traditions is that repetitions of words and gestures may become mechanical and lifeless. For Friends, the risk is that we may become lost in our own woolgathering or thought processes, or lost in pursuing our own agendas. We may mistake our thoughts or agendas for the movement of the Spirit, or we may become so involved in them that we are oblivious to the motions of the Spirit.

Queries

You might review your current practice in worship or the history of your practice in worship. How have you been moved to worship at different times? When have you been most open to divine guidance in the process of worship itself? What has diverted you from that openness? Do you sense any new openings or leadings in worship at the moment? How might you be more supportive of the corporate dimension of worship?

The gathered meeting

The experience of gathering, or covering

The most precious experience in Quaker worship has been that of the "gathered", or "covered", meeting. The gathered meeting is a profound interior experience of the mystical reality of the communion of worshipers with one another and with God in Love. If our attentiveness in worship is a kind of listening, what we hear when we are gathered is our oneness in the Light, the Life, Truth, Love. As with any other movement of worship, Friends do not hold expectations that the experience will necessarily be part of *every* meeting for worship. Friends are aware of other important work being done by God in other meetings for worship. But it is natural for those who have felt the gathered condition to hope devoutly for it. People may pray fervently for it for themselves and for the meeting; but, in the same manner that they wait on the promptings of the Spirit, they receive and experience gathering as a gift: as the grace, the mercy, the favor, the work of the Holy One.

Those who are sunk in personal meditations rather than corporate worship may miss it altogether. God generally seems to await our invitation to enter, before meeting us more than halfway. Those who discount the intimations of their intuitive nature, or subject their experiences to the reductionist exercises of rationalism, might unwittingly brush aside the overtures of the Spirit. But even they may be stirred sometimes by the Spirit that seems to pass from Friend to Friend in a gathered or covered meeting. For many, there is an almost palpable, electric sense of Presence, of Life, of Power, of spiritual movement among them.

The experience of gathering is a reminder that for all the restraint and decorum of modern, liberal Friends, we are the spiritual heirs of people closer to Pentecostals than to those Protestants who hear God's voice in The Book, or to Catholics, who find the Real Presence localized in the Eucharist.

Like Pentecostals, we anticipate and treasure the living movement of the Spirit among us. We wait on it to gather us up, to change us and to guide us. We no longer quake, cry out or engage in ecstatic behavior as some of the earliest Friends did. Indeed, some *do* question whether we might not be limiting the ways in which we respond to the Spirit in the interests of an all-too-human cultural preference for decorum. But at the rise of a gathered meeting, many eyes are moist. Many cheeks are streaked with marks of heart-breaking, heart-opening joy. Many closing hand-shakes are given with intensity born of awareness of the Ultimate Reality in which we are One. Many glances search each other in awareness and affirmation of the intimacy and ineffability of the shared experience.

Although mystics are seldom thought of in the same context as Pentecostals, gathering is also akin to the mystics' sense of union. Some have said we are the only people— other than certain Sufi ecstatics, some Native American peoples, or some Anabaptists—who practice group mysticism. In the shared experience of Life and Power, worshipers come to know their oneness with one another in God at levels not altogether conscious. Deeply entered, this noninductive knowledge is life-changing, although not in the manner of an evangelical conversion. The change is more a matter of ongoing reconfiguration of the elements of one's life around the new center or focus. The knowledge imparted unfolds and is integrated over time, as the individual responds faithfully. It bears outward fruit in God's time—and it inspires a continuing hunger for renewed experience of gathering.

In the Quaker practice of group worship on the basis of silence come special times when the electric hush and solemnity and depth of power steals over the worshippers. A blanket of divine covering comes over the room, ... A quickening Presence pervades us, breaking down some part of the special privacy and isolation of our individual lives and blending our spirits within a super-individual Life and Power. An objective, dynamic Presence enfolds us all, nourishes our souls, speaks glad, unutterable comfort within us, and quickens us in depths that had before been slumbering. The Burning Bush has been kindled in our midst, and we stand together on holy ground.

Thomas Kelly

The ground of community

Earlier Friends spoke of this communal experience as sharing the Bread of Life. To them it *was* communion. It was neither just remembrance of an event in the past, nor just a visible sign of an inward reality. It was *participation in* the inward, immediate Reality itself. It was more abundant Life, a gift of the Spirit itself to the community. To have shared this Bread not only enhanced the sense of closeness to and devotion to God; it also enhanced the sense of closeness to, and tenderness for, fellow worshipers.

If listening is what they were about, then in these favored times of worship, they heard, in their bones, that they were inextricably joined with each other as well as with God, with each other in God, with God in each other. They felt that they knew both God and their fellows more fully and dearly in some indefinable, immediate, non-cognitive way. The sense of oneness, knowledge and tenderness that is planted and tended in the times of gathering has been the ground of Quaker community, organization and conduct of life together.

If we work with the traditional Christian definition of a sacrament as an outward expression of an interior spiritual reality, then the communal life itself is the sacramental expression of the reality of union with God and one another in the gathered meeting. This is consistent with the Quaker sense that the immediacy and availability of Divine Presence makes all of life fraught with sacramental possibility, if we but lift it and our intentions from the secular into the spiritual. Like others, we tend to localize that Presence in—without limiting it to—human relationships. The Presence is God with us, among us, between us, guiding us into fuller, more loving life together.

The true fruit and sacrament of the gathered meeting is love, rather than illumination. Some mystical traditions articulate their goal as an experience and knowledge of God. To that end, people purify their lives and their practice, often with quite austere disciplines. Friends' greatest wisdom and strength—although perhaps a one-sided emphasis—is their experience that God empowers and guides ethical transformation: that the transformed life under God's guidance and in God's service is the *result* of mystical union, rather than a condition for it. The people who have experienced themselves united with God's will are drawn to manifest it as love in the world. As William Penn says,

> True godliness [doesn't] turn [people] out of the world, but enables them to live better in it, and excites their endeavors to mend it: not hide their candle under a bushel, but set it upon a table in a candlestick.

> *William Penn. LYM.*

In the first instance, we experience communion, community and efforts in the transformed life with our fellow worshipers. Communion in God becomes the ground of our life together, the thing that shapes it and makes it possible. In a lengthy section exploring Quaker Myths, Conflicting Myths and Fundamental Cleavages, Michael Sheeran, the Jesuit observer of discernment among Friends, says "Quakerism builds all upon the experience of the gathered meeting." Later, he goes on to say,

> When Friends reflect upon their beliefs, they often focus upon the obvious conflict between Christocentric and universalist approaches. ...

> the reporter ... began to find that the Christocentrics ... and some universalists would typically recall a meeting conducted in the Light. If asked to recall the business

decision that meant the most to them, they would often describe how some incident led the group to a gathered condition. ... [O]ther universalists and Friends favoring what we have called the social action and democratic myths might recall the same decision ... or express their pride in a decision well made, but would be apparently unaware of the special atmosphere experienced by the others. ...

Put simply, the real cleavage among Friends is between those who experience the gathered or covered condition and those who do not. The former can differ markedly in the language they use to verbalize the event. For one, the group is gathered in Christ; for the other, the force at the root of the universe or in the depth of every human is expressing itself in the covered assemblage. In either case, the words and concepts are secondary; the event, the experience, is what counts.

... [T]he universalist humanism of the person who experiences the covered condition will lead in a quite different direction from the individual who does not have this experience. In the experience, the former finds guidance, motivation to reconsider preferences, a sense of obligation to the decision reached in this atmosphere. None of these factors directly affects the person who has identical belief but lacks the experience. In this very important sense, those who share the experience, be they Christocentric or universalist or whatever else, are the coreligionists.

Michael Sheeran

The quality of our life as a spiritual community depends upon the degree to which we are inwardly reaching, stretching toward, re-orienting our personal and corporate being toward a deeper sense of our unity in God. Without that intentionality or directionality, without the experience in which it is grounded and toward which it aspires, community can only be constructed laboriously by human effort, with primarily secular models from which to work.

With no spiritual ground, we can have no truly spiritual community. With no spiritual ground, we cannot aspire to relationships that transcend the desirable, but purely human, possibilities of mental health, sociological soundness and good political process. We will lack the vision, the empowerment and the guidance to move beyond the limitations of our conditioned pasts to the new ways of being and behaving in the world that Friends have felt were their divine calling. Some of the challenges of our life in community stem from very different understandings, visions of and aspirations for Quaker community—and from very different ways of articulating and interpreting them.

In terms of our ground in a spiritual experience of unity, the question of whether our experience is expressed in the cherished categories of Christian thought, or in more neutral, universalist terms, is clearly secondary. Early Friends placed more emphasis on the immediacy of spiritual experience than on theological articulations of it. The community of liberal Friends today includes both Christian and universalist Friends, who both experience the gathered condition although they express it in different terms. The tension about the language in which the experience is expressed is less fundamental for the functioning of Quaker community than is the tension concerning the reality and importance for the Quaker gestalt of the experience of gathering itself.

Queries

Do you feel your unity in God as the overriding fact of your life in community? Can you work with people whose experience differs from yours or is expressed differently from yours? Are you able to be with and act from your experience without labeling it? Are you able to permit others to express their experience without requiring that they conform to your standards of expression?

Have you experienced the gathered, or covered, condition? Have you been aware of it as part of the Quaker experience? Do you wait for it? Pray for it? For yourself or for the community? Does either the experience or the awareness of the possibility inform your sense of community and its possibilities? On what basis do you find unity with people for whom the references and claims to spiritual experience are opaque and don't sound altogether desirable?

If you have no experience of gathering, are you open to it? How do you enter into community with people for whom it is the basis of their life together? What is your sense of the basis for Quaker community?

May they all be one, just as, Father, you are in me and I am in you, so that they also may be in us, ... With me in them and you in me may they be so perfected in unity that the world will recognize that it was you who sent me and that you have loved them as you loved me.

John 17:21, 23. NJB

In the two chapters that follow I'll be tracing some of the ways the gathered meeting—

like the interior posture of listening—is foundational for our faith and practice together.

References and resources for meeting for worship and gathering

Full publication information is in the Bibliography at the end of this book. For abbreviations, see p. xix.

Margaret Hope Bacon, ed.
Wilt Thou Go On My Errand? passim.

Robert Barclay.
The Apology in Modern English.
Dean Freiday, ed.
Propositions 11 and 13, esp.
pp. 257, 250.

Howard Brinton.
Friends for 300 Years.
chs. 1-4.

Howard Brinton.
Quaker Journals.
ch. 6.

Howard Brinton.
Prophetic Ministry.
PHP, no number or date.

Wilmer Cooper.
A Living Faith.
chs. 2-4, 7.

George H. Gorman.
The Amazing Fact of Quaker Worship.

Thomas F. Green.
Preparation for Worship.

Douglas Gwyn.
Apocalypse of the Word.
ch. 9.

Douglas Gwyn.
"John 15 and its Community".
QRT, spring 1980.

Brenda Clifft Heales & Chris Cook.
Images and Silence.
chs. 1-2.

Francis B. Hall, ed.
Quaker Worship in North America.
esp. chs. 5 & 7.

Thomas Kelly.
The Gathered Meeting.

Thomas Kelly.
A Testament of Devotion.
The Light Within.

London Yearly Meeting.
Christian faith and practice in the experience of the Society of Friends.
chs. 4 & 6.

William Penn.
A Collection of the Works of William Penn.
as excerpted in LYM #395;
DR p. 305.

Isaac Penington.
The Light Within and Selected Writings.
Extracts from a Treatise Concerning the Worship of the Living God; Silent Meetings; Prayer.

John Punshon.
Encounter with Silence.
chs. 1-9.

Michael J. Sheeran.
Beyond Majority Rule: Voteless Decisions in the Religious Society of Friends.
ch. IV. Quaker Myths in Perspective: Primacy of the "Event", Conclusion, esp. The Future of Quakerism, and Quakerism's Message for the American Future, pp. 81, 86-7.

Douglas Steere.
Prayer and Worship.

Douglas Steere.
Where Words Come From.

Caroline Stephen.
Quaker Strongholds.
Worship.

William Taber.
Four Doors to Meeting for Worship.
PHP # 306.

Evelyn Underhill.
Worship.

Lloyd Lee Wilson.
Essays on the Quaker Vision of Gospel Order.
Waiting Worship.

John Woolman.
The Journal and Major Essays.
pp. 185-6.

Chapter 2

Listening for the Spirit among Us as It Shapes Our Human Relationships in Community

Introduction

In spiritual formation, great emphasis is placed on personal practices—especially prayer and devotional reading—as the openings through which the Spirit of God, Christ's Spirit, the Holy Spirit shapes us inwardly toward a more perfect image of God. In our inward relationship with God, we are drawn from our egocentrism toward a life centered in the Divine. We are freed from desperate efforts to deny our finite human condition by trying to assert ultimate control over our lives. Bit by struggling bit, over a lifetime, we are detached from fears and desires that possess us.

An important part of the Quaker gestalt, however, is an implicit assertion that God's work in us is not confined to the solitude and privacy of our inward relationship in prayer and worship. A major arena for that work among Friends has been life together in spiritual community, in both worship and fellowship. The inward work of the Spirit continues in the meeting for worship—with the important difference that it's a corporate experience in which God works with us collectively as well as individually. As we give ourselves over to the Divine Work in these times, we are knit together inwardly. Our vision is opened to include movement of our personal relationships with God toward wholeness, within the movement of the sum of all relationships toward God.

Meeting life was an important part of spiritual formation among Friends until the fragmentation resulting from the inroads of privatization and individualization.

Friends have sensed the Spirit working within our meeting relationships in such a way that we assist—sometimes inadvertently—each other's spiritual formation.

This certainly doesn't mean we set out to make each other over in ways more comfortable to ourselves. Quite the reverse, it means learning to live lovingly with and through the human frailties of others. Most especially, it means allowing our own frailties, faults and sins to be illuminated in the encounter with others—accepting the guidance of the Light to lead us out of our own darkness. A major point of our faith is that God is often to be found working with and in us in dark times of frustration, disagreement and betrayal. Paradoxically it is the bleak times, rather than the rosier ones, that offer the greatest opportunity for spiritual growth and self-transcendence. It can't be done by gritting our teeth and forcing ourselves to "be nice" any more than we can force ourselves to accept a theological dogma that has no meaning or logic for us.

Rather, Friends rely on the Holy Spirit moving within and among us, in our weakness, to form us in greater humility, yieldedness and authenticity of love as we confront the vicissitudes of human life together. This is the ground in which God's Love has the chance to grow within us and among us, transforming us collectively into a loving community, even as we are changed individually.

This chapter deals with the ways in which the Quaker gestalt opens us to listening communally for guidance, strength and courage to change, to be formed and transformed toward more abundant life—with and through each other.

> ... [Y]ou are no longer aliens or foreign visitors; you are fellow citizens with the holy people of God and part of God's household. You are built upon the foundations of the apostles and the prophets, and Christ Jesus himself is the cornerstone. Every structure knit together in him grows into a holy temple in the Lord; and you too, in him, are being built up into a dwelling-place of God in the Spirit.
>
> *Ephesians 2:19-22. NJB*

This passage from the Letter to the Ephesians is attributed to Paul, but almost certainly was written after his time by someone who had assimilated not only his thought but his verbal expressions. It speaks of the reconciliation of formerly alienated or hostile Gentiles and Jews in church community—an area of great strife in the early church. Hence, it is full of imagery that emphasizes reconciliation, joining together people who were separate, and being knit together and built up into one edifice.

The author fills it with some of Paul's favorite metaphors for the community, mixed and flowing into each other, in Paul's own impassioned, oral style: fellow-citizens, a household, a dwelling place, a structure, a holy temple of God. The mixture of both organic and architectural metaphors expresses different aspects of Paul's sense of the way we are united in spiritual community.

Fellowship is an outward expression, a celebration and a reminder of our eternal oneness in God's love "already" experienced in the gathered meeting. In the temporal "not yet", in which we move and are conscious much of the time, our living and working together with other people is the great reminder that God is present—working creatively through very different people to challenge one another's egocentrism, willfulness and cultural assumptions.

Community provides a challenge for each of us to change, to work and stretch toward our truest selves as unique manifestations of God's love in interpersonal relationships. It can be the opening for us to cooperate with the transforming work of the Spirit within us. It can open us to give over our centeredness in self in order to grow toward the fullness of our unity with diverse people in God's Love. We express our profound oneness and simultaneously grow toward more perfect expression of it by means of loving care of others—and by attentive listening for God speaking through others, through relationships and human situations, as well as within ourselves.

It's easy to sentimentalize this communal life. In fact, there are times of great sweetness, comfort and warmth in it, even though we live this life together with people we might not have chosen for our beloved community. The mystery is that people's inevitable differences give us openings for spiritual growth and maturing in ways that are sometimes uncomfortable, if not downright painful. The harmony, peace and tenderness we experience in favored times of worship are usually actualized only at the cost of revelatory confrontations with, and healing of, our own wounds, brokenness, willfulness and egotism—in encounter with the wounds, brokenness, willfulness and egotism of others. The willingness to stay with conflicting senses of God's will and Truth testifies to our trust in the healing and revelatory work of the Spirit of God within our very conflicts. Friends have cherished the meeting community, both for the Life in it and as a prophetic witness to the rest of the world about the nature of God and the effect of God's transforming love. It is at once hard-won and a gift of grace.

Mutual commitment to life together as a school of the Spirit

Pseudocommunity

The highly mobile and privatized society in which we live tempts us to cut and run when personal encounters become difficult. For those of us who live in densely populated areas, there are always new groups of people available with whom we can maintain more distance, and more carefully managed relationships. In the middle-class culture, a plethora of worthwhile activities is pressed upon us, demanding our time and energy or offering relatively painless paths to self-fulfillment. When difficulty arises, we can always move on and begin again at the safely superficial level of relationship that M. Scott Peck refers to as "pseudocommunity". If life in our meeting community seems too demanding, we can always dilute the intensity by making meeting just one in a number of optional activities tailored to suit our interests and provide personal fulfillment.

Many people make apparently satisfactory lives in this way. Life lived at this level, however, usually fails to satisfy those touched by the vision, the memory, or the longing for union in a gathered meeting or beloved community. In them there grows an alternative vision of life with others, focused on listening for God's guidance into the unity that arises in a gathered meeting. There is a readiness, even a hunger, for a life committed to what has been called the "school of the Spirit". This is a school in which we listen with our whole being for the Spirit, responding with transformed attitudes and behaviors. The transformations are often painfully worked out with one another. Many of its disciplines are parallel to the personal practices explored in Volume I of *Listening Spirituality*. A significant and fundamental discipline is commitment to community as well as to God.

Commitment to God and to community

Commitment is difficult enough in each individual's personal practice. When undertaken with others, it becomes even more strenuous. The parallels with marriage are unmistakable. The divorce rate indicates that we are a people much less willing than our forebears to persist in, work with and learn through difficult relationships. Although the level of intimacy is lower in community than in marriage, the sources of potential difficulty are multiplied. Sometimes we are unwilling to try to resolve our differences until they have grown too big for simple resolution. Or we may unilaterally decide to sever difficult relationships, rather than acknowledge our own role in them or make any of the adjustments necessary for them to continue. Or we may shrink from permitting others to be privy to our efforts at reconciliation or from being involved in other people's efforts at reconciliation.

Spiritual life is a life of commitment to being present to what is, and open to the potentiality of the Spirit within it—rather than attempting to reshape the world to suit our personal desires or extract from it our self-fulfillment. Lived in community with others, spiritual life requires a similar commitment to remaining with what is and open to the creative potentiality of the Spirit within difficult situations. That does not mean we submit passively to destructive, abusive or unjust situations. But it does mean that we labor lovingly with others until we have truly exhausted what loving commitment and reconciliation can do to bring us into unity—trusting that the Spirit of God is working in them as well as in us, more deeply and creatively than we are able to.

Quaker folklore is full of tales of Life-giving resolutions that came, feeling like gifts, when people had labored long and with apparently little effect. Such tales are cherished among Friends and retold when they gather. The presence of so many stories of this kind is emblematic of the high value Friends place on reconciliation: on both the human activity and the divine. Emphasis is often given to the superiority of God's solution to any proposed by conflicting parties. Often the willingness to stay alive to the question over time seems to have been the preparation for discerning and receiving the utimate resolution.

We also tell stories of people having been disowned by the community. We take most of them from those periods of our history when disciplinary rules were applied judgmentally and unilaterally, without openness to the possibility of some unperceived dimension of the issue. We often use these stories to make the point that disownment, separation and judgment are wrong or "un-Quakerly". I don't mean to say it's always possible to find "a third way", or that mollifying people is more important than any issue. Human limitation sometimes means we may reluctantly have to accept separation, to let people go. Yet it does seem important first to have tried as many alternative ways as possible of remaining together in mutual love.

One problem with this point of view is that not everyone in the meeting has the same level of commitment to remaining present and open to Divine Guidance, the same level of yieldedness of ego and willfulness. Our meetings include both those who long for a centered and committed spiritual community, and those for whom the meeting is an optional item, poorly integrated into, or simply tacked onto a life filled with a variety of other activities. We have those who feel that community should be a place of unfailing, undemanding, loving acceptance and those who feel that community is the place where we are challenged and supported to grow to our fullest potential in God.

These very different understandings of what constitutes spiritual community create many of our failures in communication and in caring for one another. Much disillusionment or burn-out occurs because some people have given themselves wholeheartedly to the work of the community, only to find others withhold themselves or work from a more limited and secular vision.

For each meeting it is a serious matter to decide whether to promulgate a vision of community, or what vision of community to promulgate. In places where the numbers of people available to sustain community life are small or dropping, members often fear placing expectations on newcomers lest they be frightened away. Even where numbers are not a problem, the desire to be hospitable and welcoming can lead to avoidance of making demands, or of considering what demands might be appropriate to make. In many meetings, there is a tendency to encourage people to become members at the earliest moment they feel a measure of comfort with the group. The addition of people who may not be committed to, or may not even understand, the underlying religious experiences and assumptions of the community can have a great impact on the nature of the meeting's future life.

Commitment and membership

When people do apply for membership, the burden of discerning the rightness of their application is often placed on the applicants, rather than on the clearness committee nominated to evaluate the application. As I have been invited to various places for workshops on discernment, I've often heard people voice disappointment about their clearness committees for membership or for marriage. They're distressed that events which are so momentous in their lives, that have occasioned such soul-searching and are significant for the life of the meeting, are more or less given a rubber stamp by members of the meeting's weightiest committee. They are distressed not to have been assisted in deepening their own sense of the meaning of the action, or pressed to bring forward and test the fruit of their own interior searching. One person spoke of being tempted to withdraw her application, if it meant no more than the delighted addition of a name to the meeting's rolls.

Often, the problem is that committee members themselves have no clear sense of either the basis of membership or the source of the spiritual authority for such a decision. To assume spiritual authority personally is quite rightly uncomfortable. We sometimes forget, however, that we may always turn to the Source of authority. As a poor compromise, we sometimes try to establish rules of thumb: length of attendance, experience in a Quaker school, classes attended, books read. But none of these is an accurate guide.

Some people arrive among us having been brought by God to a readiness surpassing that of most of our members. Others persist their whole lives in views of Quakerism interpreted through secular institutions and notions. In reviewing an application for membership, committee members need to hold both extremes before themselves in their discernment process.

It is not reasonable to impose upon applicants a much more rigorous standard than could be satisfied by existing members. Yet, the consequence of having no standard is that the meeting conforms to the vision of the people who have been admitted— rather than having the new members gradually transformed into Quakers. In our folklore, we have tales of people who have waited five years, ten, as many as forty years before requesting membership. For some people, these are merely amusing stories of dithering or lack of interest. For others, hearing of such deep seriousness in seeking and finding strikes a resonant chord. It reminds them of their own seeking and finding, of the central place of the attendant meanings in their lives.

It takes time to know whether we belong, not only in the sense of being able to join comfortably in group activities, but in the sense of belonging deeply to one another, to God, and to one another in God. I, for one, have experienced the grace of being supported in Quaker community, as I crawled from one end of this spectrum toward the other. Another, perhaps fuller, metaphor might be crawling toward the center in God, upheld along the path by community life.

Mutual support and accountability of individual and meeting

If our yearning is to grow toward personal spiritual maturity and corporate unity in spiritual community, the mutual support and mutual accountability of the individual and the community are indispensable. It's important for both the individual and the meeting to be clear where they are in regard to these questions. Does the meeting aspire to be a spiritual community in the sense of being committed to mutual support and accountability in the struggle to be reconciled and woven together in Love? Is it willing to hold out the vision and be held accountable for living into it? Is this vision seen as a basis for membership? Is growth in this direction to be encouraged after membership has been approved? Is the meeting willing to support its members in this aspiration by creating and fostering opportunities for its members to move in this direction?

In an earlier time, when the gathered meeting was an indisputable Quaker experience, the community was comfortable with spiritual aspirations. Embracing the lowest common denominator of spiritual aspirations—lest anyone feel left out—would have been unthinkable.

Today, committed spiritual formation groups, prayer groups, worship groups or worship sharing groups can provide opportunities for people who yearn to move from peripheral spiritual concern toward the center. The presence of such groups in the meeting may also raise the possibility of a life centered on God for people who have been only slightly aware of it among us in the past—for people who think of us primarily as an ethical culture society, as a pacifist lobbying group, or as creators of excellent, elitist schools. The spiritual maturing experienced by members of listening groups, who yearn for gathering, may leaven the meeting as a whole through example, vision, or contagion—so that those who choose not to join do not resent, resist or label them "in-groups", "holier-than-thou", etc.

Such groups also become, at least temporarily, one of the concentric rings of spiritual community for their members. They may be one of the places where people find shared commitment, vision, mutual support and mutual accountability, if it is lacking in the larger meeting community. If disregarded, these mini-communities, or *ekklesiolae*, as Thomas Kelly might call them, can be marginalized or even encouraged to make their own community elsewhere. This might leave the meeting with less diversity to accommodate; but it will also be left without some of its more spiritually grounded members.

Meetings must consider what they expect of the membership process, of members, and what they expect in the way of continuing transformation. Individuals, too, need to assess their motives when entering into membership. If the meeting community, to some extent, is to be accountable to support the maturing spiritual life of the individual, then the individual also becomes, to some extent, accountable to conduct her life in community from a spiritual center.

First of all, prospective members must be aware that mutual accountability in all its dimensions is important—especially in the membership process. People coming from churches where clergy bear the weight of such responsibility are often oblivious to the spiritual demands of a church that has abolished the laity. Secondly, we must recognize how difficult this kind of accountability is for any of us in a culture that encourages rugged individualism and makes a fetish of privacy, while it maintains hierarchical structures in most institutions.

In this era of rampant individualism, there are many people who feel either that there is no need for formal membership or that membership involves too much sacrifice of personal autonomy or identity. Some people reject membership with self-satisfaction in the fact that they are "free spirits", not "joiners". This stance shows no sense that the ground of Quaker community is God-given gathering together. It also shows a lack of willingness to enter into the complexities of life that community entails. We must not, however, despise such a declaration. In it the person admits that he's a product of the surrounding times and culture. He may be more realistic and more fully aware than others that the wider culture enshrines the individual will, sapping people's willingness and ability to give themselves to community. We must respect the declaration, praying that the quality of our own lives in community may open others to transformation.

We must not minimize how difficult it is for us, having absorbed the individualistic values of our culture, to give any authority to community or to expose our private selves to others. At the same time, we must be aware that spiritual community requires of us precisely such trust, openness and yieldedness. The community, in turn, must work to be worthy of that trust, openness and yieldedness. Accountability runs in both directions. In order for an individual to be accountable to a community for her spiritual growth, the community must be accountable to its individual members as a place of loving support for spiritual growth—with some genuine humility about its fallibility.

Finally, we must be aware that quite a few of us hang back from applying for membership from a sense of unworthiness. In my own case, I know I had a vague sense that I must somehow make the entire spiritual journey from self-centeredness to God-centeredness, from individualism to communal life, from privatism to self-giving in intense social activism before I could qualify as a member of the Religious Society of Friends.

No one told me this. I never articulated it for myself. I simply looked at the shining faces of the *de facto* elders and ministers, heard of the self-sacrificing deeds of the social activists in the meeting, read John Woolman and the mystics and knew I had a long, long way to go before application for membership was thinkable. When an articulation of this sense was finally drawn from me in a Yearly Meeting workshop, I practically had my fellow attenders rolling on the floor with laughter. I was gently encouraged by some "elders" to apply for membership shortly thereafter.

What was missing in my experience, of course, is missing in most modern meetings. There is rarely a clearly articulated sense that spiritual maturing or transformation is a life-long process. It is not mentioned that membership is simply a rite of passage in that process, the moment of adult declaration that this is the church structure, this is the spiritual community within which we feel called to live out the process of our spiritual maturing. This is the trellising that best supports the growth of our interior relationship with God and our exterior relationship with the world. These are the people with whom we will live out the vicissitudes of our inner and outer lives.

Worthiness has nothing to do with membership. God has already accepted us in our imperfection and is loving us forward toward a more perfect image of God's self. The real issue in membership is commitment on the part of both the meeting and the applicant to remain faithful to the development and requirements of the process within Quaker tradition.

Queries

As you ponder how you might embody this spiritual practice of commitment and mutual accountability, it may be useful to begin by reflecting on the times when you have felt most lovingly supported in community—and when you have felt most let down, alone or bereft. What do these occasions tell you about the community? ... about yourself? On reflection, were your expectations reasonable within the tradition? Or were they shaped by the secular culture? When are you most inclined to flee community? What gives you the hope and strength to stay and work for its improvement? ... for your own improvement?

Does your meeting attempt to discern the rightness of membership for applicants, or simply accept all comers? How does either of these policies affect the quality of the meeting for worship? ... meeting life? ... its functioning as community? If you are not a member of the meeting, how do you feel about the meaning of membership, and its advantages or disadvantages? If you are not a member of a meeting, what would be required for you to make a commitment? Is there some helpful way the meeting might reach out to you? Is there some way you might reach out to the meeting?

Does your meeting attempt to prepare people for membership in the community? If you are a member, how did you discern whether or when it was the right step for you? If and when you were admitted to membership, were you visited in the manner that Richard Claridge was visited in about 1697?

This was the way that Friends used with me, when I was convinced of truth, they came oftentimes to visit me; and sate and waited upon the Lord in silence with me; and as the Lord opened our understandings and mouths, so we had very sweet and comfortable seasons together. They did not ask me questions about this or the other creed, or about this or the other controversie in religion; but they waited to feel that living Power to quicken me, which raised up Jesus from the dead. And it pleased God so in his wisdom to direct, that all the great truths of the Christian religion were occasionally spoken to. Now this was Friends way with me, a way far beyond all rules or methods established by the wisdom of this world, which is foolishness with God: And this is their way with others that are convinced of the truth.

LYM. #369

What was the membership process like for you? Did it assist your own clearness as to what was involved in the present and what might be hoped for in the future? Are you satisfied with the degree of seriousness and care taken? How might it be improved? What might be the most helpful kind of process for the individual? For the community? If you have served on a clearness committee for membership, how did you discern whether it was right, or the right time, for the person to be received into membership?

Whether or not you are a member, have you experienced meeting life as a community? ... as an institution? ... as a disparate collection of individuals lacking an inner unity in love? ... as an in-group of old friends, unreceptive to newcomers? What are the touchstone experiences for your view of meeting life?

Transformed relationships in community

Mutual love, care, tenderness, respectfulness and humility

And in the measure of the Light, ... all wait and dwell, ... where the unity is, whereby you all may know that you are true disciples, in that you love one another ... .

Therefore, dear Friends, abide in the Cross, and keep your minds to that which is pure; ... and consider one another, and provoke one another to love and to good works; not forsaking the assembling of yourselves. ... And dwell in love and unity in the pure eternal Light: there is your fellowship, there is your cleansing and washing. Keep you all here faithful to your own measure.

Margaret Fell (Barbour)

Over and over, earlier Friends found their own experiences expressed in the New Testament exhortations to the early churches. They were one of the touchstones for Friends' sense that their experience was the same as that of the primitive church. The diction of their letters to one another was shaped by that of passages in the epistles. Margaret Fell's letters from her home at Swarthmoor were a major formative, stabilizing and encouraging force for the first generation of Friends as they traveled on foot and horseback all over England and beyond, and passed in and out of prisons. The above excerpt from one of her letters is couched in phrases clearly reminiscent of the Letter to the Hebrews, as well as of John and some Pauline letters. At the same time, it's evocative of the living experience of gathering among Friends, holding before them its gifts and implications for their behavior and relationships.

The experience of unity in the Light is the ground and source from which we draw the understandings and strength necessary to move more deeply into true fellowship. Margaret Fell is confident that if Friends "wait and dwell" in the Light, they will find their fellowship there and will know their love for one another as their true discipleship (John 13:35).

Waiting and dwelling in the Light, they will also experience "cleansing and washing": a metaphorical baptism or dying to self-will and egocentrism that will enable them to maintain their unity centered in God and love for one another. Conversely, life in community will inevitably provide continuing occasions for baptisms, or deaths, of self-will. Above all, faithfulness to mutuality will provide many openings to baptism.

Mention of the Cross in the context of community is a slightly different allusion to the death of self-centeredness and self-will that liberates people to keep their minds "to that which is pure"; to "consider one another, and provoke one another to love and to good works"; and to keep "faithful to your own measure". "Baptism" and "abiding in the Cross" lay the basis for a resurrected heart, free of the things that enslave us. Crucifixion of self-will also lays the basis for a resurrected mind, open for God and for each other rather than filled with self-preoccupation and overmastering desires.

"To your own measure" is also a reminder that this is not done by artificial straining to live up to some abstract principle of virtue or perfection. One's own measure refers to the measure or amount of Light or guidance given to each person at any given time. There is complete confidence that, if only we can become attuned to it, we will be drawn and guided into loving, virtuous conduct rather than artificially coerced into it by ourselves or by others. That doesn't mean loving conduct will be painless or without difficulty. It means that we will be drawn by Light and Love rather than by desire for the good opinion of others or ourselves.

Sometimes tenderness and consideration simply well up in us, given as grace. More often we are conscious of falling short or erring on one side or another—particularly with difficult people. Love is both a gift and a discipline. Yet the discipline is subtle. Self-coercion rarely works for long. Its fruit is often anger at the suppression of one's impulses, or bitterness if one's loving gestures are met with unlove.

In the kindergarten of the School of Love that we attend with one another in community, we can lead one another on by meeting love with love. With grace, we may even be able to meet unlove with love. In this way we may eventually be able to provoke one another to love, rather than to the exasperation usually signified by that verb in modern vernacular.

Un-self-centered behavior is hard for humans. It's especially hard today because popular modern psychology, reacting to the repressive era in which it was born, encourages self-fulfillment and self-assertion as priorities that—without great care—can foster self-centeredness. These cultural priorities are one reason for the need for communities with a commitment or covenant to aspire to self-transcendence rather than self-fulfillment, to mutuality as well as a personal relationship with the Divine. Spiritual communities are where we practice the counter-cultural behaviors of living love with others committed to the same struggle, where we encourage and admonish one another in tenderness.

Even this measure of kindness and gentleness requires the grace that Fell suggests Friends have found in their relationship with divine Light. By bringing to one another—and to the situations in which they find themselves—the same open, attentive and willing listening they bring to worship and to contemplative personal prayer, Friends have received the freedom and strength to love one another. Excessively strenuous efforts of the will to improve behavior usually only feed self-will and often result in a backlash of resentment from the recesses of one's self. It seems we receive this transformation—like others—from God, as part of the overall spiritual maturing process.

As we expand our attentiveness to include more than our own inner self and personal concerns, our being begins to be centered elsewhere. We become more free and open to see and hear the people before us. When we listen with our whole being—as we must when we listen for the Spirit—preconceptions begin to slip away, analysis diminishes, our perceptions become more simple and direct, less intellectualized. Part of the amazing grace of this kind of listening is not only that we feel more tender and cherishing of the person with us, but with time the person may also begin to feel more loved and loving.

Both parties feel more connected, joined in the Ocean of Love and Light that is beyond as well as around and between us. This isn't a technique. It's rarely possible to turn it on and off. And it can't be faked. Although some psychotherapists simulate it, most only sustain the appearance when they authentically move into the reality. It's truly a part of a way of being as we move more fully into a life centered on God. In the re-centering, the focus moves and widens from exclusively within ourselves toward that of God in the other, and finally toward the Spirit moving between us, uniting us in Love.

The experience of the divine Life, Light, Power, Love between us evokes mutual love and its attendant behaviors between us. Love begets love. Light shows us light. Life draws us into more abundant life. Divine power empowers us to do what we might not be able to do on our own.

Below are some exhortations from the letters to early churches that speak of the behaviors expected from members. They are not here to invoke scriptural authority, but to show how the same vision of anticipated behaviors has arisen over and over, how the same need arose to hold out the vision of life in the school of the Spirit, the need to exhort people to renewed commitment and effort. This vision inspired many of the letters of early Friends.

If our life in Christ means anything to you—if love, or the Spirit that we have in common, or any tenderness or sympathy can persuade you at all— then be united in your convictions and united in your love, with a common purpose and a common mind. That is the one thing that would make me completely happy. There must be no competition among you, no conceit, but everybody is to be humble: value others over yourselves, each of you thinking of the interests of others before your own.

Phillipians 2:1-4. int

My sisters and brothers, you were called to freedom; but be careful, or this freedom will provide an opening for self-indulgence. Rather, serve one another in works of love, since the whole of the Law is summarized in a single command: "Love your neighbor as yourself." If you go on snapping at one another and tearing each other to pieces, be careful, or you may end up destroying the whole community.

Galatians 5:13-15. int

Instead, I tell you, be guided by the Spirit, and you will no longer yield to self-indulgence. The desires of self-indulgence are always in opposition to the Spirit, and the desires of the Spirit are in opposition to self-indulgence: they are opposites, one against the other; that is how you are prevented from doing the things that you want to. But when you are led by the Spirit, you are not under the Law. When self-indulgence is at work the results are obvious: sexual vice, impurity, and sensuality, the worship of false gods and sorcery; antagonisms and rivalry, jealousy, bad temper and quarrels, disagreements, factions and malice, drunkenness, orgies and all such things. And about these, I tell you now as I have told you in the past, that people who behave in these ways will not inherit the kingdom of God. On the other hand the fruit of the Spirit is love, joy, peace, patience, kindness, goodness, trustfulness, gentleness and self-control; no law can touch such things as these. All who belong to Christ Jesus have crucified self with all its passions and its desires.

Galatians 5:16-24. NJB

So since we live by the Spirit, let us follow her lead. We must stop being conceited, contentious and envious.

Sisters and brothers, if one of you is caught in any sin, the more spiritual among you should correct the offender in a spirit of gentleness—remembering that you may be tempted yourselves. Bear one another's burdens, and thus fulfill the law of Christ.

But if you think you're important when you're not, you're deceiving yourself.

Galatians 5:25-6:3. int

Queries

Is there someone in your meeting whose life speaks especially powerfully of the gifts of the Spirit? Is there someone in your meeting whose demeanor or behavior is especially challenging to your growth in the gifts of the Spirit? Is there someone who makes it easy for you? It may be useful for you to examine what helps you and what hinders you in being loving: not just in others but also in yourself. How might you be being called to enter more fully into love and humility in community? What might be your practice or your reminders?

Forgiveness, reconciliation and learning peace-making

As the chosen of God, then, the holy people whom he loves, you are to be clothed in heartfelt compassion, in generosity and humility, gentleness and patience. Bear with one another; forgive each other if one of you has a complaint against another. The Lord has forgiven you; now you must do the same. Over all these clothes, put on love, the perfect bond. And may the peace of Christ reign in your hearts, because it is for this that you were called together in one body. Always be thankful.

Colossians 3:12-15. NJB

Live in peace with one another.

We urge you, sisters and brothers, to warn the idlers, cheer up the fainthearted, support the weak and be patient with everyone. Make sure that no one repays one evil with another. Always seek what is good for each other—and for all people.

I Thessalonians 5:13b-15. int

Remember this, my dear brothers [and sisters]: everyone should be quick to listen but slow to speak and slow to human anger; God's saving justice is never served by human anger: so do away with all impurities and remnants of evil. Humbly welcome the Word which has been planted in you and can save your souls. ...

Nobody who fails to keep a tight rein on the tongue can claim to be religious; this is mere self-deception; that person's religion is worthless.

James 1:19-21; 26. NJB

So from now on, there must be no more lies. Speak the truth to one another, since we are all parts of one another. Even if you are angry, do not sin: never let the sun set on your anger or else you will give the devil a foothold. ... No foul word should ever cross your lips: let your words be for the improvement of others, as occasion offers, and do good to your listeners; ... . Any bitterness or bad temper or anger or shouting or abuse must be far removed from you—as must every kind of malice. Be generous to one another, sympathetic, forgiving each other as readily as God forgave you in Christ.

Ephesians 4:25-27, 29, 31-32. NJB

The preceeding passages focus on some of the hardest aspects of life together in spiritual community. The letters were written to young churches suffering from grievances, complaints, lies, deceit, bad temper, anger, shouting, abuse, malice and bitterness. These are attitudes we rarely discuss in church life. We prefer to hold up the vision of our meetings practicing listening, compassion, generosity, humility, gentleness, patience—and, most of all, forgiveness, love and peace. When we focus on our oneness and unity in the Love that is God, it's tempting to believe that we will all live happily ever after together, with never an unkind word or misunderstanding, much less legitimate complaints, anger or real nastiness. The challenge, of course, is to hold up and live out the vision while acknowledging and accepting the reality of our own flawed humanity and that of those we live with.

In relation to romantic visions, the same challenge bedevils marriage in our culture, focusing all the attention on the wedding as a glorious once-for-always union, befogging the view of subsequent life together. The inevitable, subsequent difficulties are often felt as a shock, if not a betrayal. The couple has often made no commitment to the hard work of reconciliation. Even more disempowering, they usually have no sense of how to go about it. When most of us are so ill-prepared to work realistically and lovingly within the most intimate relationship of our lives, it is small wonder that our commitments to, and ideas about, such work in spiritual community tend to be even more shaky, and individualistic rather than shared.

Of all the negative feelings mentioned in the above excerpts on community, conscious malice is surely the rarest. We are almost invariably confident we're behaving well, in just the way a reasonable person might expect. At bottom, we feel ourselves to be innocent and right. When others behave very differently or experience our behavior as wrong, hurtful or reprehensible, our first impulse is usually to wonder what's wrong with them. Fault is mostly felt to lie outside ourselves; so our sense of the other person's wrongness and blame is generally compounded when we see that they experience the fault as in us. This is fertile ground for a cycle of blame, conflict, anger and bitterness. Our temperament and early patterning are the main determinants of whether we respond to this cycle by flight or by fighting.

In his treatment of community making and peace, the psychiatrist M. Scott Peck outlines a dynamic of response to differences that he has found in therapy groups over the years. People's initial response as they discovered their differences was a determination to deny or overlook them. The resulting behavior was the artificial niceness, mentioned near the beginning of this chapter, that Peck calls "pseudocommunity". This is superficial, utterly inauthentic behavior, based on sweeping differences— sometimes deeply felt differences—under the rug for the sake of an appearance of compatibility or agreement.

It's possible to read the above excerpts in a way that supports such behavior. We can take being "clothed in heartfelt compassion, in generosity and humility, gentleness and patience ... [and] love" as advocating a superficial covering for whatever discordant feelings lie beneath the surface. We can hear the exhortations, "Be slow to speak" and "No foul word should ever cross your lips", as advocating suppression of hard feelings. Even "never let the sun set on your anger or else you will give the devil a foothold" may be read as advocating a forced and false reconciliation.

In the contemporary psychotherapeutic climate, it's often felt that the only way through the tumultuous feelings that can arise in circumstances of conflict is to act them out, or at least vent them, if we're not to create problems by suppressing them or by letting them explode. Among Friends, who place high value on peace, harmony and unity—and see conflict as a symptom of being "out of the Life"—venting is felt to be unloving and self-indulgent. The alternative response is often to create artificial peace, brittle pseudocommunity, by suppressing anger or by withdrawing from the situation.

Such efforts are not mere hypocrisy but often a sincere and painstakingly disciplined, if misguided, effort to preserve harmony in a community where discord is felt to be unacceptable. Suppression of anger is, as one Friend puts it, the underside of our vision of oneness. The peace it preserves is superficial, often fragile. It can be sustained only if we keep our relationships superficial, distant, relatively uncaring or uncommitted. More often this peace or pseudocommunity is the precursor of covert hostility, passive aggression or an explosion when the stress of containing anger finally becomes overwhelming. Alas, like much that passes for peaceableness among us, it is more a matter of dodging conflict than of the authentic peace that is the fruit of the Spirit.

In Peck's natural history of community making, he sees no way through our differences other than through the condition he calls "chaos". The evolution he has seen reenacted over and over in his groups has been that eventually the strain of suppressing differences through the behaviors of pseudocommunity becomes insupportable. One or more members of the group will finally feel driven to make themselves more comfortable by trying to make over in his or her own image those people who are uncomfortably different: by healing, fixing, saving, converting or otherwise straightening them out. As others resist or retaliate, a chaotic condition arises in which each person is either withdrawing or fighting for control on some level or another. There is no longer an appearance of community or even coherence.

In spite of the high value Friends place on harmony, I've lived through this condition in meetings I've loved and been part of. Once it went on for two years. I'm talking about fighting, about a relentless insistence on one's own way that grants no quarter—much less the possibility of moral integrity—to the other view. Here and there I've seen most of the shades of manipulation, vehement confrontation and bland coerciveness. Peck feels it's necessary to let the chaos work itself out, wear itself out, empty itself of energy and of the hope of having its own way. He calls this impasse which is born of exhaustion "emptying". In being emptied of our own projects, plans and views; of our claims to intellectual, moral or spiritual rightness; of our certainty of bearing the prophetic word of God in this matter—we find there arises the possibility of hearing, or being willing to hear, a voice other than our own. In the hearing, community is born.

It would seem that Peck is right about the natural order of things. Our cherished differences will become emotionally unbearable. The excruciating, chaotic process of fighting exhausts our self-will. Fighting empties our self-will sufficiently to extend our horizon, so we can begin to find the center of the universe somewhere outside ourselves, to find the Light in which we can hold things. It is a hard, bitter way to become fitted to enter into more authentic mutualities, reciprocities and harmonies of life committed to community with others. It may be the only way in the natural order of things.

I believe there is a better way in our tradition. Embedded in the hard-won and long-tested traditions of Quaker practice, there is the possibility of a more direct way to emptying. It lies in our practice of intentionally being open to what is, of being attentive to difference, to listening for what underlies it in ourselves, in others, and in the Spirit moving between us. This means we *begin* by intentionally emptying ourselves to wait on, rather than avoid, the excruciating pain of living with and listening to people whose views, stance, preferences and very way of being are different from and challenging to our own. When we are sufficiently prayerfully opened, we are tendered by what we hear. We often find the error of our preconceptions and have our boundaries of acceptability extended. We can grow more deeply into a sense of our common humanity and seek the way to allow the humanity of all parties to be stretched in love.

It is important to cultivate the return to listening when we find ourselves confronted with hard differences. It is in the midst of such listening—holding differences in the Light, finding the gifts in them and the way beyond the differences—that Friends have found it possible to receive community as a gift from God they cannot achieve by their own resources.

If we are to learn to open ourselves to the gift of peace among us, there are other parts of our tradition we must take care not to trivialize or secularize. First of all, we must become more careful about the precise nature of the harmony and unity we seek. It is not mere decorum. Peace is a fruit of the Spirit, not of proper behavior. It is not what Dietrich Bonhoeffer called "cheap grace", won simply by having good intentions and being nice.

Secondly, as in the analogy of marriage, we must not expect that life together will always be peaceful or without differences. Even anger is sometimes legitimate. If we are truly, humbly respectful of what really is, we can count on having painful, upsetting differences. Spiritual maturity requires a commitment to face them with a minimum of fear and bitterness.

It's impossible to undertake never to differ or be angry. Our spiritual responsibility is to acknowledge our differences within the context of serious commitment both to one another and to finding our way to authentic unity even when there is no apparent way. If we do not have faith in this possibility or are too impatient to wait on its unfolding, we will be driven back on purely human solutions: fight, flight or negotiated settlement. If we can stay with the reality of the difference and allow its unfolding without rancor, the painful crucifixion of our wills may be crowned with resurrection. We may not escape without anger; but we need not allow our actions to take their shape from it. We may be given deeper insight into whatever is at issue, personal growth beyond some enslaved behaviors, and more profound intimacy with those who have endured the discipline with us. We may receive peace and harmony as a gift.

The way does not lie through venting our anger, letting it all hang out in a fight, or in acting on the desire to take revenge or to "teach someone a lesson". It lies in acknowledging and exploring, inwardly and with others, our anger and what it tells us—precisely in the context of our faith and hope in the possibility that we will be guided into harmony and love. The way lies through our willingness to shift the focus of our attention and listening from ourselves to the Spirit of God.

We can renew our commitment to one another in the disciplined practice of humble listening to one another. Our humility lies in submission to the reality that hard differences, and conflicting views or desires are part of the human condition. Our differences aren't a matter for shame or guilt unless we are unwilling to learn from them and move beyond them. It's our glory and surely God's intention that we are inevitably different. No two galaxies or snow flakes are the same. Each has its place in the midst of differences and it's to the glory of God that we find our way through differences into harmony with one another and with God's will.

We begin by listening, listening in humility before what is: not to critique, argue or refute, but to hear at the most profound level what is on one another's heart, and to be heard. We listen—and are listened to—in trust that it's natural and inevitable to differ and to be angry when we can't have things as we think they should be; and that differing need not alienate us from one another. We breathe deeply and allow ourselves to open to the truth of each other's being in God beneath the words. We listen in confidence that God can and will bring something out of our faithfulness to this listening, although it may not happen all at once. It may be that we need to learn something different from what we had thought was the object of the exercise. It may be that we need time to let a shift take place in our depths, or for us to begin to be willing to let a shift take place. Occasionally, one of us will find it's right to give way to the other. It's much more likely that both will come to know *how they must give way to each other*.

It's been my own experience, and that of many others, that listening in this way opens us to a new respect, tenderness and even love for the person we attend to. Hearing under the words can lead us to a better grasp of the intellectual and moral integrity of the other. It can also carry us to a more profound sense of the reality of the other as a subjective entity like ourselves, as another manifestation of the infinite diversity and mercy of God. With that as a ground, our relationship can never be the same.

As for myself, the special, graced times when I have been listened to in this way, the times when I have been the recipient of this attention empty of preconceptions, prejudice and desire to change me have been my most profound experiences of being loved. The love with which God loves me seems to flow through the transparent intentionality of my friend to me. I am filled with gratitude and reciprocal love even at the remembrance.

The listener's very relinquishment of any desire to heal, fix, save, convert or straighten me out allows me to speak and to hear myself, without the need to defend my position, myself, my sense of rightness or my integrity. Paradoxically, the freedom to speak and hear myself in this undefended way is what has sometimes allowed me to hear what needs to be changed in myself and to begin to let go of it or change it. Sometimes, in the spaciousness of that open listening, the view, of which I have been possessed, simply seems to have been struck off like manacles. I am free of it, free to receive some new thing that may arise between us.

The new thing will not necessarily be an agreement of views. There are inevitably different perspectives on some issues. On some issues, the truth embraces contradiction and paradox. Listening, however, can help us go below dichotomies to deeper truth, can open us to the grace that will restore our mutual respect, love and harmony to allow us to go forward together. It can help us to let go of whatever stands in the way of going forward together.

All these challenges—letting go of whatever stands in the way of going forward together; emptying of rancor and bitterness; giving over unalterably fixed views— amount to nothing less than forgiveness. So often, forgiveness is thought of as a kind of absolution granted from a position on high. Such forgiveness isn't forgiveness at all. It condescends from a prideful sense of being right and clings to—insists on—the other's being wrong. It cannot be called forgiveness if it preserves divisions, superiorities and inferiorities, and defends the state of affairs from which all the trouble began. True forgiveness is another face of reconciliation, peace making or binding up whatever has been broken in the world. True forgiveness is much more costly to the self, as well as more healing, than absolution born of condescension.

People sometimes speak with shocking glibness of forgiveness and enemy love. They are perhaps the hardest things in the world. They are superhuman tasks which—like marriage or community—we can manage only with divine assistance. Yet the above passage from Colossians tells us this love and peace are precisely our tasks: "... it is for this that you were called together in one body."

Both Colossians and Ephesians tell us we are to forgive because God has forgiven us. They conjure an image in which the Spirit flows into us as the forgiveness with which we have been forgiven, and through us as the forgiveness with which we forgive—just as the love with which we love is that with which we have been loved. Just so the prayer we pray is the Spirit praying in us that we may be joined to one another and to God in perfect reconciliation, love and peace. Somehow in the passage through us of forgiveness, love and reconciling prayer, the transformative work of the Spirit takes place—healing, purifying, saving us from ourselves, our pasts and the deformations of the world.

It is all a work of grace to which we are invited, in which we may participate, with which we may cooperate in co-creating a new order of being. The cost is opening ourselves to the forgiveness that heals us and enables us to give over our strongly held views. The cost is to give over that pride which is our pernicious need to be right, or superior, or in control—everything that alienates us from one another and from God. This struggle takes place whenever we find ourselves experiencing antipathies, disapproval, distress or enmity toward another. Wherever there is alienation, judgmentalism or unlove, there is an opening for God's healing and reconciling love, if we will turn toward it and open to it. It is in reconciliation of differences and healing of offenses within the community that we find the primary exercise of the peace testimony (Cronk).

To forgive, to reconcile, to make peace, to find our unity at a level beneath our differences is to be faithful to our experience of the Divine Center within. To forgive is to pass through the center of ourselves and beyond. It is to be gathered together into the Divine Center and know that we are gathered. It is to taste to the full the loving implications and ethical imperatives of our gathering. Sometimes nothing will do but to throw ourselves on the mercy of God and ask to be permitted to experience being gathered into immediacy and truth.

Sometimes it is enough to remember having been gathered. The abundance of Life in the memory alone may be sufficient to pull us out of the constriction of our own egos and open our eyes and ears in tenderness for the living reality of one another. When even the remembrance of gathering feels beyond us, it can be sufficient to renew our intention to live out our knowledge of gatheredness by humbly listening.

Queries

Who are the people in your community with whom you would not have chosen to live? Have you found yourself in the conflict avoidance and pain-ignoring of pseudo-community with them? Are you attempting to heal, fix, save, convert or argue them into the blessedness of being more like you? Is there someone with whom you have struggled through these conditions and come to be able to cherish in her or his difference?

Are you able to be the first to forgive and seek reconciliation, even when you feel innocent of fault? What is required before you can forgive someone? Possibly more difficult: what is required before you can ask for or accept forgiveness from someone else? Can you ask for or accept forgiveness from God? Do you feel that you require forgiving at all? What does being forgiven mean to you? How does it work for you? It might be fruitful for you to journal in detail about your responses and motivations in one relationship involving forgiveness.

In the passage from Colossians the communal virtues are stressed again, this time with an emphasis on the dimensions of love and an extraordinary statement about peace. Have you felt that it is peace for which you have been called into community? If so, what does that mean to you? Have you considered that forgiveness is a primary community virtue? ... that forgiveness is one of the ways in which we manifest the Divine Nature and our own transformed life? What do forgiveness and peace have to do with each other?

The passage from the First Letter to the Thessalonians lays greater emphasis on the spiritual community as a place of peace and peace making. Hear it in relation to the ways in which spiritual community is cultivated.

What part is purely human "community building"? Where does God's gift come in? Where is the movement of the Spirit?

What does forgiveness have to do with peace and peace-making or reconciliation? Sandra Cronk speaks of the meeting as a school for peace making. What might she mean by that? How might a school for peace making be different from what M. Scott Peck calls pseudo-community? What might it have to do with Friends' peace testimony or peace activism in the world?

Mutuality and the care of the meeting

Bearing one another's burdens

> The whole group of believers was united, heart and soul; no one claimed private ownership of any possessions, as everything they owned was held in common. ...
>
> None of their members was ever in want, as all those who owned the land or houses would sell them, and bring the money from the sale of them, to present it to the apostles; it was then distributed to any who might be in need.
>
> *Acts 4:32, 34-35. NJB*

The selection from Acts speaks of different dimensions of caring for one another. Friends have not held personal property in common; however they have taken very seriously the responsibility of caring for the needs of those in fellowship with them. In the persecutions during the English Commonwealth and Restoration, they provided for the needs of members whose goods had been seized, or for children whose parents were jailed. Being under the care of the meeting was related to the fellowship that arose from gathering and unity.

In *Friends for 300 Years*, Howard Brinton lists excerpts from the minutes of various meetings "that indicate the character of economic interdependence developed in meeting community." They include the meeting's taking responsibility for hiring a cow for a widow, purchasing warm winter clothes for someone judged poor, making restitution for losses in a fire, and "visiting every family among us where ... there is occasion to suspect they are going backward in their worldly estate." To this day, there is a fund in Philadelphia Yearly Meeting established for the relief of "Friends in Necessitous Circumstances". The fund is derived from the income of property willed to the Yearly Meeting by a Friend who had been assisted in this way. Friends have taken the blessedness of mutuality and equality with the utmost seriousness. Our life together in community, mutuality and reciprocity makes us responsible for one another.

Mutuality of receiving and giving

> ... [D]uring supper, Jesus ... rose from the table, took off his clothes and wrapped a towel around his waist. He then poured water into a basin, and began to wash the disciples' feet, and dry them with the towel that was around his waist.
>
> When Jesus came to Simon Peter, Peter said, "Rabbi, you're not going to wash my feet, are you?"
>
> Jesus answered, "You don't realize what I am doing right now, but later you'll understand."
>
> Peter replied, "You'll never wash my feet!"
>
> Jesus answered, "If I don't wash you, you have no part with me."
>
> Simon Peter said to Jesus, "Then, Rabbi, not only my feet, but my hands and my head as well!"

Jesus said, "Any who have taken a bath are clean all over and only need to wash their feet—and you're clean ...

After washing their feet, Jesus put his clothes back on and returned to the table. He said to them, "Do you understand what I have done for you? You call me "Teacher" and "Sovereign"—and rightly, for so I am. If I, then—your Teacher and Sovereign—have washed your feet, you should wash each other's feet. I have given you an example, that you should do as I have done to you.

John 13:2-10; 12-15. int

At its best, the mutuality and equality that come of oneness also eliminate the subtle ascription of superior and inferior positions to care-givers and care-receivers—the barely conscious presumption or condescension that subverts much helping in "the world". In the footwashing passage in John 13:2-15, listen carefully to Peter, who often speaks for ordinary folks in the gospels. His position is heightened by the reverence in which he holds Jesus; but he also illustrates the difficulty most of us have in accepting the loving care, the service—even the love—of anyone else.

Having been schooled to rugged individualism by the wider culture, most of us have trouble receiving help gracefully—much less asking for it, even when we are in great need. Mixed in here are feelings that our character, our adequacy, our self-worth, our very identity may inhere in self-sufficiency, in doing without whatever we cannot provide for ourselves. This kind of individualism not only denies our ultimate oneness but is destructive of it.

On the other hand, being wholly dependent upon others and unwilling to do anything for oneself also denies mutuality, and is unhealthy. There is, however, a great difference between complete dependency and interdependence or mutuality that acknowledges, fosters and expresses our sense of ultimate unity with one another in the love of God. To nurture and build up spiritual community, it is as necessary to learn to ask for help and receive it gracefully as it is to give ourselves in service to others.

I was once given the spiritual discipline of saying, "Yes, thank you," whenever someone offered me anything—no matter what. It was the most difficult and most educational spiritual practice I've experienced. It was nearly a year before I could simply draw a deep breath and control the reflexive impulse to say, "No, thanks. I can manage it myself" or "That's not necessary" or "I couldn't possibly accept. It's much too kind or generous or" ... or dozens of other demurs. In those breaths, I learned to see defensive distancing in myself. I'd responded as if I were being threatened rather than being offered a kindness. The threat, of course, was to my ego, to my tenacious, culturally-correct self-image.

Once, with the same spiritual guide who gave me this discipline, I was talking about the vision of love as the life's blood of the mystical body of which we are all part. She said, "Then how can the love circulate and nourish the whole body, if one part refuses to accept it?" It was staggering to think that this refusal of loving help could make me an occlusion in the body, rather than a useful part. It was humbling to realize that the pride implicit in my efforts at taking care of myself closed me off from the flow of Life that could sustain my own efforts to care for others.

It's so difficult to see just where pride stops being a healthy respect for ourselves as unique beings God has intentionally created. It's difficult to see where it goes over into an unhealthy effort to stand on our own, apart from the rest of the created community, from those springs through which God's love wells up for us and for others through us. It's necessary to be aware of the importance of constantly discerning the difference.

Unwholesome pride also makes us want to always occupy the position of the care-giver but never be the recipient of care. We do ourselves no spiritual good by wanting always to take the generous part while denying others opportunities to live outwardly their own generosity of spirit.

If we are to care for one another, it's fundamental that we be open to asking for—and receiving—care. Having participated in both dimensions of mutual care sensitizes us to the feelings of F/friends who are in the reciprocal role to ours at any given time. As we are helping, we know what it is like to be helped. As we are being helped, we know what it is like to give help. We can be more tender of those who are experiencing the difficulties of receiving. We can be more thoughtful of those who are extending themselves to give us help. We can learn how much we truly receive in both positions—and how much we give in both positions. In a sense, both giver and receiver are under the care of the meeting for their mutual good and their mutual learning in the School of Love.

References and resources for the spiritual dimension of community

Full publication information is in the Bibliography at the end of this book. For abbreviations, see p. xix.

London Yearly Meeting.
Christian faith and practice in the experience of the Society of Friends.
1972. ch. 7: #320-324 self discipline; 365-375 membership.

London Yearly Meeting.
Church government.
ch. 23: #831-834; Membership; 844-846; Termination of membership.
ch. 26: #881-884; 894; 906-907; Marriage.
ch. 27: #931-934; Burials and cremations.
ch. 28: #941-944; Outward affairs: wills, oaths and legal action by Friends.
ch. 29: #951-953; 956; Finance.
ch. 30: The meeting and its members.

Hugh Barbour, ed.
Margaret Fell Speaking.
PHP #206. pp. 24-25.

Dietrich Bonhoeffer.
Life Together: a discussion of Christian fellowship.
esp. chs. 4-5.

Dietrich Bonhoeffer.
The Cost of Discipleship.
ch. 1, esp. p. 45.

Howard Brinton.
Friends for 300 Years.
pp. 127-28.

Howard Brinton.
The Quaker Doctrine of Inward Peace.
PHP #44.

Sandra Cronk.
Peace Be with You: A Study of the Spiritual Basis of Friends Peace Testimony.
The Meeting as a School for Peacemaking.
pp. 23-28.

Adam Curle.
True Justice: Quaker Peace makers and Peace making.
pp. 56-63.

Richard Foster.
"The Agony and the Ecstasy".
Faith at Work.
May/June 1987.

Damon Hickey.
Unforeseen Joy: Serving a Friends Meeting As Recording Clerk.
pp. 5-6.

David Holden.
Friends Divided: Conflict and Division in the Society of Friends.

Thomas Kelly.
"The Blessed Community",
in *The Eternal Promise.*
p. 72-89, p. 81.

M. Scott Peck.
The Different Drum: Community Making and Peace.
esp. ch. V, pp. 86-90.

Andrew Bard Schmookler.
Sowing and Reaping: the cycling of good and evil in human systems.

David Spangler.
The Call.

Douglas Steere.
Where Words Come From.
esp. pp. 1-27.

Lloyd Lee Wilson.
Essays on the Quaker Vision of Gospel Order.
The Meeting as Covenant Community.

Chapter 3

Discernment: the Heart of Listening Spirituality

Discernment of spirits and Divine Guidance

Introduction

This chapter is divided roughly into three parts. The first part discusses primarily but not exclusively the nature of discernment which is the heart of "listening" in this book and, in my opinion, the heart of Quaker spirituality. The second part discusses some of the practical ways in which discernment or listening is pervasive in meeting life and the conduct of business. The third part is an example, drawn from the *Journal* of John Woolman, of the way in which a leading may be discerned and grow into a concern that may draw others to get under its weight until ultimately it becomes part of the Quaker testimony to the Truth of the relationships of God and humans, and of humans with one another.

In his list of gifts useful for building up the church in I Corinthians 12:8-10 Paul includes the gift translated by the *inclusive new testament* as "distinguishing one spirit from another." Distinguishing or discerning spirits has had a variety of interpretations in Christian theology. Some interpretations have focused on distinguishing between evil and good.

Among Friends the power to make spiritual distinctions has focused less on good and evil than on the central importance of right discernment of Divine Guidance and in discerning God-given gifts, leadings, work and roles among us. In a "listening spirituality"—without the guidance of dogma, catechisms and liturgies—our individual and corporate ability to discern, distinguish or sift Divine Guidance from other promptings is critical. Rather than drawing a dualistic, yes/no distinction beween good and evil, Quaker spirituality demands of us a commitment to a much more subtle and strenuous effort to discriminate movements of the Spirit among the complex motivations, forces and dimensions of experience within and around us.

In the New Testament mingling of psychology, sociology and spirituality, "spirits" often refers to the source or motivation of an impulse or urge. To distinguish the spirits in motivations is to discern where particular impulses come from: whether from various kinds of social conditioning and pressure, from the deformed needs, desires or fears of the unhealed self—or from the Love that is the gift of the Spirit and can work through each of us for all of us.

With more sophistication in modern psychology, we are less apt than either the early church or early Friends to expect totally pure motives from one another. Our embodiment of the Spirit for one another is always in process, imperfect, growing. Our history has taught us over and over again how far we may stray from Paul's portrait of the patient, forbearing love necessary for life in community (I Cor. 13) when we attempt to hold one another to rigorous standards of purity. Indeed, the failure of love over against judgmentalism seems to be the distinctive flaw of the churches of the radical Reformation. Their demands for purity can become the shadow side, if you will, of their great aspiration for a life of perfect discipleship.

Today, we are more apt to be compassionate toward each other's imperfections, at least when others seem committed to cooperating with the Spirit's maturing work in them. Yet, the desire to be tolerant is misguided if it leads us to abandon spiritual responsibility by willfully refusing to discern or distinguish where things are coming from among us. Such abandonment can damage rather than build up our life together.

Discerning a dynamic rather than a map or plan

Among earlier Friends, faithful responsiveness to inward prompting was experienced as obedience to the requirements of a transcendent, yet utterly present, deity. In the twentieth century, the response has often been felt more nearly as cooperation—sometimes articulated as co-creation—with God. Co-creation implies a still unfolding creation in which the Creator continues to work with and through us when we respond in faithfulness to the promptings of Love and Truth in our hearts.

Both interpretations reflect Friends' felt sense of the Divine as a dynamism rather than as an entity. By and large, Friends have sensed God not only beyond history but also moving within history and nature—rather than standing outside and giving orders, pulling strings or whispering instructions in order to stage-manage history. The sense of the dynamic, ongoing work of God within and through us and the rest of creation is part of the Quaker experience of "God with us". Friends have expressed this as God among us, within us, moving with us, moving us with God's own self, through the complex situations and interactions of life, nature and history.

In one of Thomas Merton's taped talks to novices in the Cistercian monastery at Gethsemani, he speaks to his students of the idea people often have that God stands totally outside time. Such a God is often thought to have constructed a detailed plan of what is to happen, or what we are to do in our lives, or a map of where each of us is to go. He jokes with his students that they waste a lot of time thinking the map is in a drawer somewhere and all they have to do is find the drawer and see what they are supposed to do, how their lives are supposed to unfold.

He tells them there is no map or pre-designed divine plan. Rather the movement of the Spirit is unfolding in a kind of great improvisation in every instant as history goes on. We participate by moving with the dynamism, Spirit or Life, trying to discern the direction of the movement and to stay with it. Our cooperation or lack of it is part of the creation of the next instant.

In Quaker tradition, this effort to "stay with it" is evident in the classic Quaker vocabulary of waiting for Way to Open, seeing where Way is Opening, following Way Opening. Implicit in this phrase is a sense of unfoldment in and of time, in which we are called to take part by feeling, by being alive to, the movement and the way it draws us. The capacity to distinguish this movement of the Spirit from impulses arising elsewhere is among the "gifts of the Spirit" that Paul lists. It is also invited, cultivated and lived into by the disciplined practice of living close to God over time in prayer.

Motions, leadings or concerns versus principles or values

Spiritual discernment is the primary, underlying stratum of the "listening" on which this book focuses. It is the same gift or capacity whether it's functioning in personal prayer practices, in discernment of true leadings, or in corporate practice of worship, ministry, pastoral care, or the conduct of business. It is a growing ability to distinguish the spiritual intentionality, directionality of being, or tropism toward God in ourselves, in words, or in a speaker, from other impulses, words or speakers that are perhaps worthy but arise from a different source. The inability to distinguish the Spirit was surely one of the factors that led to the chaos in the church in Corinth that Paul addressed. This insensitivity to distinguishing the spirit impelling us is also a plague in many Friends meetings today.

The leading to speak in meeting—or "appear in the ministry", as it was traditionally called—is only one of the innumerable ways in which Friends have felt led, moved or drawn by the Spirit. The fullest Quaker life would be one lived in attentive listening for the murmurings of the "still, small voice" (I Kings 19:13 KJV) in all dimensions of life. Movement into service of any kind traditionally has not been a matter of personal desire or a career decision but the result of a concern laid upon the heart. It is not momentary. It won't go away until it has been satisfied.

This has been true of service either within the meeting or in "the world". There is much talk today of "Quaker principles or values" as a kind of general set of rules against which Friends might measure themselves or a proposed activity. Earlier Friends, did not deduce their service from established principles or laws. Like Paul, they felt liberated from rules and laws into the freedom to follow the Spirit of God. A leading into service was a matter of "living" concern sometimes experienced as a particular "charge" or "burden" in an equally particular matter, given to them personally, of which they must clear themselves before they could find peace. Notice the intuitive, physical or visceral vocabulary that Friends have traditionally used to express their discernments.

Intuition versus technique

The question was how to determine whether the prompting was in fact a "living concern", a true leading of the Spirit, an authentic charge from God—whether it had Life in it. If analysis and deduction from principle are not adequate to determine whether one is in harmony with Divine Will or guidance, then how can one be sure? So much havoc and pain have been wreaked in the world by people who were certain they were performing God's will that it's very important to have safeguards for the process of distinguishing a true leading from a false one. Yet it is part of Quaker experience and tradition that discernment is a matter of intuition, rather than technique, and human intuition is notably fallible.

Thomas Green is a Jesuit, whose order is much given to matters of discernment, albeit in a somewhat different manner from Friends. He likens discernment to the way his mother learned how to buy neckties for his father over the years. After much trial and error, she began to get a feel for what impulses to follow if she wanted the tie to be worn rather than to languish in the back of the closet—a feel for what would please him rather than satisfy some other intention she might have for him and his ties. In short, she developed a capacity for discerning what would be pleasing to her husband, just as a Quaker hopes to develop and be guided by a capacity for discerning what is pleasing to God.

Another purely secular analogy to spiritual discernment is an "ear" for music or an "eye" in the arts. On a crude level, it is artistic discernment or feeling that enables us, when we have looked enough, to distinguish a Rembrandt from a Raphael. With very intense looking over time, we might even come to distinguish a true Rembrandt from a fake one. With enough listening we know reflexively a symphony by Tchaikovsky from one by Beethoven. Over time we may come to be able to distinguish among works by a given composer, or the orchestras playing them, the influences or nuances in the interpretations, true or false notes. These are kinds of artistic discernment, born of long attentiveness in the medium that draws us.

My favorite story about secular discernment was told me years ago by Helen Waldo, a gifted elementary school teacher who had taught my son. Helen told me of

a man who had worked successfully for many years to acquire a fortune. He finally felt he had riches enough to put aside time for something different, that he had long wanted to do. Accustomed to being able to afford and command the best, he sought out the person who had the greatest reputation for his knowledge of jade. He offered him as much money as he wanted to teach him about the stone and the work done in it.

After much persuasion, the connoisseur finally agreed. The two arranged that the wealthy man would come one night a week for an indefinite period to learn about jade. When the wealthy man arrived for the first meeting, the connoisseur took his coat and hat, led him to a room unfurnished except for a table, a chair, a lamp and a small silk pouch—and left him. When the millionaire opened the pouch, there was a stone inside that he knew must be jade. To his surprise, he was left alone in the room with the stone for a long time. When the connoisseur finally returned, he brought the man's coat and hat, put the stone back in the pouch and escorted his student to the door, bidding him farewell until the next week.

The next week, the student of jade was treated in the same way except that the stone was a different one. And so it went on for some time. Often he would not even see the connoisseur, but would be admitted and escorted out by a servant, always left alone in the bare room with a different stone.

At last the millionaire could contain his outrage at this treatment no longer. As he left one evening, he complained to the connoisseur, "I am paying you a very large sum of money for instruction in jade; and you have barely spoken a word to me in all this time, much less taught me about the types of jade, the ways of working it, the various artistic traditions and periods. Now, to cap the whole fraud, the stone you gave me tonight wasn't even jade!"

The connoisseur just smiled—and finally the wealthy man understood that learning jade was not a matter of a course of instruction or cognitive understanding.

Earlier Friends often spoke of "feeling after" Truth, which is analogous to the above secular examples of developing "an intuitive feel" for some kind of object, situation or work. It is a non-inductive kind of knowledge born of intimate experience. As an analog to Thomas Green's mother and the neckties, the discernment that we hope to develop or be granted as a gift is a feel for what is pleasing to God. As an analog to the aesthete's ear or eye, we hope to develop an ability to sense the sacred or secular origins of diverse things. As an analog to the connoisseurship of jade, we long to know the real thing when we confront it. This sense seems to be a gift that comes of disciplined faithfulness in our relationship with God. That happens only out of long, intimate acquaintance with the Divine in prayer and worship, as Green's mother had with her husband in her marriage, as the aesthete has from years of attentive looking or listening or as the millionaire had through intimate familiarity with the look and feel of real jade.

The gift can develop by trial and error, as John Woolman relates of his early response to a call to minister and his chagrin when he realized he'd gone beyond what was required of him and expounded his own ideas. Others also relate their experiences in suppressing the call to speak with subsequent internal suffering or even reproach by "connoisseurs" in the meeting who had the capacity to discern that they had failed to respond to a true leading to speak (Woolman; Bacon). These Friends took very seriously the prospect that—as they lived closer to the transforming Light of God—they would grow in their capacity to discern for themselves what is the will of God, what is good, acceptable and mature (or "perfect", as the King James Version translates it).

The main theme of the Letter to the Galatians is the contrast between a life lived in Christ, and a life lived by laws and rules. Galatians and the Letter to the Romans, are the great encouragements to the strenuous life lived in response to the Spirit's guidance.

Fruit of the Spirit, Life, and other tests of leadings

Caution is important if we are not to mistake every inward impulse for spiritual guidance. The positive counterpart of caution is encouragement to grow into the "fruit of the Spirit". The fruit of the Spirit are described in Galatians 5:13-26 quoted in the previous chapter. This passage distinguishes the difference between the true freedom that the guidance of the Spirit brings and the illusory freedom of self-indulgence. Self-indulgence—far from freedom—usually involves permitting ourselves to be overmastered, controlled or even compelled by our desires or other passing emotions (Gal. 5:16 NJB, int). Self-indulgence or overmastering desires are also sometimes translated as "self". The traditional translation, "flesh", is misleading in modern English.

"Fruit of the Spirit" is not meant as yet another set of laws or rules to live by. Rather the fruit are the evidence we are to seek for the presence of the Spirit of Christ in our feelings, in a situation, or in the outcome of a course of action. Friends and others have taken these fruits as authenticating signs of the presence and the leadings of the Spirit in a given instance.

Although ultimately leadings are intuited in a listening spirituality, Friends and others have used some safeguards to test an individual's sense of divine guidance. Paul mentions two kinds of gifts. First, there are the graced natural abilities or talents required for the functioning of the spiritual community. Second, there are the spiritual gifts or the fruits—faith, hope and love—that hold the multifaceted life together, keep it going and give it possibilities and dimensions of meaning and worth, beyond those of a well-run institution or business. The spiritual gifts or fruits of the Spirit have often been used as tests of the authenticity of a leading, whether into vocal ministry or some other kind of ministry or guidance.

The "fruit of the Spirit", listed in Galatians 5:22-23, is an expanded version of faith, hope and love in I Corinthians. The *inclusive new testament* translates the fruit of the

Spirit as "love, joy, peace, patient endurance, kindness, generosity, faithfulness, gentleness and self-control." It contrasts this list with all manner of self-indulgence, going on to say,

> Those who belong to Christ Jesus have crucified their ego, with its passions and desires. So, since we live by the Spirit, let us follow her lead. We must stop being conceited, contentious and envious.
>
> *Galatians 5:24-26. int*

Crucifixion of self, self-will or ego was certainly part of the early Quaker sense of how one comes to live in the Spirit. Testing our leadings or their potential outcomes against these fruits, we begin with love as the first fruit. The question is, "Does this action spring from, express or increase the Love of God in the world?" Giving over ego, passions and desires is certainly one rule of thumb for discernment of a leading.

Another old, Biblical Quaker test of a leading is, "Is there Life in it?" This touchstone is in accord with the Old Testament commandment to "choose Life!" as that which is in harmony with the will of God. "Choose Life!" also accords with the New Testament sense of the Spirit as bringing or leading us into New Life in love and harmony with God and one another. We must be careful to distinguish or discern this sense of Life from the vitality and excitement that can come from participation in a group. The latter are not to be despised, but may not be adequate as a test of Life (Deut. 30:15-20, esp. 20, and Paul, *passim*).

Another way Quaker traveling ministers of the eighteenth and early nineteenth centuries tested the authenticity of their leadings was by wrestling with them as Jacob is said to have done with an angel in Genesis 32:22-33. The journals of these ministers record many struggles against an impulse to minister, whether it was a general leading to minister vocally, a leading to travel in a particular ministry, or a sense of guidance to visit some particular meeting or to deliver some especially hard message. Sometimes the minister's resistance went on until he or she became seriously ill before yielding to the leading as being authentically of God (Bacon).

One element in this wrestling was often holding in the Light a concern for the needs of spouses and children. Another was the awe in which ministry was held. This awe led to questioning seriously whether the minister was actually fitted for service in light of his or her awareness of shortcomings and human failures. To yield too readily to the impulse might indicate that the impulse was born of human need or desire rather than a sense of how the Spirit was moving in the meeting. To wrestle with all one's strength against it, like Jacob wrestling with the angel, might result not only in illness but in blessing as a servant of God.

None of these tests is a substitute for that connoisseurship of the Spirit, the Grace-given, time-tested power to distinguish intuitively what comes of God and what comes of our purely human needs, desires and fears. The ability to discern true jade from false comes only as a result of having spent significant time with the real thing. When we can say with honesty that we have spent that time, then we will have some touch-stone experiences to help us discern the signs of the Spirit of Christ working in us from all the other things that work in us. We can compare our experiences of later knowing, as Woolman did, that we've made a mistake, with experiences of later receiving the "penny of peace" that some Friends felt was the reward of faithful servants in the vineyard at the end of the day (Matt. 20:1-16).

Sensitivity to changes: new openings in leadings, ministry or mission

When one lives in confidence of the presence and guidance of God in all the vicissi-tudes of life, discernment is not a one-shot experience focused on some major turning point. If we are faithful to the guidance we are given, it is an ongoing process in which we may grow into more and more sensitivity to the "drawings in the mind", "the promptings of Love and Truth in the heart", "the nudges of the Spirit", "the require-ments of God" in our daily lives.

That means we need to develop the capacity to be flexible, to bend with the winds of the Spirit, to change course and chart new territory as Way Opens before us, slams shut behind us or in our faces, or takes the occasional sharp turn to left or right. Lloyd Swift observes that many elderly Friends show a grace-ful flexibility that has grown over a lifetime of bowing to the leadings of the Spirit against their own personal proclivities.

Among Friends a ministry is usually very particular, and defined by circumstances. As a rule, it has a beginning, a middle and an end—although those are usually only discernable as they arise rather than as part of a projected plan with pre-set limits. The important thing is to keep discerning "whether there is still Life in it", rather than letting it become a "dead form" running on like a juggernaut.

When the Life is exhausted, when the charge is fulfilled, when the burden is discharged, we can say with George Fox, "I am clear of it." We can lay it down and await the next thing, confident that God's work goes on. If we are faithful servants, we are bound to be called upon for some new, perhaps unexpected service that may be different from what we have been led to before. The willingness to be guided by the Light, to discern and be faithful are what must remain the same. I remember a question period in which Douglas Steere once spoke quite movingly of having a clear sense of leading into a particular action that appeared right to himself and others. Yet the plan never came to fruition in spite of their best efforts. Only in retrospect did he see that out of that aborted mission had grown the shoots and tendrils of another totally unanticipated action that turned out to be full of Life and spiritual fulfillment.

Queries

Do you seek the will of God in all things? ... some things? ... sometimes? What governs your desire? Do you find yourself impatient with those who fail to see your point of view? ... impatient with waiting to come to unity? ... impatient to get on with it?

Have you experienced being led, in any way, by the Divine? Is there something within your experience, without which you would not feel led to act? Is there something, the presence of which would fill you with confidence? Examine your experience of those times when you have felt sure of your inward guidance. Have you continued to feel sure of your leading as the experience was played out? If so, see whether you can identify any characteristics of the experience which might be a touchstone of authenticity for you.

Can you find the evidences of the "fruit of the Spirit" in your touchstone experiences? It could be useful to record your findings in your journal.

Structures for discernment

Nurturing the spiritual life of the meeting

Even before there were formal monthly meetings organized for the conduct of local business, there were meetings of those who served as ministers and elders, although they did not yet have this name. They were not without agenda. They parcelled out among themselves the responsibility for vocal ministry among the various meetings in the period of rapid growth in Quakerism. However, the purpose of their coming together was to worship. In some sense, they "met to meet" in openness to whatever the Spirit would draw forth. Their concerns for the care of the meeting and the attendant business arose and were discerned out of the silence. These were certainly part of the genesis of the later meetings for business in the monthly meetings. Note, however, that such meetings for business took place not among the general membership but among those with a special calling to care for the meeting as ministers or elders.

In time, some meetings separated the elders' responsibilities for the spiritual life of the meeting from their responsibility for the pastoral care of the meeting—for the material and moral life of the members. This gave rise to parallel Committees of Overseers and Committees for Worship and Ministry. In other cases the responsibilities remained together under Committees for Ministry and Counsel, or Ministry and Oversight. In all cases, it was understood that the purpose was to meet together to feel the concerns for the life of the meeting arise and to discern what was authentically laid upon them by the Holy Spirit and what might have more human origins.

Vocal ministry

Over time and geography, Friends have made various provisions for the nurture of the spiritual life of the meeting. The particular responsibility for building up the community was originally seen to rest with vocal ministers. These men and women were inwardly called by God to a sometimes itinerant preaching and teaching ministry. Occasionally there was some formal discernment of spirits, modeled to a degree on the apostolic preaching portrayed in the Book of Acts and implicit in the authentic Pauline letters.

Considered from the standpoint of discernment, the most important dimension of vocal ministry to be addressed is the seriousness with which Friends have traditionally taken an utterance in meeting for worship. Until late in this century, every effort was made to safeguard vocal ministry as a prompting of the Holy Spirit for the good of the community. This required discernment or distinguishing of the "spirits", motivations or sources of the impulse to speak. Mere desire, agitation or aptness of thought was inadequate reason to risk breaking rather than fulfilling the silence. The service of the vocal ministers was not only to bring words to the meeting, but to discern where the words were coming from before permitting themselves to rise to speak. In case of doubt, they restrained the impulse to speak no matter how *à propos* the message.

Elders

The discernment performed by elders was present among Friends from the very beginning even though elders were not formally named. Soon however, elders took their place alongside the ministers—both in the early church and among Friends who saw themselves as "primitive Christianity revived". In both cases, this development took place as the dynamic early movement settled into an institution and began to be assimilated to the repectabilities of the wider society around them. In the case of Christianity, this was the society of late antiquity; in the case of the Religious Society of Friends, it was Restoration England (Fiorenza; Gwyn).

As meetings became settled, elders performed a variety of functions, according to their gifts and leadings. Some elders were primarily nurturers and companions of ministers. Some had a more discerning role, encouraging and guiding people "young" in the ministry, and discouraging people whose ministry did not seem to come from the Center. Other elders functioned primarily in relation to the meeting as a whole, some taking on various dimensions of pastoral care. Some felt led to nurture the spiritual lives of individual members in ways outside the vocal ministry, perhaps by spiritual counsel, by prayer in and for the meeting, by nurturing the spiritual lives of children or in other ways.

In any case, all gifts and ministries were for building up the spiritual life of the meeting and the Society: directing and re-directing people to the Spirit of God, to the Inward Christ, the Light, the Inward Teacher, the Guide, the one true Priest and Shepherd. It was clearly understood that any member of the meeting might be called to some part of this service, but that some were specifically led by the Spirit at any given time. Some were called more often so that the meeting recognized and named their calling.

Discernment of spiritual gifts and leadings was not left to the individual who felt led, but was the work of elders who nurtured, encouraged and discouraged fledgings. Just as "wanting to" do some service is not enough, it may also not be valid to hold back from service out of timidity or feelings of unworthiness. A gifted elder might be able to name an emergent gift, as yet undeveloped, that—with nurturing—can grow to fullness in God's service. Eventually the meetings of elders and ministers recorded the names of those whose gifts and ministry consistently bore marks of authenticity over time.

Queries

Do you feel any leading into building up the spiritual life of the meeting? If so, how does that manifest itself in you? Into what kind of nurture are you led? Have you discerned this in company with others with a gift of discernment? ... possibly with others who have more spiritual maturity than yourself?

Are you aware of anyone in your meeting who seems to have a gift for building up the spiritual life of the meeting? How does that manifest itself? How does this person prepare or open him or herself to this ministry? How does the meeting support the right use of this gift?

References and resources for nurturing the spiritual life of the meeting

Friends Consultation on Eldering.
Quaker Hill, 1985.

London Yearly Meeting.
Christian faith and practice in the experience of the Society of Friends.
ch. 24: #854-860; Eldership and oversight: the common responsibility.

Margaret Hope Bacon, ed.
Wilt Thou Go on My Errand? Three 18th Century Journals of Quaker Women Ministers.
passim.

Sandra Cronk.
Gospel Order.
PHP #297.

Suzanne Farnham, *et. al.*
Listening Hearts: Discerning Call into Community.

Elisabeth Schüssler Fiorenza.
In Memory of Her: A Feminist Theological Reconstruction of Christian Origins.
esp. Part 3.

Thomas H. Green.
Weeds among the Wheat: Discernment, Where Prayer and Action Meet.

Douglas Gwyn.
The Covenant Crucified: Quakerism and the Rise of Capitalism.
passim.

Jan Hoffman.
Clearness Committees and their Use in Personal Discernment.

Patricia Loring.
Spiritual Discernment: the context and goal of clearness committees.
PHP #305.

Parker Palmer.
"The Clearness Committee: A Way of Discernment".
Weavings.
(July/August 1988). pp. 37-40.

Lloyd Swift.
"On Discipline".
FJ. March 1989. pp. 6-7.

Jan Wood.
"Spiritual Discernment: the Personal Dimension".
CD.

John Woolman.
The Journal.
Moulton ed. esp. p. 31.

Attending to business
Nominating committees as structures for discernment of gifts

Committees evolved from groups of people who felt themselves and each other to be profoundly drawn into the nurture of meeting life. If prayerful discernment was neglected in favor of pursuing an agenda, the committee's spiritual authority could degenerate into authoritarianism. Sometimes concentration of responsibilities in the hands of a few people for life—or even passed on in families—exacerbated the situation.

More recently, partly in revulsion against the abuses of concentrated power, many meetings have turned to a universal obligation to committee membership that draws in people in all degrees of spiritual maturity and commitment. They are rotated through the various responsibilities of meeting life so that all may be seasoned in responsibility and have a perspective on all aspects of service to the meeting.

In the process we often move from appointments discerned by the community in order to answer and develop the spiritual gifts and callings of individuals, to a process of self-selection by inclination rather than discernment. This process leaves us open to being governed by personal agendas or needs, rather than by discerned guidance. Today's Friends need to focus on discerning and encouraging spiritual gifts in service of the meeting. One danger is permitting service to be automatically prolonged past authentic leading or converted into a position of a more worldly kind of power rather than of servanthood. Another danger is rotating people out of a particular service while there is still Life in their work there.

The discernment of gifts by the nominating committee for the use of the meeting is closely related to the discernment and carrying out of leadings and concerns. Leadings and concerns are usually, in some way or other, a function of the convergence of a person's God-given gifts and personal history. Both may be seen as ways in which the Light is diffused and refracted into the world through the unique configuration of individual personality. Friends found that recognition of, respect for and cherishing of individuality and differences was a way in which the Spirit carries out the numerous and various purposes of God in the community and the world. That discovery was also part of Paul's legacy to the early church. Biblical validation of their own sense of ways the Spirit moves is one of the many ways that Friends have used Biblical descriptions and exhortations to the early church as their model for church government.

Discernment of gifts requires open, prayerful attentiveness to another person: to the fullness of his or her personality, history, fears and desires. It requires distinguishing the authentic self from that self falsified by efforts to conform to the expectations of others or of society. It requires recognizing a self falsified by efforts to avoid possible failure that might come from stretching beyond present competence. It requires the same prayerful listening we have found to lie at the heart of other Quaker practice.

The object of this discernment of gifts is not career choices, affirmation of the individual, or enhancement of ego. The ultimate focus of all discernment is the will of God as dynamically revealed in the ongoing life of the person within the particular circumstances. Similarly, the purpose of the gift is not enhancement of the individual or his or her life but enhancement of spiritual community in the love of God, whether in church community or the wider society.

In present day meetings in the Friends General Conference tradition, the responsibility for this discernment of gifts and encouragement of their use in service of the meeting community generally devolves on nominating committees. Their task is frequently not understood by the meeting even when it is understood by committee members themselves. In smaller meetings, where there are barely enough people to fulfill the minimum functions, discernment often feels like a luxury. Everyone must simply pitch in if Life is to be sustained in the meeting.

Larger meetings are often located in urban areas, where people feel drawn or compelled to participate in the plethora of available outside activities and are reluctant to give themselves to committee work in the meeting. In the face of a lack of understanding of the fundamental importance of both commitment and mutuality of service in Quaker corporate life, a harrassed nominating committee often finds itself desperate to "fill slots" rather than to name gifts and open opportunities for their use in mutual service.

An additional problem with rotation of service is that often people are just beginning to understand and live into one function in the meeting when they are shunted into another (Swift). In spite of overlapping terms of service, meetings lose much corporate memory and competence in this way. Sometimes those who are truly gifted in service on one committee are arbitrarily shifted to another on which they have little to offer.

At its best, nomination to committees and offices in the meeting is a fundamental use of discernment about who we are and how God is bringing us together in the meeting.

Queries

Elizabeth O'Connor has been involved since its foundation with the Church of the Savior—a Washington DC church centered around carrying out the gifts and leadings of its members as missions. She writes of the importance of a listening, seeing person in our lives. Have you had such a person in your life? If so, how has that affected you? If not, have you learned to "listen at the altar of [your] own [life]"? How do you do that? What do you learn there? Are you able to be a listening, seeing person for others? ... for your children? How does being a listening, seeing person affect your relationships?

Jean Vanier is the French Catholic founder of L'Arche communities, in which handicapped and non-handicapped live together in mutuality and equality. He asks, have you meditated on or prayed for the gifts of others in your community? Have you felt a responsibility to evoke or affirm the gifts of others? ... anyone's in particular? Have you felt accountable to others for the use of your own gifts? ... felt able to go forward in spite of your own inadequacies? Vanier remarks on how both envy and adulation can poison the use of our gifts. Does this illuminate any of your own experiences?

How is the vision presented here of nominating people to positions different from simply asking people "what they would like to do" or from "filling slots"? What might be the difference to the meeting? ... to the person nominated? ... to God?

Do you have, in your meeting, people gifted with the ability to discern the gifts of others? Notice that even the nominating committee can use a variety of gifts and the ability to work together in mutual service.

Do you feel that your committee appointment evokes your gifts for building up the community? Do you feel stretched? ... under-used? Do you work "to the glory of God"? Does your committee work get the left-overs from a crowded life?

Meeting for business as a place of discernment

In common parlance, a distinction is sometimes made between the meeting for worship and the meeting for business. In earlier times the latter was sometimes called meeting for discipline. Among modern Friends, the corporate activity of giving one's self over individually and as a group to divine guidance is emphasized by using the formal name, the meeting for worship with attention to business. The most fully developed meeting for worship is that in which the guidance of God is overtly sought for the conduct of community affairs.

The meeting for business is a meeting for worship in which we seek to be governed as a corporate body, through the same prayerful listening that we enter in worship. In the meeting for business the Quaker sense of the connection between the interior work of the Spirit of God in both individuals and the corporate body is most fully manifested. At its best, the meeting for business is a disciplined exercise in corporate discernment of Guidance in particular matters of personal conduct, relationships and outward work. Unity is not a unity of opinion. We sense our unity when we have entered into our most profound experience as a corporate body. It sometimes has been called group mysticism. We come to know our oneness in God's presence. Our hesitations, doubts, quibbles, and agendas fall away. In that state we can see the decision or stance that expresses our fullest sense of the unity and peace of the meeting.

In his pamphlet, *Beyond Consensus*, Barry Morley develops a very helpful set of distinctions between consensus and the sense of the meeting. He distinguishes, in a variety of experiential ways, the movements of the heart in the evolution of the "sense of the meeting" traditionally sought by Friends. It helps to distinguish the traditional discernment process from the intellectual agreement or negotiated settlements resulting from discussion or from the process known as consensus. The sense of the meeting is an intuitive sense of the interior dimension of the situation. The sense of the meeting is as inclusive of the spiritual state of the meeting within the process as it is of the outcome of the process. It requires a profound examination of one's own heart as well as of the heart of the meeting.

Some issues are relatively routine and do not require the full weight of a discernment process to decide them. Nevertheless, we try to sustain our stance of worshipful discernment as we move among matters of varying weight.

In a number of liberal Friends' meetings, secularization or accommodation to the understandings and practices of the wider society around us have been at work in our conduct of corporate affairs. As is to be expected in such an inward spirituality as ours, the difference between a spiritual approach and a secular one depends primarily on the understandings, attitudes, intentions and openness to the Spirit of those who gather. If the spiritual ground of the work is not understood, the meeting can be a flat human exercise in getting through an agenda and getting things done with only a "moment of silence" as a passing nod to the Divine—or possibly only a nod to quaint tradition. At its worst, a secularized meeting for business can be a place where the unhealed and undisciplined egocentrism or willfulness of the individual members come into sharp conflict or accommodate each other in human-made compromises.

Modern Quakers of the Friends General Conference tradition are more apt than Conservative Friends to have imported business procedures from their committee and organizational work in the wider world into the setting of the meeting for worship with attention to business. The tension of having one foot in the world of institutions and businesses and the other in demanding spiritual discernment can be confusing as we try to remain in the stance of worshipful seeking together for the will of God.

It's all too easy to revert to the human organizing, manipulating, maneuvering and deciding that are often required in the ways we conduct our affairs in other groups. We can resist this temptation only to the degree that we mutually support each other in listening for intimations of Divine Will. This is what Friends have traditionally been about as we've come together to conduct business.

In *Encounter With Silence,* John Punshon makes a subtle but crucial distinction between a minute which is the servant of the meeting and the meeting which is the servant of the minute. It is worth reflecting on the significance of that distinction in relation to the will of God. The idea that the meeting should be the servant of the minute reflects the traditional Quaker sense that the minute sought is an expression of God's will for this meeting in the particular matter at hand at this time. To search and labor after just the right formulation of the minute that expresses God's will is to be a servant of God. To search and labor after a formulation that expresses a consensus of the diverse wills of members of the meeting, or is the result of a negotiated settlement accommodating the various views of members, is to make the minute the servant of the meeting rather than of God.

The Jesuit order is another group that historically has practiced communal discernment. Their vocabulary is Roman Catholic, but it is worth making the effort to translate it into Quaker terms for the light it can shed on Quaker process. Thomas Green speaks of the necessary groundwork for communal discernment in the communion, charism, core vision or common vocation of the particular community making the discernment. Among the basic Quaker expressions of "communion" or "core vision" is certainly the experience of being gathered or united in the Love or Will of God. Our "charism" or particular gift and calling as a community may well be our dedication to patterns of listening inwardly and outwardly for where the Love or Will of God is guiding us in any particular case. In Jesuit terms, our discerning listening and our cherished experience of being gathered and united in the Love or Will of God can be said to be the necessary groundwork for communal discernment.

Queries

Do you find it more difficult to listen prayerfully one-on-one or in a group? Do you find it more difficult to listen in an open, humble and respectful spirit to personal matters or to issues of business that challenge your own views? Are you able to retain your sense of love and unity with someone whose views diverge from or challenge your own? Are you able to give them credit for purity of motive? What seems to disrupt your sense of unity? ... to support it? Do you find yourself impatient with those who fail to see your point of view? ... impatient with waiting to come to unity? ... impatient to get on with it?

You might want to compare Barry Morley's development of "sense of the meeting" with that in London Yearly Meeting's *Christian faith and practice* and *Church Government*. What has any of this to do with unity or the gathered meeting? Be aware of where and how the spaces are made in the meeting for business for the movement of the Spirit and for the turnings to God. What are the spiritual functions of the three inner movements Morley identifies in the meeting for business?

As you reflect on listening and discernment in the meeting for business, this might be a good time for you to reflect and journal on what you have experienced and learned of prayerful listening and how it connects with your personal experience of the meeting for business. If you have been attending meetings for business for some time, it may be useful to journal about some episodes in your experience that illustrate the inner movements Morley describes and their consequences ... or episodes in which these movements did not take place, and the consequences. In any case, it's important not to reduce these three interior movements to purely human techniques—like consensus—for reaching agreement. Stay alive to ways in which the process is open to the Divine, and the ways in which it is vulnerable to human manipulation.

Notice that the meeting for business is not only a particular instance of the meeting for worship but also a particular instance of seeking to be guided by God. Do you seek the will of God in all things? ... some things? ...

sometimes? What governs your desire? Is there a pattern in what's given over, and what's withheld?

Does your meeting have a commitment to carrying out the will of God as discerned communally, whatever it may be? Do you bear your part of the responsibility for discerning whether the minute in fact expresses the sense of the meeting? ... for participating in carrying it out?

Clerking

The very name, "clerk", reflects the humble origins of the one who presides at meetings for business. It implies a recorder, a keeper of records. In a Quaker meeting for business, such a person would have been the one who wrote down the minutes of the meeting. If we bear in mind John Punshon's helpful distinction between a minute that is the servant of the meeting and a meeting that is the servant of the minute, being the recorder of Quaker minutes becomes a much more complex task than simply writing down what people said.

Punshon's distinction helps us see why traditional Quaker minute-keeping is so different from secular or historical minute-keeping. Quaker minutes have traditionally omitted any record of the discussion leading up to the minute and any mention of names of participants. If God's will itself is what we are seeking to express in our minutes, when it is found, all the fumbling search leading up to it falls away. Who said what becomes irrelevant. To record only the minute itself is an assertion that the minute alone—as an expression of God's Will for the meeting—is of importance. The human, historical process is not seen as what actually shaped the minute. It is regarded as incidental to the Spirit of God herself drawing us forward, shaping the minute in and through us as we listen faithfully to the process among us. As in meeting for worship, the ministry—not the ministers, or their particular roles and interactions—is of ultimate significance.

The distinction also helps us see why it is that the clerk, as formulator and recorder of minutes in a Quaker meeting, cannot be merely a scribe. The clerk must be a discerner, a listener with keen sensitivity to how the Spirit is moving among the group, where it might be headed at any moment, whether that is merely an interim direction or exploration after Truth—or if it is nearing the minute sought after. The clerk must be a discerner of spirits, of where the words are coming from in each case, of when the majority may be off track and a single voice closer to the trail, of where the reconciliation of differences might lie, of what may have to be laid aside, who might have to stand aside. In this sense the clerk is the servant of the meeting which is attempting to be the servant of the minute. And exacting work it is, too, when we struggle to get past our human preconceptions as to process or outcome in order to be faithful to the Word spoken in our hearts.

Mark 10:35-45 speaks about the servanthood of leaders:

> Zebedee's children, James and John approached Jesus. "Teacher," they said, "we want you to grant our request."
> "What is it?" Jesus asked.
>
> They replied, "See to it that we sit next to you, one at your right and one at your left, when you come into your glory."
>
> Jesus told them, "You do not know what you are asking. Can you drink the cup I will drink or be baptized in the same baptism as I?"
>
> "We can," they replied. Jesus said in response, "From the cup I drink of, you will drink; the baptism I am immersed in, you will share. But as for sitting at my right or my left, that is not mine to give; it is for those for whom it has been reserved."
>
> The other ten, on hearing this, became indignant at James and John.
>
> Jesus called them together and said, "You know how among the Gentiles those who exercise authority are

domineering and arrogant; those 'great ones' know how to make their own importance felt. But it can't be like that with you. Anyone among you who aspires to greatness must serve the rest; whoever wants to rank first among you must serve the needs of all. The Promised One has come not to be served, but to serve—to give one life in ransom for the many."

int

As the designated (but not the only) discerner, the clerk is a servant rather than the master of the meeting. Hear the echoes of the foot-washing passage from John 13 as well as of the passage from Mark on servant leadership. Mark's story seems to encapsulate the same lesson taught by Jesus' enactment of foot-washing. Hear echoes of Punshon on the meeting as servant of the minute. This kind of servanthood to the meeting, to one another and ultimately to God is an important part of the traditional Quaker sense of discipleship.

The position of the clerk is a pivotal and precarious one for both the clerk and for the other members present. Ideally, the clerk is chosen for a special gift of discernment; however that does not mean that the rest of the meeting relinquishes the task of discernment to the clerk. Knowing the difficulty, fallibility and fragility of discernment, it is their task to support the clerk's discernment in whatever manner seems to be required in particular instances to the best of their capacities. It's axiomatic that the clerk clerks best when everyone is clerking together.

The meeting members' support may be by inwardly upholding the prayerful attentiveness of the group or by outwardly recalling the group to the prayerful basis of their work together should they waver. This latter is often done by a simple request for silence, understood as a return to prayer. It may be done by offering a vocal prayer for guidance or tentative discernments of the sense of the meeting when the meeting or the clerk seem unclear of guidance. It may also be by questioning the discernment of the clerk when it feels wide of the mark or seems to be overlooking some crucial element.

One risk of clerkship for both the clerk and the meeting is that members will acquiesce too easily in the clerk's sense of the meeting, without having tested it adequately within themselves. Such carelessness, such abdication of spiritual responsibility, and such failure of mutual service has sometimes handed over to clerks power that belongs to God alone in a Friends' meeting. In the past this sometimes led to hierarchical rather than mutual forms among Friends—to paraphrase Mark, this is "behaviors of the Gentiles".

Another risk is that sometimes Friends usurp the function of the clerk by formulating their own particular version of the minute, before they have prayerfully listened to the clerk's words. This undermines the clerk's servanthood by failing to consider whether s/he has correctly discerned the sense of the meeting. While it is important to take sufficient care to have the words express precisely the sense of the meeting, Friends should refrain from expanding a minute to cover all future cases. We have found God in the particulars rather than in global statements.

Queries

What do you sense to be the lessons for yourself and your meeting in the stories in John 13:2-10, 12-15 and Mark 10:35-45?

Do you sense growing within yourself any of the gifts of clerkship? Are any notably lacking? Could you be content to clerk as a servant of the meeting rather than seeking to exercise authority? In what ways might you have to grow to become a clerk in the traditional Quaker model?

Are you exercising your own capacity for discernment in support of the clerk during the meetings for business? While a minute is being written, do you hold the process in prayer?

References and resources on discernment in attending to business

Howard Brinton.
Guide to Quaker Practice.
PHP #20. Structure. Meeting
for Business.
Business before Meeting.

Howard Brinton.
Friends for 300 Years.
ch. 7.

Howard Brinton.
*The Quaker Doctrine of
Inward Peace.*
PHP #44.
The Philosophical Basis;
Inward Peace as a Test.

Wilmer Cooper.
A Living Faith.
chs. 2, 6.

Sandra Cronk.
Peace Be with You.
The meeting: the place of
discernment.

Matthias C. Drake.
"Beyond Consensus:
The Quaker Search for
God's Leading for the
Group."
in *CD*, also excerpted in *FJ*, 6/86.

Margaret Fell.
Womens' Speaking Justified.

Thomas H. Green.
*Weeds Among the Wheat:
Discernment, Where Prayer
and Action Meet.*

Douglas Gwyn.
Apocalypse of the Word.
ch. 10.

Robert Halliday.
*Mind the Oneness: the
foundation of good Quaker
business method.*

Alistair Heron.
Gifts and Ministries.
A discussion paper on eldership.
QHS.

Damon D. Hickey.
*Unforeseen Joy: Serving
a Friends Meeting as
Recording Clerk.*

Rufus Jones.
"The Sense of the
Meeting",
in Jessamyn West, ed.
A Quaker Reader.

Thomas Kelly.
A Testament of Devotion.
The Simplification of Life.

Paul A. Lacey.
*Quakers and the Use
of Power.*
PHP #241.

London Yearly Meeting.
*Christian faith and
practice.*
(1952). ch. 7: #325-332;
333-337; 338-340; 341-348;
#349-354; 358. The meeting
as fellowship.

London Yearly Meeting.
Church government.
(1952). ch 17: #711-726.
General counsel, sense of the
meeting, attendance, clerkship.
ch. 17: #727-729. Appointments; nominations committees.
ch. 17: #735-736. Concluding
general counsel.
ch. 20: #781-788. History of
yearly meeting.
ch. 21: #811. History of the
meeting for sufferings.

Patricia Loring.
*Spiritual Responsibility
in the Meeting for
Business.*

Barry Morley.
Beyond Consensus: Salvag-
ing Sense of the Meeting.
PHP #307.

Elizabeth O'Connor.
The Eighth Day of Creation: Discovering and Using Your Gifts.
p. 17.

John Punshon.
Encounter with Silence.
chs. 11-12.

George Selleck.
Principles of the Quaker Business Meeting.

Michael J. Sheeran.
Beyond Majority Rule.
esp. chs. 3, 5.

Douglas Steere.
"Some Dimensions of the Quaker Decision-Making Process".
FJ. 1982.

R.W. Tucker.
"Structural Incongruities in Quaker Service".
QS.

William Taber, Jr.
"The Friends Discernment Process: One View of Gospel Order".
CD.

William Taber, Jr.
"On Ministering to the Meeting for Business".
Address to PYM Worship and Ministry Retreat, 3/25/87.

William Taber, Jr.
Introduction to Samuel Bownas. *A Description of the Qualifications Necessary to a Gospel Minister.*

Jean Vanier.
Community and Growth: Our Pilgrimage Together.

Lloyd Lee Wilson.
Essays on the Quaker Vision of Gospel Order.
Taking on the Risks of Ministry.
The Meeting for Business.

Roger C. Wilson.
Authority, Leadership and Concern.

Discernment of personal concerns and leadings

Another area of discernment in meeting life is distinguishing among personal concerns, leadings and what Paul Lacey has helpfully termed "bothers". In his pamphlet, *Leading and Being Led,* Lacey describes bothers such as the multitude of things that pain, disturb or nag us, yet are not truly concerns that have been laid upon us by God for intensive action, either personally or corporately. Spiritual responsibility rests upon both those who discern leadings and those who follow them to be careful whether we are dealing with a leading or a bother.

Concerns are ultimately quite personal, arising within an individual in ways that are intimately connected with his or her personal nature, gifts and history. Both despite and because of that fact, we must be particularly careful about how much of our broken or needy humanity and how much of the Divine we are sensing when we feel led. We Friends, with our interior spirituality, have found it important to turn to the community for assistance in discerning the Spirit-led quality of our leadings and concerns. Instead of the checks of authenticity that others find in dogma, catechism, liturgy—or the ultimacy given to literal interpretations of the Bible—Friends turn to the guidance of the Spirit moving in one another. Leadings and concerns, especially those that will involve or reflect on the corporate body, are discerned corporately.

In this era of rugged individualism, many who feel strongly concerned or bothered on issues, or inspired by an idea, sometimes want to bypass or short-circuit the corporate process of discernment in their own affairs. The experience embodied in our tradition, however, has been that the Light refracted through a variety of personalities, perceptions and gifts can usually illuminate more widely and deeply than that focused through a single lens.

Our fears of and impatience with the restraint of the corporate body are very often just the willfulness, or overemphasis on product, that is encouraged by the wider culture. Submission to corporate discernment is an exercise in patience, trust and openness to Divine Guidance. First, we trust in the capacity of our fellow members to discern that Guidance and to be as yielded as ourselves in hearing it arise in the individual instance—especially as it touches us personally. Ultimately, our trust is in the Spirit of God moving among us, opening us, illuminating us, showing us the Way forward, and drawing us into heartfelt unity. If we are to expend time and energy in corporate discernment, we must be willing to accept the resulting Guidance.

In order for us to be able to accept corporate authority as genuinely spiritual and God-given, the members of the corporate body must put from themselves any authoritarianism, pet theories or other attitudes that would hinder the movement of the Spirit or foreclose the possibilities before us. We must be able to trust them. A membership known to be committed to listening together for the guidance of the Holy Spirit is naturally easier to trust. The Spirit, however, is powerful and can often work with unpromising material. Over and over Friends tell stories of how we have surprised ourselves by coming to a place of yieldedness, insight and harmony that we hadn't thought possible in such trying circumstances.

Where concerns affect the meeting or its relations with the rest of the Religious Society of Friends, those bearing them have traditionally taken them before the meeting for business for corporate discernment. The classic example in Quaker history, and one being revived in some meetings today, is traveling in the ministry. In the "middle period" of Quakerism, the chief way Friends were held together in faithfulness to our traditional ways of coming to God, across oceans and distances, with no modern transportation or media, was through Friends under concern to speak to the spiritual life of other meetings. A Friend with such a concern or leading was usually someone recorded in his or her own meeting as a minister.

The person feeling led to travel among Friends, in fairly specific geographical regions or circumstances, usually allowed his leading to be inwardly seasoned and tested for months or years before bringing it to the meeting for business for discernment. My favorite example is John Wilbur whose journal records the first "drawings in his mind" to visit Friends in England some seventeen years before he brought the leading to his meeting.

The leading was tested, its specificity, spiritual implications and questions were brought forth, the qualification of the individual in question to carry it out was examined, in whatever ways the meeting felt moved. If the leading was discerned to be truly of God, then the meeting would record that discernment in a "traveling minute" to be presented to meetings where the minister traveled. The minute would signify to the other meetings that the person bearing it was not there at his own behest but was a recognized, valued member of his meeting whose leadings to speak could be trusted to bear some mark of Divine Wisdom for those to whom they were addressed. Inasmuch as the leading was felt to originate with the Spirit, both the individual and the meeting were obliged to leave no stone unturned to see it carried out. In turn, the visited meetings instructed their clerks to endorse the traveling minute with their sense of the fruit of the visit. The home meeting was kept in touch with other meetings by the members who traveled.

The same process has been employed by and for those traveling under other concerns, whether for the spiritual or humane welfare of others. A recent example in my own yearly meeting has been a member who has traveled extensively under concern for issues related to the population explosion. The corporate body is important both in fostering and in authenticating individual concerns. There is a fruitful tension and interaction between corporate and individual authority. Each in its own way represents Divine Authority—the only authority Friends traditionally recognize. At times a single individual performs a prophetic role by hearing, more clearly than the corporate body, the will of God in a particular instance—a prophetic role that raises the corporate consciousness. At other times, the body functioning together as an organism hears more clearly than the individual caught in her own personal agenda, however altruistic it seems. Each must be responsive to and nurturing of the other, yielding to the other as guided by the Spirit.

Some scholars feel that part of the problem of the gifted minister, James Nayler, that led to his blasphemy trial was confusion about outward checks on inner guidance. (See Bittle for the story if it's unfamiliar to you.) London Yearly Meeting's *Christian faith and practice* extract #22 contains Nayler's statement of his "utter dependency upon God, without recognition of any human medium or instrumentality." His unwillingness to challenge his enthusiastic followers' sense of guidance, his unwillingness to hold them accountable to any outward discernment and his yielding to their sense of what was right *for him* led to his martyrdom. The subsequent persecution of Friends led the young movement to consider more carefully how leadings might be authenticated.

Some early steps were "settling", or establishing, meetings and a beginning recognition of the need for corporate authority grounded in loving unity as the best outward approximation of the inward authority of God.

Clearness committees

In the twentieth century, a new structure for discernment has been evolving among Friends for discernment of leadings. At times it has been used for leadings in purely personal matters. It may also be used for a preliminary testing of leadings before bringing them to the meeting for business.

The clearness committee is nominally an old structure among Friends: a small committee first used for "clearing" marriages in the sense of going sufficiently into the details of the lives of the partners to be sure there were no impediments to the marriage. The other old use was to make sure a Friend's business affairs were cleared up before he was granted clearness to move to a new location. Applications for membership are also "cleared" or explored by use of clearness committees. All these committees present their findings to the meeting for business. Clearness committees have also been used for preparing business before it comes to meeting by investigating ahead of time any details that the meeting might require to come to its discernment.

The novelty in its present use is that it is coming to be an instrument for personal discernment. A small group of people, usually four to six, meet as a discernment group similar to those described in Volume I, chapter 7. Their focus is the person who experiences a sense of leading, for the purpose of assisting her clearness as to its nature and as to the authenticity of its spiritual origin. Either the individual's personal discernment process may be helped or the group may be discerning on behalf of the meeting. In either case, the person who feels led is the focal point of the group.

The first step is for the focal person to prepare a statement of the sense of leading and any pertinent questions or issues that may help the process. Before meeting, the committee members read the statement with prayerful openness as often as possible. The meeting itself has some of the characteristics of worship sharing. After a time of centering silence to support prayerful listening and prayer for guidance and right hearing, the focal person speaks of the issue to be discerned.

Then, after a time of recentering and refocusing, the committee may ask questions for clarification, then evocative questions meant to draw forth further spiritual implications of what they have heard. If the focal person wants to hear any opinions, advice, guidance or speculation from the committee, he will ask. Otherwise, the committee should be careful not to impose its views on him. If the committee is simply assisting the focal person's own discernment, their work is only to assist his awareness of the movements of the Spirit in his life. As the focal person's process is completed, it is wise to give the committee members an opportunity to speak of their sense of how they have heard the Spirit moving in the process. If someone's sense differs significantly from that of the focus person it is important he not go forward without knowing it.

A clearness committee and a support committee are different. In the former, the group needs to discern and reach clarity that the focus person is correct in rightly understanding God's guidance. In the latter, the group has already discerned that, and has moved on to discerning ways to help him move forward with the ministry of the leading. If the committee is discerning on behalf of the meeting, it will probably want to meet separately afterward to discuss Friends' sense of the question examined and their recommendations to the meeting.

It is not a discussion of the issues. Silence that allows the issues under the issues to be heard should flow around the speech—or rather the speech should be as much a part of the silence as authentic vocal ministry is of the silence in meeting for worship. Insofar as we are listening for God, a clearness committee will be a form of contemplative prayer or worship.

Discerning meeting or group missions

Sometimes, as a person speaks of his concern before a clearness committee or a meeting for business, others are gathered into a sense, not only of the authenticity of the leading but of shared concern. This is one of the ways a meeting may be led to "get under the weight of" a leading or concern that can then become a meeting mission rather than simply a personal concern. Sometimes a personal concern over time gradually gathers others in the meeting into shared concern, again making it a meeting mission.

Sometimes, people—especially people newly come to Friends—are disappointed when Friends fail to join them in concerns which may well have considerable ethical force or merit. The expectation arises from a misunderstanding that Friends act concertedly from a generalized moral obligation to do anything that falls under one of their testimonies.

For Friends, however, there are numerous actions that fall under one of the testimonies that may not be discerned to be laid upon their particular meeting at that time. No meeting could possibly hope to perform all the actions that might lie under the testimonies. Discernment looks for the specific guidance of God in particulars, rather than for generalized moral obligations. In each instance we find our peace in discerning God's will for us in this case at this time, regardless of the merit of the proposal. Logic, moral persuasion, or pressure, although they may pull at us, do not have the force of discernment in deciding whether we are drawn corporately into the flow of someone's concern.

Some of our greatest difficulties arise when we revert to the easy idea of "Quaker principles" or "Quaker values" rather than discernment. In an effort to avoid the laborious and uncertain, intuitive process of discernment, modern Friends often advert to Quaker principles or values. The principles are usually a reduction of one of the testimonies to a generalized moral obligation rather than to a statement of the vision of life attuned to Divine Love that comes of the gathered meeting.

To attempt to turn the testimonies into principles is to disregard the specificity of the concerns and leadings that are laid on us as particular individuals. It is also to create a set of ethical demands for action in the world that is impossible for any individual or organization to live up to. These demands in turn create a constant anxiety that is contrary to the peace of God given us when we are faithful to specific tasks given us as individual people or meetings.

For the same reason, traditionally Friends have not come together to draw up "mission statements" for their meetings out of an undefined sense that "we ought to be doing something about some of the evils in the world." Leadings and concerns arise within the individual, just as the primary contact with the Divine in Quakerism is always within the individual. It may become shared as a meeting mission, analogously to the way we are gathered in the Spirit of God.

However, some leadings and concerns remain individual, just as we all retain our individual gifts, histories and personalities within our union in the meeting. Indeed mutuality of service would be a senseless exercise if our gifts and leadings were identical. The work of the world could not be done without the diversity of our callings.

Queries

Are you able, in our social milieu of rugged individualism, to accord the corporate body the authority described here? From what does that authority seem to be derived in your meeting?

Do you tend to discern your concerns or leadings or to generalize them from your knowledge of tradition and testimony?

References and Resources for discernment of concerns and leadings

Exod. 40:34-38.
Isa. 11:1-9.
Matt. 25:31-40.
Luke 4:14-21; 10:25-37.
Gal. 5:22-23.
James 3:13-4:2.

British Yearly Meeting.
Quaker faith and practice.
#13.01-13.13; Concern.
13.20-13.27 Traveling in the
ministry.

William G. Bittle.
James Nayler, 1618-1660.
esp. ch. IV.

Suzanne Farnham, *et al.*
*Listening Hearts: Discern-
ing Call in Community.*

Jan Hoffman.
*Clearness Committees
and their Use in Personal
Discernment.*

Paul Lacey.
Leading and Being Led.
PHP #264.

London Yearly Meeting.
Church government.
ch. 25: #861-868; 872-878.
Concern and minutes of
support.

London Yearly Meeting.
*Christian faith and
practice.*
ch. 1: #24-25; #50; #72.
Spiritual experiences.
ch. 7: #359-364. The meeting
as a fellowship.
ch. 8: #376-378; 383; 385-
393. Publishing truth.
ch. 13: #579-596; #600; 602;
604. National responsibilities.
ch. 14: #605-606; 609-611;
613-616; 623-624; #625-626;
629; 633-34; 636-638 (only
para 1-3); 641-642; 645- 646;
648-651; 654; 657; 659; 661;
663-666; 668-9. International
responsibilities.

David Lonsdale.
*Listening to the Music of
the Spirit: The Art of
Discernment.*

Patricia Loring.
*Spiritual Discernment:
the context and goal of
clearness committees.*
PHP #305.

Parker Palmer.
"The Clearness
Committee: a Way of
Discernment".
Weavings. July/Aug. 1988, pp.
37-40.

Jan Wood.
*"Spiritual Discernment:
the Personal Dimension".*
CD.

Peter Woodrow.
Clearness.

John Woolman: an example of the evolution of discerned leadings, concerns and testimonies

Historically widening circles of concern

John Woolman is the exemplar *par excellence* of a life lived under guidance, "close to the Root", seeking and responding to intimations of God's will in daily prayer and self-examination.

His ability to articulate his inner experience and the faithful record he kept in his *Journal* provide a prime example of the way an individual leading can develop into a personal concern, the personal concern can become a call to others to get under the weight of the concern, and finally the shared concern can grow in the hearts and awareness of the members of the meeting and the larger Society of Friends. When the concern illuminates the Quaker witness to our experience of oneness in the Love of God, it becomes an aspect of our testimony to what we have learned when we have been gathered at the feet of the Inward Teacher.

In the following excerpts from his *Journal*, we have a taste of Woolman's personal experience of transformation, guidance and the ways in which his own life—and the lives of others—were changed as he obeyed his guidance. Notice that his discernment of his leading comes out of an encounter with a concrete situation. The generalizations and intellectualizations come later, after painstaking, prayerful examination of his own interior responses.

As you read these excerpts, be aware of the visceral and intuitive language Woolman uses to describe the ways he becomes aware of guidance—and his sensitivity and attentiveness to such intimations. These passages provide an excellent example of the traditional Quaker vocabulary of discernment mentioned above. The vocabulary, in turn, provides insight into the nature of the discernment process as it developed among Friends. Notice how Woolman feels his way among the intimations and considerations that press themselves upon his mind. These are examples of "discernment of spirits" or of "where the words come from".

In his journal for 1742, John Woolman first writes of a leading that points to the concern that would be the central issue in his life, from which others opened. We can see how it began with him and how it went on:

My employer, having a Negro woman, sold her and directed me to write a bill of sale, the man being waiting who bought her. The thing was sudden, and though the thoughts of writing an instrument of slavery for one of my fellow creatures felt uneasy, yet I remembered I was hired by the year, that it was my master who directed me to do it, and that it was an elderly man, a member of our Society, who bought her; so through weakness I gave way and wrote it, but at the executing it, I was so afflicted in my mind that I said before my master and the Friend that I believed slavekeeping to be a practice inconsistent with the Christian religion. This in some degree abated my uneasiness, yet as often as I reflected seriously upon it I thought I should have been clearer if I had desired to be excused from it as a thing against my conscience, for such it was. And some time after this a young man of our Society spake to me to write an instrument of slavery, he having lately taken a Negro into his house. I told him I was not easy to write it, for though many kept slaves in our Society, as in others, I still believed the practice was not right, and desired to be excused from writing [it]. I spoke to him in good will, and he told me that keeping slaves was not altogether agreeable to his mind, but that the slave being a gift made to his wife, he had accepted of her.

Journal. pp. 32-33

In 1743, while traveling in the ministry in Virginia, Woolman speaks of a further unfolding of his concern in relation to the circumstances in which he finds himself:

> Two things were remarkable to me in this journey. First, in regard to my entertainment: When I eat, drank and lodged free-cost with people who lived in ease on the hard labour of their slaves, I felt uneasy; and as my mind was turned inward to the Lord, I found, from place to place, this uneasiness return upon me at times through the whole visit. Where the masters bore a good share of the burden and lived frugal, so that their servants were well provided for and their labour moderate, I felt more easy; but where they lived in a costly way and laid heavy burdens on their slaves, my exercise was often great, and I frequently had conversation with them in private concerning it. Secondly, this trade of importing them from their native country being much encouraged amongst them and the white people and their children so generally living without much labour was frequently the subject of my serious thoughts. And I saw in these southern provinces so many vices and corruptions increased by this trade and this way of life that it appeared to me as a dark gloominess hanging over the land; and though now many willingly run into it, yet in future the consequence will be grievous to posterity! I express it as it hath appeared to me, not at once nor twice, but as a matter fixed on my mind.

Journal. p. 38

By 1753 he had achieved greater clarity about where his motivations lay in writing instruments conveying slaves. He "discerns the spirits" at work within himself:

> About this time a person at some distance lying sick, his brother came to me to write his will. I knew he had slaves, and asking his brother, was told he intended to leave them slaves to his children. As writing is a profit-

able employ, as offending people is disagreeable to my inclination, I was straitened in my mind; but as I looked to the Lord, he inclined my heart to his testimony, and I told the man that I believed the practice of continuing slavery to this people was not right and had a scruple in mind against doing writings of that kind: that though many in our Society kept them as slaves, still I was not easy to be concerned in it and desired to be excused from going to write the will. I spake to him in the fear of the Lord, and he made no reply to what I said, but went away; he also had some concerns in the practice, and I thought he was displeased with me.

In this case I had fresh confirmation that acting contrary to present outward interest from a motive of divine love and in regard to truth and righteousness, and thereby incurring the resentments of people, opens the way to a treasure better than silver and to a friendship exceeding the friendship of men.

Journal. pp. 45-46

In the account of 1756 we find the summarizing passage that is printed in books of discipline. It had taken fourteen years for this process to evolve in Woolman's heart and clarify in his mind:

Scrupling to do writings relative to keeping slaves having been a means of sundry small trials to me, in which I have so evidently felt my own will set aside that I think it good to mention a few of them. Tradesmen and retailers of goods, who depend on their business for a living, are naturally inclined to keep the good will of their customers; nor is it a pleasant thing for young men to be under a necessity to question the judgment or honesty of elderly men, and more especially of such who have a fair reputation. Deep-rooted customs, though wrong, are not easily altered, but it is the duty of every-

one to be firm in that which they certainly know is right for them. A charitable and benevolent man, well acquainted with a Negro, may, I believe, under some certain circumstances keep him in his family as a servant on no other motives than the Negro's good; but man, as man, knows not what shall be after him, nor hath he any assurance that his children will attain to that perfection in wisdom and goodness necessary in every absolute governor. Hence it is clear to me that I ought not to be the scribe where wills are drawn in which some children are made absolute masters over others during life.

About this time an ancient man of good esteem in the neighborhood came to my house to get his will wrote. He had young Negroes, and I asking him privately how he purposed to dispose of them, he told me. I then said, "I cannot write thy will without breaking my own peace," and respectfully gave him my reasons for it. He signified that he had a choice that I should have wrote it, but as I could not consistent with my conscience, he did not desire it, and so got it wrote by some other person. And a few years after, there being great alterations in his family, he came again to get me to write his will. His Negroes were yet young, and his son, to whom he intended to give them, was since he first spoke to me, from a libertine become a sober young man; and he supposed that I would have been free on that account to write it. We had much friendly talk on the subject and then deferred it, and a few days after, he came again and directed their freedom, and so I wrote his will.

Near the time the last-mentioned friend first spoke to me, a neighbor received a bad bruise in his body and sent for me to bleed him, which being done he desired me to write his will. I took notes, and amongst other things he told me to which of his children he gave his young Negro. I considered the pain and distress he was in and knew not how it would end, so I wrote his will, save only that part concerning his slave, and carrying it to his bedside read it to him and then told him in a friendly way that I could not write any instruments by which my fellow creatures were made slaves, without bringing trouble on my own mind. I let him know that I charged nothing for what I had done and desired to be excused from doing the other part in the way he proposed. Then we had a serious conference on the subject, and at length, he agreeing to set her free, I finished his will.

Journal. pp. 50-51

His refusal to write wills conveying his fellow human beings as property is one striking case of the negative leading that Friends have sometimes called "a stop in the mind". Woolman's intellectual and social considerations show the very kinds of inward voices and factors that often tempt us to roll right over such tender "stops". Discernment requires very respectful consideration of "stops" unless or until it is absolutely clear that they are evasions rather than faithfulness.

This is another instance in which we may be called to run counter to a culture that urges us not to dither but to go full speed ahead with whatever may bear the kind of cultural stamps of approval Woolman experienced and rejected. You can see that the concern arose and was further refined and clarified in each instance of encounter with a violation of Woolman's inner sense of rightness. It was attentiveness over years that honed Woolman's sense of right action in relation to conveying slaves.

His unease about receiving hospitality from slave owners who lived in luxury and idleness on the fruits of their slaves' labor was ultimately resolved in a similar refusal recorded in 1757:

... When I expected soon to leave a Friend's house where I had entertainment, if I believed that I should not keep clear from the gain of oppression without leaving money, I spoke to one of the heads of the family privately and desired them to accept of them pieces of silver and give them to such of their Negroes as they believed would make the best use of them; and at other times I gave them to the Negroes myself, as the way looked clearest to me. As I expected this before I came out, I had provided a large number of small pieces, and thus offering them to some who appeared to be wealthy people was a trial both to me and them. But the fear of the Lord so covered me at times that way was made easier than I expected, and few if any manifested any resentment at the offer, and most of them after some talk accepted of them.

Journal. pp. 60-61

The concern that manifested itself as a "stop" in Woolman's mind in 1742 had been seasoned and produced in 1746 the essay "Some Considerations on the Keeping of Negroes". It wasn't until 1753 that he presented the essay to the publications committee of Philadelphia Yearly Meeting, which, after revision, printed it in 1754. By the publication of this essay and one of its own, Philadelphia Yearly Meeting embraced the belief that slaveholding was sinful (Soderlund). In 1758 Philadelphia Yearly Meeting made slave trading a disownable offense. The Yearly Meeting appointed Woolman and others, including some of the Philadelphia elders and ministers who had revised his essay, to carry the concern for slavery. Individually and together, they labored with slave-trading and slave-holding Friends in their own meetings and when traveling under concern in other yearly meetings. Anthony Benezet was led under concern to open schools for freed slaves or their children. Woolman completed another essay on slavery in 1761, which was published by the Yearly Meeting the following year.

In 1742 the twenty-two year-old man had been hesitant to express scruples about his complicity in conveying slaves. By 1746 the "stop in his mind" had become positive action, blossoming into his essay. He waited, however, until the Yearly Meeting had united with his concern in 1754. By 1757, his *Journal* records Woolman's increased boldness in having conversations with individual slave owners specifically about freeing their slaves.

Philadelphia Yearly Meeting, however, did not minute its unity on freeing slaves until 1776, four years after Woolman's early death. The lag of the Yearly Meeting's testimony behind Woolman's concern still put them nearly 75 years ahead of most of their fellow citizens. It's often hard to keep in mind that Woolman's discernment and struggle was taking place—not in the abolitionist period before the Civil War in this country—but before the Revolutionary War and the establishment of the United States.

When Friends in Virginia and the Carolinas finally came under the weight of this concern, theirs was no mere intellectual assent to an idea. Their lives and economic status testified. Without slaves many were no longer able to farm in the manner the land and crops required. Giving up slaves also reduced their capital and wealth considerably and placed them outside the society of their former neighbors and peers. In the end, many gave up their plantations and joined the migrations to the wilderness frontiers on the eastern edge of what is now the Midwest.

The treatment of ethics in Volume III will examine ways in which the leadings and concerns of Woolman's life formed an integrated testimony to the oneness of humanity and all the creation in God's Love. His life also testified to the necessity for the integrity of our inward experience and outward action. For example, his life attests to the connection between the inward testimony to peace and the outward payment of taxes to support wars; for the inward testimony to economic simplicity and the outward interconnections of all our possessions and their modes of production. In his later essays, Woolman testifies to the connections of our possessions with peace, with war and with the humane treatment of all human beings and all parts of the creation.

The vindication of Woolman's work is sometimes seen in the triumph of a national emancipation of slaves. The carnage of the Civil War that brought about the emancipation would have horrified and grieved him deeply. Woolman himself, no matter how devoutly he hoped and worked for such an outcome, would not have measured the ultimate value of his work in its effectiveness. Our own faithful listening and responsiveness, our humane treatment of all human beings and animals, reflected in sparing use of the goods of this world and the labor of others, would be a more accurate measure of living close to the Root, in Woolman's eyes.

The beginning of the passage concerning Woolman's trip to Indians at Wyalusing as the French and Indian War was becoming threatening in Pennsylvania, is a classic, clear and much loved statement of how a particular leading can originate.

> Having many years felt love in my heart toward the natives of this land who dwell far back in the wilderness, whose ancestors were the owners and possessors of the land where we dwell, and who for a very small consideration assigned their inheritance to us, and being at Philadelphia ... on a visit to some Friends who held slaves, I fell in company with some of those natives who lived on the east branch of the river Susquehanna at an Indian town called Wyalusing, about two hundred miles from Philadelphia. And in conversation with them ... I believed some of them were measurably acquainted with that divine power which subjects the rough and froward will of the creature; and at times I felt inward drawings toward a visit to that place, of which I told none except my dear wife until it came to some ripeness.

> ... Love was the first motion, and then a concern arose to spend some time with the Indians, that I might feel and understand their life and the spirit they live in, if haply I might receive some instruction from them, or they be in any degree helped forward by my following the leadings of Truth amongst them. And it pleased the Lord to make way for my going at a time when the troubles of war were increasing, and when by reason of much wet weather travelling was more difficult than usual at that season, I looked upon it as a more favourable opportunity to season my mind and bring me into a nearer sympathy with them. And as mine eye was to the great Father of Mercies, humbly desiring to learn what his will was concerning me, I was made quiet and content.

Journal. pp. 122-23, 127-28

Woolman's account of the journey itself is filled with honesty about his fears of going into country where Indians were on the warpath, hostile forces were afoot in the forest, and the weather was truly miserable for sleeping rough. There is an utter absence in his account of the sense of necessity of evident results. It is an exercise in faithfulness to a leading, with the consequences left to God. Indeed there are no outwardly noticeable results of this trip, apart from the gift to us of Papehuneg's statement that he "loves to feel where the words come from." Nothing could be further from our contemporary, secularized cost accounting and desire for effectiveness.

Woolman's life can be read as a homily on the treasured story of the first time Margaret Fell heard George Fox speak in Ulverston church. On that occasion, Fox said,

> "The Scriptures were the prophets' words and Christ's and the apostles' words, and what as they spoke they enjoyed and possessed and had it from the Lord. ... Then what had any to do with the Scriptures, but as they came to the Spirit that gave them forth. You will say, Christ saith this, and the apostles say this; but what canst thou say? ..."

Fell was stricken by this statement and responded to herself,

> "We are all thieves. ... we have taken the Scriptures in words and know nothing of them in ourselves."

> *LYM*

Fox and Fell were pointing to the tendency to quote others concerning God's requirements, without consulting the movements of the Spirit within ourselves.

Woolman's life is a wonderful example of the interplay between the exercise of his sensitivity and attentiveness to inward experience—and of his remarkable intellectual gift for meditating on the implications of his experience. In other words, Woolman was not a "thief", because he always listened first to the immediate promptings of the Spirit within him. He used Biblical pronouncements and social norms as secondary sources of direction.

Verbal testimony to the experience of the living God is a counterpart to testimony in action: a life that speaks. Both are obedient to the promptings of the Spirit. In earlier periods of Quakerism, the testimonies testified or attested to the nature and requirements of God. Individuals testified to what they had experienced livingly—rather than to what they agreed with intellectually, or deduced from principles. Today, we often flounder. We often fail to distinguish between testimony and principle. A testimony has spiritual force in discerning leadings. Its spiritual force comes from the experience of the Spirit to which it testifies. It comes from an experience of God breaking into the particularities of our lives, disquieting our hearts. They will not be stilled until we respond as required.

Principles have moral force; but they carry no personal experience of leading. Principles can be arrived at by a purely intellectual process. Modern media bombard us with vivid impressions of agonizing situations that plainly violate the insights of one or another of the testimonies. Principle indicates we should do something about these situations, geographically distant from the circumstances of our lives. Many Friends experience acute pain not only at the far-away situation but also at the lack of any clear, interior Guidance as to how they might be led to act in relation to it. When we begin from principle, or a moral generality, it is more difficult to know which circumstances of our lives constitute an encounter in which guidance by the Spirit is occurring.

We are all familiar with the make-do solutions to out-of-reach moral issues: letters to government representatives; checks to organizations whose charters address the situation; and retracing and rediscerning—as Woolman did—our personal economic and social links with the situation through possessions, purchases and relationships. These measures seldom feel like enough. Yet we are reluctantly forced to recognize that the multiplicity of such situations in the world drains so much attention, energy and time that it is not humanly possible for each of us to address them all.

Feeling the obligation of principle, rather than waiting on specific leadings by God often leads to constant pressure to act on situations all over the world. This ceaseless agitation can lead to psychological numbing. Numbing of personal pain, leading to numbing of compassion, was first recorded by psychologists and sociologists writing of the surprising lack of concern in the general population about nuclear escalation. Among people who feel helpless in the face of overwhelming challenges, the mind usually defends itself by a numbness to the threat. The price of this numbness is diminution of other feelings, among them compassion for others who suffer. Assaulted by incessant violations of our testimonies to the requirements of God's Love, we risk suffering psychic numbing in many areas of our lives. Numbing is accompanied by loss of compassion for others, or even loss of the very capacity to know our own feelings (Lifton; Soelle). We do well to attend to the fact that both our apathy and our distress are considerably eased when we are overtaken by a compelling leading and commitment to some one concern.

It is also significant that we will be led to be present for our concern, rather than assigning it to proxies. It may be that we will be uprooted and moved to an appropriate place to carry it out. Most of us will probably be overtaken where we are. Guidance usually comes in the unique particularity of our lives. Both the historic circumstances and our unique constellation of gifts are involved in our leadings, concerns and prophetic witness. This stance requires enormous faith that others will be raised up to do the work to which we haven't been specifically led, work that is, for one reason or another, beyond our scope.

Queries

Notice that Woolman is less interested in conveying something to the Indians than he is open to receiving instruction from them. Compare your own experiences of leading with his. Have you ever been led to simply be present with someone, rather than to try to change them in some way? What might Woolman's Wyalusing experience add to your repertoire of touchstone experiences (past discernments that have proved right over time and illustrate how God works in your life)?

Have you ever been led to do something that placed you at physical risk? How did you discern the rightness of it? Did you include your family in the discernment? How did it turn out?

Do you wait on ripeness when you sense a leading growing in you?

Do you have immediate experience, comparable to Woolman's, of being changed, transformed and guided, in which to ground your principles? Do you seek to be sensitive to it?

Elizabeth Watson's caveat about leadings into vocal ministry may be broadly applicable to other leadings: For those who are shy or hesitant, even the smallest intimation of Divine Leading should be taken very seriously. For those who speak or act quite easily, intimations of Divine Leading should be waited with and examined more carefully before acting. Have you any experience of feeling led but being hesitant or hanging back—only to realize later that the leading was authentic? What would make you more confident in your leadings?

Resources and references for the evolution of a testimony

Friends Consultation on Discernment.

Friends Consultation on Testimonies, Queries and Advices.

London Yearly Meeting.
Christian faith and practice.
#20.

Irwin Abrams. "A Word about Listening".
FJ, 6/1/87.

Lewis Benson.
Catholic Quakerism.
chs. 5, 6.

Howard Brinton.
Friends for 300 Years.
ch. 9.

Howard Brinton.
The Quaker Doctrine of Inward Peace.
PHP #44.

Howard Brinton.
The Sources of the Quaker Peace Testimony.
PHP #27.

Wilmer Cooper.
The Testimony of Integrity.
PHP #296.

Sandra Cronk.
*Peace Be with You:
A Study of the Spiritual Basis of the Friends Peace Testimony.*

Adam Curle.
True Justice: Quaker Peace makers and Peace making.

Ram Dass and Paul Gorman.
How Can I Help? Stories and Reflections on Service.

Ram Dass and Mirabai Bush.
Compassion in Action: Setting Out on the Path of Service.

Douglas Gwyn.
The Apocalypse of the Word.
Chs 7, 8 & 11.

Jan Hoffman.
Clearness Committees and their Use in Personal Discernment.

Jack Kornfield.
A Path with Heart: A Guide through the Perils and Promises of Spiritual Life.
esp. ch. 20.

Thomas R. Kelly.
"The Eternal Now and Social Concern".
A Testament of Devotion.

Paul A. Lacy.
Leading and Being Led.
PHP #264, esp. p. 4.

Robert Jay Lifton.
A psychologist with a body of work on human psychology as cause and effect of war. His work on the emotional numbing that took place for those living in awareness of the ongoing threat of nuclear holocaust is of great importance to our self-understanding.

Patricia Loring.
Spiritual Discernment: the context and goal of clearness committees.

Wolf Mendl.
Prophets and Reconcilers: Reflections on the Quaker Peace Testimony.

Elizabeth O'Connor.
The New Community.
An account of the evolution of the Church of the Savior in Washington DC into a group of worshiping mission groups organized in support of the callings of individuals in response to the needs of inner city people, learning to incorporate the "helped" into the planning of the "helpers".

Sterling Olmstead.
Motions of Love: Woolman as Mystic and Activist.
PHP # 312.

Parker Palmer.
"The Clearness Committee: a Way of Discernment".
Weavings. 7/88.

John Punshon.
"The Peace Testimony".
QRT. Summer 1988.

Jean R. Soderlund.
Quakers & Slavery: A Divided Spirit.
p.26.
Scholarly study by the librarian of Swarthmore's Peace Collection, that traces the mixture of feelings and motives and the uneven progress of the anti-slavery movement among Friends prior to the American Revolution.

Dorothee Soelle.
Suffering.
esp. ch. 2. One treatment of the inverse relationship between numbing and compassion, in a religious context.

Jean Vanier.
Community and Growth.

Lucinda Vardey.
God in All Worlds: An Anthology of Contemporary Spiritual Writing.
esp. Part IV. Surrender.

John Woolman.
The Journal.

Conclusion

A problem for a spiritual comunity is that of discerning the discerners. The discernment process is inevitably fallible and frequently flawed. Yet the darkest periods in our history have come when we've tried to circumvent it. Our greatest failures have arisen when we've assumed we already know in principle what God requires of us and have no need to discern it in particular instances. We've failed when we've been insufficiently attentive to the spiritual dimensions of this process, or when—not trusting our capacity to discern—we've tried to substitute human forms and processes for spiritual discernment.

In the wrong hands, the power of naming gifts and appointments to meeting functions became a rigid instrument of all too human control and authoritarianism. Elders who were in tune with Spiritual Authority, rather than being authoritarian, empowered people to grow into authentic spiritual gifts. Elders who were spiritually experienced, intuitively wise and loving, gently discouraged people from using ministry for self-fulfillment, self-aggrandizement, compensation for wounds, or promulgation of personal views.

The great problem for modern Friends has been staying alive to the movements of the Spirit in particularities rather than in generalities. We must stay alert to misguided efforts to streamline or make more efficient our processes by adapting them to techniques or methods of "the world". To remain alert requires a base-line sense of what has traditionally been involved in discernment among Friends. We need to guard against assuming that what God requires of us is too obvious to require attentive listening in each particular instance, or that techniques that serve secular business will serve spiritual business as well.

Chapter 4

Listening for Spiritual Gifts and for Divine Guidance into Service in the Meeting

Being led into particular ministries in meeting life

Gifts and the meeting as organism guided by the Spirit

The ways we are called to be present for and with one another in spiritual community are various, and frequently nameless. I spoke earlier of ways in which our very brokenness and wounds may evoke either ministry or challenge to spiritual growth in one another. This chapter is concerned with spiritual gifts within us that draw us into particular ministries in addition to the countless unnameable ways in which we minister every day. Being gifted by the Spirit for work does not mean we are without wounds or brokenness. Spiritual gifts are not a mark of holiness. Our wounds are inevitably part of our existential human condition. Our gifts are part of the challenge to growth and yieldedness in our relationship with God.

The very namelessness of some of our ministries can keep us closer to the vital freshness of their inward promptings as Life, Love and Truth in our relationships—rather than inviting us to take on roles or personae. The circulation of Love among us is reminiscent of nothing so much as the current of lifesblood in an organism constituted of individual cells or organs that all function together better than any does apart, each supplying some lack of the others.

The following long excerpt from Paul's first letter to the church in Corinth is his fullest development of the analogy of the spiritual community to a unified organism animated and guided by the Spirit, by means of spiritual gifts.

There is a variety of gifts, but always the same Spirit. There is a variety of ministries, but we serve the same One. There is a variety of outcomes, but the same God is working in all of them. To each person is given the manifestation of the Spirit for the common good.

To one, the Spirit gives wisdom in discourse, to another, the word of knowledge through the same Spirit. Through the Spirit, one person receives faith; through the same Spirit, another is given the gift of healing; and still another, miraculous powers. Prophecy is given to one; to another, power to distinguish one spirit from another. One receives the gift of tongues; another, that of interpreting tongues. But it is one and the same Spirit who produces all these gifts and distributes them as she wills.

The body is one, even though it has many parts; all the parts—many though they are—comprise a single body. And so it is with Christ. It was by one Spirit that all of us, whether we are Jews or Greeks, slaves or citizens, were baptized into one body. All of us have been given to drink of the one Spirit. And that Body is not one part; it is many.

If the foot should say, "Because I am not a hand I do not belong to the body," does that make it any less a part of the body? If the ear should say, "Because I am not an eye I do not belong to the body," does that make it any less a part of the body? If the body were all eye, what

would happen to our hearing? If it were all ear, what would happen to our sense of smell? Instead of that, God put all the different parts into one body on purpose. If all the parts were alike, where would the body be?

They are, indeed, many different members but one body. The eye cannot say to the hand, "I do not need you," any more than the head can say to the feet, "I do not need you." And even those members of the body which seem less important are in fact indispensable. We honor the members we consider less honorable by clothing them with greater care, thus bestowing on the less presentable a propriety which the more presentable do not need. God has so constructed the body as to give greater honor to the lowly members, that there may be no dissension in the body, but that all the members may be concerned for one another. If one member suffers, all the members suffer with it; if one member is honored, all the members share its joy.

You, then, are the body of Christ, and each of you is a member of it. Furthermore, God has set up in the church, first, the apostles; second, prophets; third, teachers; then miracle workers, healers, assistants, administrators and those who speak in tongues. Are all apostles? Are all prophets? Are all teachers? Do all work miracles or have a gift of healing? Do all speak in tongues, or do all have the gift of interpretation of tongues?

Set your hearts on the greater gifts. But now I will show you the way which surpasses all the others.

Even if I can speak in all the tongues of the earth—and those of the angels too—but do not have love, I am just a noisy gong, a clanging cymbal. If I have the gift of prophecy such that I can comprehend all mysteries and all knowledge, or if I have faith great enough to move mountains, but I do not have love, I am nothing. If I give away everything I own to feed those poorer than I, then hand over my body to be burned, but do not have love, I gain nothing.

Love is patient; love is kind. Love is not jealous, it does not put on airs, and it is not snobbish; it is never rude or self-seeking; it is not prone to anger, nor does it brood over injuries. Love doesn't rejoice in what is wrong, but rejoices in the truth. There is no limit to love's forbearance, to its trust, its hope, its power to endure.

Love never fails. Prophecies will cease, tongues will be silent, knowledge will pass away. Our knowledge is imperfect and our prophesying is imperfect. When the perfect comes, the imperfect will pass away. When I was a child, I used to speak like a child, think like a child, reason like a child. But when I became an adult, I put childish ways aside. Now we see indistinctly, as in a mirror; then we will see face to face. My knowledge is imperfect now; then I will know even as I am known.

There are, in the end, three things that last: faith, hope, and love. But the greatest of these is love.

So pursue the way of love, but earnestly desire spiritual gifts as well, especially the gift of prophecy. Those who speak in tongues do not speak to us but to God—for no one understands them when they talk in the Spirit about mysterious things. On the other hand, those who prophesy do talk to us—and they do so for our edification, encouragement and comfort. Those who speak in tongues benefit only themselves, but those who prophesy benefit all the church. ... I would much rather you prophesy. ... As long as you eagerly desire spiritual gifts, desire those that benefit the entire community. ... It must always be for the common good. ... Prophets can always control their spirit of prophecy. God is a God of peace, not disorder. ... Let everything be done with propriety and order.

I Corinthians 12:4-14:5, 12, 26b, 32-33, 40. int

Spiritual community, gifts, and ministry or service

The well-known passage on love in the above quotation is often read out of context, as exalting personal love. In fact, it's embedded at the heart of a passage on relationships in spiritual community. It is the ultimate expression of Paul's vision of the loving, forgiving, forbearing, "un-self-centered" behavior appropriate in spiritual community. Here love is plainly stated to be a gift of the Spirit, as it is called one of the fruits of the Spirit in Galatians. In Galatians, love is the first fruit listed. Here love is called the greatest of the gifts—and the best way of all. All three descriptive phrases express that real love is beyond simple human capacity. They hint at the mysteriousness with which it arises in us.

One of the things Paul understood superlatively well is spiritual community: its spiritual basis and lessons, as well as the human failings and problems that make it so difficult. Paul's mystical sense of living or being "in Christ" gives an added dimension to his sense of the community as the outward, visible, physical body or manifestation of the Spirit that animated and guided Jesus—present among all-too-human beings.

Paul's vision is taken to another level in this great image of the *ekklesia* (the assembly, meeting or church) as a body or organism animated and guided by the Spirit, with love at its heart. His vision also illuminates community and community interactions as another sacrament in Quaker life. We are the outward body of Christ to the extent that we come together with the individual and collective intention of being guided by the Spirit of Christ. The same reality is seen from a slightly different angle in the Quaker view of community as "Gospel Order": an ordering of common life that both permits and relies on the immediacy of Divine Guidance.

What is important here is the sense that our different abilities are functional and God-given. We are not each meant to do everything or all meant to be the same. We are meant to supply one another's lacks, evoke and celebrate one another's capacities, and work together for the good of each and all, under Divine Guidance. Paul emphasizes, especially in chapter 14, that gifts are not for ego-enhancement or self-aggrandizement, but for building up the community and nurturing the organism in the life of the Spirit. Some of the gifts he enumerates sound foreign to modern Friends. Others are clearly as important for our life together today as they were to the church in Corinth. And some unnamed or even unnameable ministries should be understood to be a tacit part of the list.

Some modern Friends resist the word "ministry" under the mistaken impression that it brings with it implications of the kinds of specialness or holiness that have been attributed to the "ordained clergy" of other churches. From the beginning of the Christian tradition, ministry—and the Greek and Latin words it translates—have referred to service. As part of the Reformation, our tradition has carried the understanding that all of us have not only the capacity but the obligation to minister, to be of service. Some, however, are more fitted than others for particular functions such as preaching, administration, pastoral care, and so on. It is often experience brought in from some other church that causes some Friends to regard a sense of leading as presumptuous, inflation of ego or a claim to holiness.

At the outset, the Reformation churches denied a sense of specialness or sacredness to their clergy. Luther insisted ministry was to be undertaken and performed faithfully just like any other job or calling. Friends, in particular, have felt it important to focus on the sacredness of what is being ministered and the ordinaryness of the one who ministers it. Friends' tradition has always been clear that we are all led to some services. God uses us in the midst of our imperfections, although following the leading can be part of the transformative process. To submit to the leading is to yield ego and self-will; and no special status is ascribed to the one who serves. Our leadership has tried to be truly a "servant-leadership". The imagery of being simply a channel for the Spirit occurs frequently in reference to Quaker ministry.

At a deeper level, ministry refers to service as ways in which each of us brings to one another the measure of the Spirit we have received, in the particular manner we have received it. We minister the life-giving Spirit of God to one another in countless nameable and unnameable ways. To call one another to live more consciously and with more commitment into our gifts and their implications is to invite one another into more abundant life. Each person who opens himself to more abundant life, opens more abundant life for the community. In terms of listening attentiveness for and to God among us, the gifts of the Spirit may be thought of as the particular ways each organ of the body attends to and cares for the others and the whole.

Another dimension of our listening is attentiveness to the specific gifts of others. Discernment and nurture of gifts were traditional gifts of elders. It's important to remember that some people really do have a special gift for it. We must remember, however, that all of us bear some measure of responsibility for discerning, evoking and encouraging one another in this way. If it is assumed to be "everyone's" task, however, it is often treated as nobody's responsibility.

Drawing forth people's capacities for building up the community, in itself, builds up community. Discerning, evoking, nurturing and supporting God's gifts in others is also a happy antidote to the temptation to self-centered fascination with our own gifts. It can help to heal us of the alienation that self-concern often brings. It can draw us into relationship, love and the wholeness of community. It isn't very helpful to try to build community from our wounds and brokenness, or our exasperation, judgment and conflict. It is more wholesome for our community to be developed from—and focused on—the God-givenness of people's being and lives.

Focusing on the gifts of the Spirit in others, on the ways in which they have been given to us and our community for our good, can actually be a very helpful element in the reconciliation of conflicts and antipathies. When we find ourselves at odds with others, it's very human to focus primarily on what we think is wrong with them, how we want them to change (while we remain perfect as we are). Our relation to the conflict may be transformed by holding them in the Light with the intention of being shown how—at least embryonically—they are gifted by the Spirit, how—at least potentially—they are organically fitted into the wholeness of our community.

Amazingly often, what causes difficulty is the defect of a virtue, the perversion or denial of a gift, the shadow cast by authentically high aspiration—our own as well as those of others. By opening to this possibility, we may be shown the way to celebrate the gifts of others rather than struggle with them.

Some caution in naming and claiming of gifts

Healing and spiritual growth can come through faithfully attending to one's own gifts, callings, concerns and leadings. In the present context, I want to add a parenthetical word of caution about too facile a naming and claiming of gifts. In our enthusiasm for laying hold of a positive orientation to others and for a celebration of giftedness in community, we sometimes slip into an unfortunate, superficial mutual admiration, fraught with potential harm for the community. Entering into the naming of gifts with insufficient awe and prayer can lead us to name skills or personal qualities that lack the weight of spiritual gifts.

The individualism of our culture actively promotes an isolated self-centeredness. It engenders a sometimes desperate and pathetic longing for marks of specialness—of which Andy Warhol's sardonic "fifteen minutes of fame" is emblematic—to which few of us are totally immune. We must take care not to overinvest in the specialness of our own gifts or those of others even as we name, celebrate and live into them together.

A former spiritual director of mine kept over her kitchen sink a plaque with eight or nine baby opposums shown hanging upside down by their tails from a branch. On the ground below them, their mother was shown admonishing them, "Always remember you are absolutely unique—just like everybody else."

Queries

Are you more comfortable with the image of the Body of Christ, with the idea of Gospel Order, or of spiritual community—or with some other image or analog for our oneness in community? How does your vision enhance your sense of life in the meeting? How does it differ from a vision of community built by human effort? How is it the same? What aspects of your meeting feel more like an institution? What aspects feel like an organism? What makes the difference? How does your community life relate to God?

Related passages on gifts occur in Romans 12:3-13 and Ephesians 4:1-7, 11-16. Notice the valuations of the various abilities. Are you able to accept a valuation so contrary to that of secular society? Do you tend to want people to be more like yourself? Do you tend to want to stand out from the community? If so, how do you respond to those feelings? How might they build up community? ... subvert it?

What gifts are you especially aware of in your meeting that build up (edify) the community? Where do they seem to be operating most freely and fully and visibly at this time? Where are they working for the good of the meeting, but hidden from sight? What obstructs the development of gifts in your community? Is there someone in your community who is particularly gifted at discerning, evoking or developing latent gifts in others?

What gifts do you bring to the community—functional or spiritual—either latently or in developed form? Are you being called to grow into some new service? Are you resisting or responding?

Have you ever felt drawn to name or support gifts in another person? If so, what did you do about it? If so, is this a frequent occurence? Might you be being nudged to attend more intentionally to this leading? Has anyone else spontaneously affirmed this gift in you? ... more than one person?

Do you hold others in the Light with the intention of seeing the giftedness and other ways the Spirit is working through them for the good of the community? Do you celebrate the spiritual gifts of others inwardly or outwardly? How? How often?

What do you feel is the difference between the love Paul describes and sentimentality? What might it mean that love—rather than our personal gifts in ministry—is the greatest gift in and to community? ... that love is a gift rather than an achievement? Relate this to your personal experience of meeting life.

Elizabeth O'Connor and Jean Vanier speak of the ways in which both envy and adulation undermine the development of gifts in service of the organism or community. Have you experienced either one in your meeting or in your own life? It might be fruitful to journal about the effects of one, the other or both of these feelings on service in the community.

Resources and references for spiritual gifts

Howard Brinton.
Friends for 300 Years.
ch. 7.

Wilmer Cooper.
A Living Faith.
ch. 6.

Sandra Cronk.
Gospel Order: A Quaker Understanding of Faithful Church Community.
PHP #297.

Sandra Cronk.
Peace Be With You: A Study of the Spiritual Basis of the Friends Peace Testimony.
The Meeting as the School for Peacemakers; ... A Center for Transformation; ... Where Forgiveness is Offered; ... The Body of Christ in the World.

Dean Freiday.
"The Early Quakers and the Doctrine of Authority".
Quaker Religious Thought.
Vol. 15, #1 (Autumn 1973).

Alastair Heron.
Gifts and Ministries: a discussion paper on eldership.

James Hillman.
The Soul's Code: In Search of Character and Calling.

London Yearly Meeting.
Christian faith and practice.
(1952). ch 7: #317-319, Unity of spirit.

Elizabeth O'Connor.
The Eighth Day of Creation: discovering your gifts.
esp. pp. 34-41.

David Spangler.
The Call.

William P. Taber, Jr.
"Worship in the Conservative Tradition",
in *Quaker Worship in North America.*
Francis Hall, ed.

Jean Vanier.
Community and Growth.
esp. pp. 31-42; and chs. 6-7.

Elizabeth Watson.
"Worship that Comes from Silence in the General Conference Tradition",
in *Quaker Worship in North America.*
Francis Hall, ed.
p.115.

Vocal ministry in service of the meeting's life

Prophecy and mysticism

In some sense, the discernment that lies at the heart of Quaker spirituality is most characteristically recognized in vocal ministry. It can be seen in the effort to distinguish an authentic leading of the Spirit to speak from the purely human desire to share, to instruct or to straighten out the previous speaker, to be thought wise, good or "spiritual", or simply from the need for attention.

You've probably noticed the similarity and differences between Quaker vocal ministry and Paul's description of prophecy in the church. Vocal ministry is classically understood to be permissible only if the minister is moved by the Spirit of God, for the upbuilding of the community—most particularly to turn people to their Inward Teacher or Guide. The authentic leading to speak usually comes through a heart, mind and life prepared by devotional reading, meditation on religious truth, prayer, faithful following of God's guidance and leadings between meetings—and a sensitivity to the work of God within the meeting for worship.

Although the message and words may have been forming for some time, perhaps years, the sense of permission or freedom to speak them must be sensed at a particular time and place lest we outrun our Guide, or mistake what has been given for our personal guidance as being for the entire meeting.

In the Old Testament, the prophets were those who heard and conveyed the guidance of God. They called to a people who had lost their Way, a people succumbing to the temptation to be assimilated to the surrounding culture, to the temptation to accumulate more than their share of the goods of this world, to forget the needs of "the little ones", widows, orphans and dispossessed, to forget love of neighbor—even to forget God. The classic, succinct, prophetic statement of God's requirements in the Old Testament was Micah's: "To do justice, love mercy and walk humbly with God." (Micah 6:8, KJV)

The New Testament extended the prophetic call from love of neighbor to include love even of one's enemies, while continuing to stress care of the "little ones". These now also included the socially outcast, the despised, the disabled and diseased. Paul expresses the expectation that, in the early Christian house churches, there would be people given the gift of prophecy for the sake of the church community.

In much of Protestant tradition, there is a line drawn between the prophet who speaks for God to the community out of ethical concern and the mystic who is said to be individualistic in his spirituality and relationship with God. As has been expressed in various places, both in this volume and in the one preceding it, Quaker spirituality does not distinguish between the prophetic tradition and mysticism (Hinshaw).

The mystic is plunged into and through the Center, back into the world as a transformed person with experiential rather than merely cognitive knowledge of the oneness of our being in God's Love. The mystic is given an unfolding awareness of the implications of that experience for his own life and for that of the community. Many Quakers have also experienced that, when we listen for God, we may be plunged through our individual centers into unity not only with God but with the whole of humanity and the creation in God's Love. Whether it is sensed in visionary, auditory, kinesthetic, intuitive or other ways, the urge to embody and speak of the consequences is a source of ministry.

A heightened sense of God's love and care for each and all of us together lies at the heart of the prophet's authority. It gave Old Testament prophets the empowerment and responsibility to begin their messages with the words, "Thus saith the Lord." In both the Old Testament prophecy to the nation and in the New Testament house churches, the prophet's message might call people to greater and more inward attention to God. Or the prophet might call his people to turn from outward idols—either in the literal sense of false images or in the metaphorical sense of the lures and addictions of money, power or sexual misconduct—to the outward expression of relationship with the Divine in ethical conduct: love of the "little ones", one's neighbors, even one's enemies.

Friends have felt their vocal ministry to be prophetic in this sense of an utterance inspired by God for the good of the community, in a meeting gathered in God's Spirit and Love. Contemplative or mystical prayer in which self or ego is given over or transcended is the ongoing, living work of the Spirit—God's Will flowing through us and the universe. In a gathered meeting for worship, it is the work of God that is experienced. In the Quaker tradition, to pray or otherwise minister vocally is to sense, to gather up the work of the Spirit in our midst. It is truly awesome to speak for the Spirit or to describe what the Spirit is doing in our midst.

Awe of vocal ministry

The Old Testament records the reluctance and even fear some of the greatest prophets expressed when they felt called by God to this ministry (Exod. 3:1-4:17; Jer. 1:4-10). The journals of Quaker ministers often express a similar sense of unworthiness, fear and resistance to a felt call into vocal ministry even to the point of illness. John Woolman describes his initial response to the call in a way that makes it clear what the trepidations and risks were in vocal ministry when it was taken with such seriousness. Few people today attempt to keep to vocal ministry that has been so carefully discerned to be of the Spirit. Few people in most meetings would understand or credit the spiritual authority such vocal ministers bear when faithful.

In the absence of an understanding of the prophetic nature of Quaker vocal ministry and its grounding in interior worship, much contemporary vocal ministry has become modeled on experiences of the attenders in other settings. In the absence of knowledge of the tradition of giving over self and will, ego and intellect to baptism in the silence, people may model their inner work and outward behavior on something else. The model might be anything from a therapy group, to a support group such as a twelve-step group, or a forum for expression of opinions, uplifting thoughts or calls to specific activities.

Some of us see in the silence an opportunity to share with the community some striking events, issues, personal problems or reflections about the week. Before we speak them into the silent prayer and worship of the meeting these events, issues, problems or reflections are best held in the Light for discernment of the work of God within them. We must question whether they have been given to build up the spiritual life of the community: whether there is anything in them consecrated by an indefinable sense of Divine Prompting—or even urging—to offer into the silence. Otherwise they will remain inauthentic ministry, not of the Spirit, no matter how uplifting, interesting or thought-provoking.

It has traditionally been an awesome undertaking to risk breaking the silence of the community's prayer and communion with God. It has been said that authentic ministry fulfills the silence of worship rather than breaks it. One speaks "out of" the silence in the sense of responding to, expressing or pointing to the depth in which we are all grounded. In earlier times, the meeting for worship was understood as the Quaker time of Communion with God and with one another in God. Earlier Friends used to distinguish between the "communion bread" that was inwardly given to us to be shared out with the community to nurture it, to enhance or fulfill its unity in God. They contrasted this with "bread for home".

Sharing, counsel and discussion

In this generation, we often experience a startlingly chatty tone in meeting that betrays a lack of depth from which the words are coming. There sometimes is an amusement and easy laughter in the listeners that suggests their separation from, rather than union with, the speaker. It indicates entertainment rather than prayer, diversion from the depths rather than directedness into it. Messages are often embedded in a wealth of personal detail that frequently draws attention to the speaker's giftedness or neediness rather than to the supposed Source of the message—even as it is rendered more comfortably folksy. Are we modern sophisticates more nervous about entering into awe itself than earlier Friends were? Are we less in awe of the Source of our being and of our words than John Woolman and countless other Quaker ministers of the past were?

In their Swarthmore Lecture, *Images and Silence*, Brenda Heales and Chris Cook distinguished two major categories of modern meetings for worship that are notable for the content of what is said rather than for where the words come from. Rather than meeting for worship of God, modern Friends often find themselves in what Heales and Cook have called "Meeting for Counseling" or "Meeting for Discussion".

In a "Meeting for Counseling", someone rises to speak in the manner of a therapy or support group, describing a personal pain or trouble. The remainder of the meeting then becomes focused on the person's pain or trouble—rather than on the still, small voice within. Speaker after speaker rises to offer consolation, advice or sympathy. Heales and Cook do not question the need for a meeting to be responsive to the pain or trouble of individuals within it. But they seriously question the meeting for worship as the setting for such response.

Human counseling and consoling in the milieu of worship betrays the fact that the meeting has failed to provide another venue for pastoral care, comfort, healing and problem-solving. Verbally bringing distress to the people present for worship—for them to undertake verbally to heal, save, fix or solve it in the time of worship—betrays a failure of the sense of the Presence of the Healing Spirit. It betrays a failure of the very sense that the nature of the Spirit is healing, if together we yield to it in a stilling of our own wisdom, labels, projects or desires. It betrays a failure of the sense that God is present with and for us in our suffering; ... a failure of the sense that we have neither to bear it alone nor rearrange it all for ourselves.

Frequently the rush to help in the meeting for worship is so heavy that there is barely space between speakers to take in what has been said. If there were someone present with an authentic message of the Spirit for the sufferer or for the meeting, they might well find no opening in which to speak it. If spoken, there might be no pause or hush in which to take it in.

In what Heales and Cook call a "Meeting for Discussion" someone rises to pose a topic or question that might be theological or to make a plea that might refer to a matter of social or political justice. Thereafter, the procession of speakers is much the same as those in the "Meeting for Counseling". This time the suggestions are more apt to be intellectual analysis or anecdotes of experiences or situations related to the subject. Again, Heales and Cook are clear that there needs to be a place in each meeting for such questions to be examined, but that worship is not the time and place; vocal ministry is not notional, political, theological or speculative. It is not a call or invitation to action with or without phone numbers and announcements.

Neither is inspired ministry the same as teaching. Teaching may emerge from prophetic ministry. But it is different from history lessons, from astute analysis of the situation, or from other lessons that arise from the rational, cognitive part of ourselves. Vocal ministry is not even for teaching about vocal ministry when the meeting has gotten out of the Life. This very restraint leaves the faithful, present to worship God, peculiarly vulnerable to invasive outsiders. We are even more vulnerable to those among ourselves who have failed to understand or to be taught the basis on which meetings for worship have traditionally been held.

Heales and Cook relate a story of people asking for silence in such meetings and being ignored. I have experienced people asking for the meeting to return to the Center to take what has been said into the Light, only to be ignored. Just as the "Meeting for Counsel" illustrates a need for more creative pastoral care in the meeting, so the "Meeting for Discussion" illustrates a need for Adult Religious Education to bring people into fuller understanding of the basis of Quakerism and its prophetic tradition of vocal ministry. It requires considerable spiritual experience, self-discipline and discernment to minister faithfully in the Quaker tradition. The occurrence of a "Meeting for Discussion" also reflects a need for forums to discuss issues of social order that are troubling to members of the meeting.

Rules of thumb

An article by "Helpful Hannah" in the *Friendly Woman* a few years ago featured a flow chart, eliminating several possible mistaken motives for speaking in meeting, in order for people to check themselves when the impulse to speak arose. It's such a useful flow chart that requests to copy flooded in and it was reprinted in *Friends Journal*. Still, useful as it is, there is no check list comprehensive enough to substitute for the development of discernment over time. One must discern whether what presents itself to be spoken out of the silence is of the Spirit for the community at this time, whether it is best kept for some other occasion or medium, or for one's own illumination. It's amazing how many messages, that at first seem to come for "them", turn out to be most meaningful when directed inward by the one to whom they are given.

"Helpful Hannah", Douglas Steere, Bill Taber and Elizabeth Watson (see resources), among others, give us many helpful rules of thumb for discerning a "true" leading to speak or not to speak from a "false" one. None of them is adequate of itself, but each is helpful when used together with other tests. There is also the Quaker test of a sense of heart-pounding, trembling awe and compulsion. Again, this alone is not adequate; but it may be when taken together with other experiences. On the other hand, the phenomenon may be as simple as tachycardia or stage fright. Some experienced ministers have reported that, with time and experience, ministry was no longer such a sweaty experience—although the awe of the Divine never wears off.

"Quench not the Spirit"

Yet there was a historical period when meetings languished and some died out for lack of vocal ministry—out of excessive awe for the service or excessively authoritarian control over who could and could not speak, what could and could not be said. To guard against silencing all ministry, I remind Friends of the fondness of earlier Friends for the passage from I Thessalonians that enjoins church members to (in the words of the King James Version) "quench not the Spirit". The passage enjoining Peter to "feed my sheep ... feed my lambs", in the epilogue to the Gospel According to John was also cherished in this connection. Metaphors for vocal ministry among Friends often hover around feeding, bread, refreshment, water of life and the like, stressing nurture for the life of the Spirit.

Friends were in the forefront of those who sought freedom to speak in Church based on the movements and revelations of the Spirit in their hearts rather than having the privilege restricted to those who had been educated in a certain way or chosen by the social elite to speak. What I urge here is not a quenching of the Spirit, but rather living closer to the Spirit in order better to know what truly comes from that Source and what comes from elsewhere. Discerning true jade is important in our vocal ministry as well as in all else. Our discernment is never infallible, although the Spirit is. We can only hope, through faithfulness, to grow in the measure of the gift of discernment we are given.

The qualities of the minister

The winds of the Spirit blow where she lists (after John 3:8). Our great task in life is to have our sails spread to catch them and allow ourselves to be propelled by them where she wills, when they come. Part of spreading our sails is a life given over to personal spiritual practices and disciplines such as those outlined in the first volume of this book. We are "tendered", as Friends used to say of being made attentive and responsive. Our minds are prepared with reading and reflection on spiritual matters, a regular time in speaking and listening, conversation or communion with God, and a life given over to following the Guidance given in those conversations. We are "tendered" into more perfect love with our flawed fellow human beings and the creation for which we have stewardship.

The minister is also helped by the self-knowledge of motivations and sources of impulses that can grow in times of retirement, of silent waiting, of watching our thoughts. Over years of practice, we come to know—more perhaps than we wanted to—about the springs of our impulses, the demands of our wounds, the distortions of our brokenness. We learn to distinguish them from, or in the midst of, the upwellings of Spirit that impel us to our feet.

In our generation we are too psychologically sophisticated to expect that our motivations will ever be purely of the Spirit. We do not expect, as some earliest Friends did, to become a hollow reed or a trumpet through which the Spirit might blow. We have come to know that the human psyche may be a legitimate medium through which God's word is spoken—as well as merely a distraction or a delusion. Our sophistication requires even more finely tuned discernment than that of our spiritual forebears. Frequently, however, we give discernment shorter shrift than their awe might ever have permitted them.

Some earlier Friends acknowledged the mixture of motives, quoting by analogy the passage from the Old Testament law that says "Thou shalt not muzzle the ox which is treading out the corn." (Deut. 25:4 KJV) In other words, it is permissable that there be something in it for the person who is serving the community. Knowledge of some potential mixture in our motivation does not, however, allow free rein to every passing impulse.

The expectation is always present that ministry is for the service of the community— not by bringing it into conformity with the wishes or viewpoint of the minister, but by bringing it closer to God. It takes more spiritual sophistication to discern when our flawed motives are sufficiently laden with the winds of the Spirit to justify speaking the words that have come to us. We must sense when our words may be of a piece with what is at work with the silence, rather than merely adding to words that have gone before, in order to satisfy something in our very human selves.

All this is helped by the personal disciplines described in Volume I, and the attentiveness to community and unity of which I've been speaking in this volume. As we prayerfully attend to the others who worship with us, both in and out of the time of worship, we may become sensitized not only to the concerns of their lives but to how the Spirit is moving in and among them. One expectation of Quaker traveling ministers in an earlier time was that they would have this capacity to sense or feel the spiritual state of individuals or of a meeting as a whole. Often their ministry arose as they sensed the Word of God addressed to this spiritual condition. The minister might articulate his sense of the Spirit moving and working within the meeting. Or as yet another part of the work of the Spirit the minister might respond in vocal prayer.

To rise to speak has been in our tradition an awesome responsibility. Yet, the first lesson of the minister may be, "Hear and obey." If our personal and corporate practice is directed to listening for the guidance of the Spirit among us, there can be no more appropriate response to that Guidance than to yield to it.

Humility is not only the ability to see the truth naked without interpretation or distortion, but also the ability to see one's own nakedness before what is. We must, therefore, be open and humble before whatever is given us to articulate for the meeting. Granted, the words will be ours. We have no other words to use for our experience than those dredged up from the rag-bag of our life's experiences and readings, patched together in a kind of simultaneous translation from a mysterious non-language into a quilt we hope will be pleasing to the Spirit who speaks to and through us. We must perform this task in humility and responsibilty and then *sit down*, resisting the urge to add to it, embellish it, round it off or complete it. That task may be given to another—or not.

I don't know whether by disciplined faithfulness we can recapture the sensitivity of this ministry of an earlier time. Our intuitions have been blunted by the rationalist education we've had and its circumscription of what is real or valid, of what true sources of words might be. In writing this book, however, I am staking my belief that we have experienced the aridity of reductionisms and circumscribed spaces; and that we thirst for something more. That something is always on offer to us if we are willing to redirect ourselves and take on a life of disciplined spiritual practice. In the midst of a surfeit of words, many meetings languish for lack of ministry that springs from a life lived with intentionality toward God. We may not all want or be capable of such a life; but even a few members may make a difference to the nourishment and life of a meeting (Herrman).

What meetings do *not* need is self-appointed saviors who are convinced of their calling and impose with excessive frequency their enthusiasms, viewpoints, assumptions of authority and demands upon the worship of the meeting. Friends' worship is particularly vulnerable to people who have special causes to press or are in need of occupying a role or status that will bolster a fragile or damaged ego. For the good of the meeting as well as of themselves, they need to be gently discouraged and helped to find what they need in another setting within the meeting community.

If all this sounds discouraging of speaking in meeting, it is because I think that, at this juncture in our history, many of our meetings are in a pendulum swing in vocal ministry. In the recent past, some meetings have had a period of insufficient vocal ministry that failed to feed the sheep and nourish the life in God. Unfortunately, in some meetings, the pendulum now seems to be swinging toward a kind of secularization of vocal ministry that may reflect either a discomfort with, or fear of, silence—or forgetting what it is that Friends found within their hearts in the silence.

In order for us to remember what we have sought and found in the silence, non-ministering Friends need also to reclaim their own capacity for spiritual discernment. We need people who are able to speak authoritatively of what is and is not of the Spirit. We must find Ground on which to stand that will give us courage to reject a spurious freedom to speak that leaves us at the mercy of any passing impulse in indiscriminate people. We need people with a capacity to be clear about whether they are quenching something that is truly inappropriate to a time of worship—or quenching the Spirit herself.

This is not a responsibility for individuals to take on themselves simply because they do not like what is said, or the length or frequency of utterance. Here again we need some organ of communal discernment of the authenticity of ministry, of the rightness of encouragement or discouragement and of who is the appropriate person to perform the encouragement or discouragement. These questions lead us to the place elders traditionally occupied among Friends.

Qualities of the listeners

With the focus of attention on the vocal ministers, we often overlook the spiritual role in the meeting for worship of those who are not called to speak. We do, of course, participate in worship simply as worship however the Spirit of God leads us in any given meeting. Part of our prayer, however, may be that God will bring to their feet the proper ministers to "feed the sheep" as they need to be fed at that time. We may pray that those who are led to speak be strengthened to respond to the call. Our prayers can help uphold the speaker to stay close to her Guide. We may also pray that those whose ministry is inappropriate for this particular occasion, or have "bread for home" remain in their seats.

Then we may pray to receive the vocal ministry given us as prayerfully as possible. We may pray to be inwardly teachable, that we not remain in our critical, surface consciousness or "tune out" at the first word that does not accord with our personal theology or political view. Rather than critiquing it, we may pray that we stay with the message, inwardly supporting the minister and inwardly seeking the way in which the message as a whole may be for our edification. We may pray to receive the message at the most profound level of our being, finding the level at which we are being addressed and redirected by God.

Regulating spiritual gifts in relation to vocal ministry

... When you come together each of you brings a psalm or some instruction or a revelation, or speaks in a tongue or gives an interpretation. Let all these things be done in a way that will build up the community. ... The prophetic spirit is to be under the prophets' control, for God is a God not of disorder but of peace. ... Do you really think that you are the source of the word of God? Or that you are the only people to whom it has come?

I Corinthians 14:26b-33, 36. NJB

Do not stifle the Spirit or despise the gift of prophecy with contempt; test everything and hold on to what is good and shun every form of evil.

I Thessalonians 5:19-22. NJB

[In the interest of keeping the focus on discipline, I omit here the controversial statement in verses 34-35, on the silence and subordination of women in the church. See Margaret Fell's reading of that passage.]

Queries

Is the vocal ministry in your meeting prophetic? Is it for the building up of the community? What other gifts have you experienced as building up meeting community?

Have you ever been moved to speak in meeting? How did you test the leading? What was your response? How did you feel about it later? Was your discernment confirmed or questioned inwardly or outwardly? What did that confirmation or questioning feel like? How have you responded to impulses subsequently? Do you come to meeting "purposing neither to speak nor not to speak"?

Have you ever "quenched the Spirit" prompting you to speak in meeting? Has anyone else ever quenched the Spirit in you? If so, what did that feel like? What has been your experience with vocal ministry since? Have you ever quenched the Spirit in anyone else?

How do you prepare yourself for meeting for worship? ... for the possibility of being useful in the service of vocal ministry?

How do you respond to vocal ministry that makes you uncomfortable? ... that seems to you to come from some source other than the Spirit?

References and resources for vocal ministry

Margaret Hope Bacon, ed.
Wilt Thou Go on My Errand: Three 18th Century Journals of Quaker Women Ministers.
passim.

Robert Barclay.
The Apology in Modern English.
Proposition 10, Ministry.

Richard Bauman.
Let Your Words Be Few: Symbolism of speaking and silence among seventeenth century Quakers.
chs. 1-3.

Samuel Bownas.
A Description of Qualifications Necessary to a Gospel Minister.

William Charles Braithwaite.
Spiritual Guidance in the Experience of the Society of Friends.

Howard Brinton.
Friends for 300 Years.
ch. 5.

Howard Brinton.
Quaker Journals: Varieties of Religious Experience Among Friends.
ch. 6.

Howard Brinton.
Prophetic Ministry.
PHP. no number or date.

Sydney Chambers and Carolynne Myall.
"Dear Helpful Hannah".
FJ, 9/91, p. 19.
Humorous and helpful flowchart for introduction to discernment of leadings into vocal ministry.

Margaret Fell.
Womens' Speaking Justified.
p. 9.

Elisabeth Schüssler Fiorenza.
In Memory of Her: A Feminist Theological Reconstruction of Christian Origins.

Garman, Applegate, Benefiel and Meredith, eds.
Hidden in Plain Sight: Quaker Women's Writings 1650-1700.
Tracts of Proclamation and Warning; Journals, Autobiographies, and Travel Narratives.

Brenda Clifft Heales & Chris Cook.
Images and Silence.
chs. 1-2.

John A. Herrman.
"A God Beyond Words".
FJ, 11/90.

Abraham Joshua Heschel.
The Prophets.

Cecil Hinshaw.
An Apology for Perfection.
PHP #138, esp. pp. 7-9.

Robert J. Leach.
Women Ministers: A Quaker contribution.
PHP #227.

London Yearly Meeting (1952).
Christian faith and practice.
ch. 5, Vocal ministry.

John Punshon.
Encounter with Silence.
chs. 10-11.

Douglas V. Steere.
On Speaking Out of the Silence.
PHP #182.

Douglas V. Steere.
Where Words Come From.

Douglas V. Steere.
Prayer and Worship.

Caroline Stephen.
Quaker Strongholds.
Free Ministry.

William Taber.
"Worship in the
Conservative Tradition",
in Hall, ed. *Quaker Worship in
North America.*

Elizabeth Watson.
 "Worship in the General
Conference Tradition",
in Hall, ed. *Quaker Worship in
North America.*

Lloyd Lee Wilson.
*Essays on the Quaker
Vision of Gospel Order.*
Taking on the Risks of
Ministry.

John Woolman.
The Journal.
Moulton, ed. esp. p. 31.

Eldering as service in the meeting's life

Committees responsible to nurture the spiritual life of the meeting

As Quaker tradition has evolved, there are often two committees that are entrusted with the care of the communal life of the meeting. One usually has responsibility for the spiritual life of the meeting: worship, ministry and the spiritual nurture of meeting members. The other has responsibility for the pastoral care of the meeting's members, both individually and corporately. There are also variations in which some other committees take on part of the responsibilities for which these two committees are responsible: for instance, Religious Education, Adult Religious Education or Care of the Elderly.

The responsibilities of these two committees lie so close together that they are sometimes fused into one committee of Overseers, or of Ministry and Counsel, or Ministry and Oversight. At the very least, the responsibilities lie so close together that they will usually find it necessary to hold joint meetings or a joint retreat once or twice a year. Other arrangements have been tried. Your meeting may not be among the above; but it will probably be some variant on them.

In the evolution of Quaker meeting structure, the major responsibility for both kinds of nurture of meeting life, spiritual and pastoral care, was part of the task of elders. As you can see, that means eldering took no single form or function, even though it is now preserved in corporate memory primarily in terms of discouragement of inappropriate ministry or breaches of Quaker decorum.

I've treated earlier some of the various functions elders perform within meeting, whether they are or are not so named by modern meetings. The elders' function is to truly nurture the many facets of meeting life. If people don't have the requisite sensitivity, especially the gift of discernment born of long and profound dedication to the inner life with God, then mere committee membership will not make an elder of them. Being given the responsibility may evoke a latent gift and leading in some. In others it may evoke only an unfortunate authoritarianism, self-importance or excessive diffidence. Distinguishing the spirits in vocal ministry is just one of the many kinds of nurturing gifts that come under the heading of the gift of eldership. It is, however, the one with which I'll concern myself here.

When they appeared among early Friends, the most visible service elders rendered was nurturing vocal ministers. Vocal ministers, as speakers of the prophetic word to the community, were regarded as the primary nurturers of the meeting's spiritual life. The elders' gift and work has been referred to as more priestly than prophetic (Cronk). Yet, as surely as a minister needed to be able to distinguish where his or her words were coming from within, the elder needed to make that same discernment from outside.

The ministry of the elder was fairly hidden by contrast with that of the vocal minister. It was the fruit of the elders' own, long, hidden life in prayer with God, with all the ups and downs of such an interior life over time. If it weren't for the fact that elders were recognized, recorded and placed on the facing bench by the meeting, just as vocal ministers were, they might have spent their years quietly on the back benches of the meeting. Those to whom they ministered might never have been totally aware of being ministered to.

Indeed that was the case for me when I first came to Friends in Hartford (CT) Meeting where there had never been recorded elders. At the coffee hour I received pastoral care as they welcomed me among them, and inquired after the well-being of my children and myself. I was given spiritual nurture when they suggested books to read and meetings I might attend that would enhance my understanding of wider Quakerism, and help deepen my inner life. Both the pastoral care and the spiritual nurture knit me more closely into fellowship with Hartford Friends.

As often as possible I was included in trips to Quarterly Meeting, Yearly Meeting Committee Day, special events held by AFSC, FWCC, or FCNL. That meant getting into a car with four or five other Friends, invariably including some elders, and spending at least an hour on the road. In that time we not only became acquainted but, bit by bit, spoke quite informally of various dimensions of Quaker life. I have no doubt that I, too, was examined most discerningly without my realizing it. My opinions were solicited and treated with utmost respect. I'm not sure how conscious any of this activity was on the part of the people involved. Like most gifts and leadings, it seemed to grow quite simply and naturally out of who they were. It was the best kind of spiritual Friendliness.

Some of these same people turned up on my clearness committee when I finally applied for membership. Only years later did I realize that what I had experienced with them was also eldering, drawing me more and more closely into the authentic life of the meeting, making sure that I understood what it was about. Only some time after that realization did I recognize they had also been preparing me for service to the meeting, although they couldn't have anticipated what form it would take. In those days I never even thought of ministering vocally, much less teaching or nurturing the spiritual life myself. These unrecognized elders simply supported me, fed me and let the Spirit take me as she would. Their work bore fruit in unanticipated service only some time after I'd left Hartford.

Historically, people whose profound life in prayer rendered them especially sensitive to emanations of that same Life in others were more apt to be recorded as elders if they outwardly manifested their inner life by nurturing others. Those whose profound life in prayer led them into deep prayer for the meeting, that was often of special assistance in corporate centering, deepening and gathering, might spend their entire lives unrecognized until their deaths shifted the inward "feel" of the meeting. They were no less nurturers than the others, but were hidden in their nurture.

The more visible elders in service to the meeting were those who recognized where the words were coming from and accordingly encouraged or discouraged the speaker, suggested to them practices and readings to open themselves more fully to their spiritual gift. Sometimes elders accompanied ministers on their travels in a supportive role helping them to remain centered and "on track". Just as often, two ministers would accompany each other in mutual support, sharing the service in vocal ministry.

Eldering in love and tenderness

The marks of authentic eldering are not repressiveness or harshness, as recounted in folk memories of worst cases. Rather, ministry born in the experience of God's love overflows with love and tenderness. Eldering is a kind of spiritual parenting that is reflected in the current term "spiritual nurture", and in the Quaker use of the Biblical expression, "nursing mothers and fathers in Israel".

Like a loving parent, the elder works from her or his own experience of being loved. An elder has lived close to God long enough to have spent time seeking his or her own cleansing, healing and purification. Alone in the quiet by themselves they've known the nature and marks of God's work and of human struggle. Before learning to discern them in others. They've learned something of where their own resistances and aversions to others come from before approaching the delicate work of helping or guiding others to "true north", the Inward Teacher and Guide.

This inward work over time is the spiritual equivalent of learning to discern true jade and develop a connoisseurship of and respect for God's work in budding ministers. The work requires openness to the possibility that the minister's leading, work, or message in meeting, is authentic even if it is couched in language that is difficult to accept or from an imperfect source who is not otherwise valued. Indeed we all need to be aware of this possibility in vocal ministry before we "tune it out" or undertake from sheer discomfort to quench the source. Being too caught in our own preferences, wounds and personal limitations may make us quick to quench the words that discomfort us. In our haste we may fail to perceive that the irritating source was The Source.

For this reason eldering, in the sense of discouragement, is usually not undertaken as an individual matter except by the presumptuous. To discourage a vocal minister or some other kind of minister is always to risk quenching the authentic Spirit. In the tradition, discerning the necessity for this kind of eldering was best undertaken only in consultation with other people of experience and discernment, grounded in the life of the meeting as a spiritual community.

Early on, this would have been the work of a Meeting of Ministers and Elders. Today where the elder system has been abolished, the responsibility has passed to committees for worship and ministry, or ministry and counsel. Those committees, in turn, may discern who among them seems to have a particular gift for eldering that comes of love rather than judgmentalism. We need people who can "elder" in such a way that the person learns something new and helpful, without having felt "eldered" in the pejorative sense.

One older woman in my meeting tells of coming to Friends as the young fiancée of a Quaker, wondering how she would fare in a church so alien to that of her upbringing. She says that as soon as she saw the faces of the elders on the facing bench, her doubts were resolved. She knew that everything would be all right. Their clear, peaceful faces brought her to greater stillness and a sense of the truth of the religion practiced there. Now she herself is one of those people with a clear, peaceful face who helps others know what can be the fruit of a life lived in faithfulness. She also names and supports gifts in others.

Queries

Have you experienced the care of people serving as elders? Have you served as an elder yourself? If so, do you feel you lived into the vision of the position given here? Had the vision ever been communicated to you? How might you grow in this service? How might you be stretched or challenged in this service? Do you feel your meeting is well served by its committees of overseers, worship and ministry, or their equivalent so that they provide the functions of good eldering? Where have you experienced the strengths, the weaknesses, and the functioning of the body of Christ?

After misadventures with power in the nineteenth century, the office of elder among many Friends in the United States became synonymous with a rigid, admonitory role. In London Yearly Meeting's *Christian faith and practice*, admonition is only one function in a generally nurturing role for elders. Compare and contrast that function, as expressed in extract #343, with the selection from Matthew 18:15-20. What vision of community is implicit in the two selections? Why should admonition be part of spiritual community? Are you comfortable with it? Why or why not?

Do you know anyone in your meeting who seems to have the gifts of an elder without being recognized? How does that person manifest the gifts? How do you respond to that person? How do you help nurture them? Have you ever been nurtured by them? If so, what was it like? Have you ever been "eldered" by such a person rather than by someone merely expressing a personal opinion? If so, how did it feel? How did you respond? Have you yielded?

Is there a committee or are there other people in your meeting who have accepted the responsibility of discerning, encouraging and discouraging vocal ministry? How do they do this? How are their efforts received?

Pastoral care as service to meeting life

Committee responsibility for the pastoral care of the meeting

The care of the meeting and being under the care of the meeting have been related to the fellowship that arises from gathering and unity. Many of the ways that Friends have cared for each other are described as pastoral care in other churches. Among unprogrammed Friends, there is no paid clergy designated to undertake these pastoral responsibilities. This is just one of the ways in which we have abolished the laity, making us all priests to one another—that is, people who stand in the place of Christ, the Good Shepherd who feeds and tends the flock.

We are a flock of sheep who care for one another under Divine Guidance. That is entirely in keeping with the early Quaker assertion that our only Shepherd is Christ. William Taber reminds us that the ultimate source of true pastoral care is in the worship, transformation and divine leading of the care-giver. In the care of the meeting, as in so much of our spirituality, we are called to give over our preconceptions of how we might help or whom we might help. We are thrown back upon attentive waiting on Divine Guidance to know what is required of us.

The entire meeting membership is usually reminded that we all share in these duties. In part, we share because the weight of responsibility is really more than can be borne by a few people. The greater reason is that in a community that is also a School for Love, organizational structure—no matter how efficient—is a hollow substitute for living attentiveness to, and living concern for one another in the vicissitudes of life.

In all the yearly meeting disciplines of which I'm aware, however, a Committee of Overseers, or a Committee for Ministry and Counsel, or for Ministry and Oversight, bears the primary responsibility for the overall care of the meeting. Some people, when they find themselves appointed to a committee charged with pastoral care of the meeting, feel overwhelmed by the prospect of giving care in situations that are usually thought of as requiring professional help.

Situations requiring professional financial, psychological, medical, legal or other kinds of specialized help should naturally be referred to competent people. My meeting works spasmodically at keeping a "Book of Wisdom", actually a listing of the secular resources we have among us in the meeting: people either willing to be called upon for their professional assistance or to be consulted by someone in need, to help them ascertain where to turn for professional help if they need it.

There remains a great area of non-professional care to be covered by loving community when people are in need, crisis or confusion. For one thing, many small acts of kindness can ease burdens in a time of upheaval. In small meetings this kind of care is usually poured out spontaneously and informally. In larger, urban meetings, where daily encounter or communication is less likely, some organization is usually required to ensure that needs will not go overlooked or unmet.

Some meetings have a "casserole ministry" for occasions like a new baby, illness or bereavement when families might find it difficult to cope with the ordinary tasks of life. Taking care of young children is also helpful at such times, if they won't feel uneasy at being away from their families when things are unsettled. We can also give care by replacing household necessities after loss, by helping to pack or to move households when it's not possible for it all to be done professionally, or by harvesting a garden. There are innumerable kindnesses that probably come more naturally to smaller, rural meetings than to large, urban ones—although the latter often have sufficient hands to make light work of such kinds of help. These deeds say that people are loved and connected with others in all circumstances—a sense easily lost in urban settings.

Listening as pastoral care

The greatest help, however, can seem either ridiculously easy or frighteningly demanding, depending on our preconceptions. In the passages of life and hard decision making often our primary need is for someone just to be lovingly present with us, to listen to us as we seek God's meanings, God's guidance within, God's way forward for us. Such times may be marriage, birth, illness, painful losses of many kinds: divorce, terminal illness or bereavement or loss of employment.

Listening can be subverted by the fact that we often feel we haven't properly cared for someone unless we've given them something: advice, our personal wisdom, our personal perception of their situation and what they should be doing about it, a plan of action, a book to read, an anecdote about successful solution in a similar situation. We may shrink from offering to listen because we have nothing to offer. In fact, unsolicited offerings are usually experienced as intrusive. They are another face of our own need to be an active giver. They are also a close relative of attempts to heal, fix, save, convert or straighten someone out. They are not behaviors that make people feel loved, valued or cared for.

In a prolonged period of ill health, I was astonished by how often people—on very short acquaintance, sometimes minutes—would undertake to suggest a regime or a change of attitude for me. They were confident that they had grasped the essence of my difficulty and could straighten it out, when I had been unable to do so over considerable time. In those encounters, I did not feel loved or even respected. I felt invaded and denied my status as an intelligent adult capable of handling my own life. Above all, I was denied the opportunity, much less invitation, to explore the deeper meaning of my condition for myself without the imposition of someone else's discoveries. Nor was it presumed I would naturally ask persons of my choice for their wisdom when I felt the need.

In times of distress, a lot of advice overlooks our shared trust in the presence and guidance of God within and between us. We need bring nothing more to our encounter than the willingness to listen together with another. Douglas Steere says,

> To "listen" another's soul into a condition of disclosure and discovery may be almost the greatest service that any human being ever performs for another. ... For in penetrating to what is involved in listening do we not disclose the thinness of the filament that separates [people] listening openly to one another, and that of God intently listening to each soul?

It may not happen all at once, or even at the first hearing; but somewhere in the process, the speaker, the one being listened to, can begin to hear the guidance in, through and beyond her own words. Somewhere in the process, being listened to openly, attentively, even reverently becomes a revelation of Love. And there is nothing more empowering than Love.

Ultimately, the greatest gift is not our advice, suggestions or reorganization of someone's life or outlook, but the gift of our time, presence and willingness to be lovingly attentive to the perceptions and explorations of others. We "listen" their souls into "disclosure and discovery", in trouble, sorrow or transition, restraining the impulse to put our own stamp on the time.

Patience may be necessary as well. Where wounds are deep, it may be necessary to permit a person to go over and over the events before both pain and healing can finally be released into the hands of God. A true spiritual friend is one who can be present for this process without trying to hurry it along. Too often, grieving people are given a time limit by which to pull up their socks, put aside memories, regrets and grief, and reenter life as usual. In fact, grieving may well be a life-long process, with variations dependent on personalities and circumstances. If we are truly to minister to one another, we must be prepared to stay a rather long course in openness to the other.

[For fuller consideration of interpersonal listening see the sections on worship sharing and its use in spiritual friendship groups and spiritual formation groups in Chapter 7 of Volume I. See also the paragraphs on the use of clearness committees and discernment groups in Chapter 3 on discernment in this Volume.]

Queries, Advice and Journaling Suggestions

Nurturing the spiritual life of the meeting is the function in which the gifts and services of Oversight and Ministry or Eldership meet and overlap. Do you feel any calling to this kind of service?

Do you feel that the committees responsible for these services in your meeting exercise them with a sense of leading to build spiritual community? Note that membership on these committees is usually reserved for Friends in full membership with the meeting and with some years of seasoning in meeting life. But also be aware that, while members of a committee have a particular responsibility for that area of service, all members of the meeting are considered to share that responsibility as they are able.

Major areas under the care of the meeting have been:
• Marriages
• Care and spiritual formation of children
• Marital and child problems
• Divorce
• Financial disaster
• Illness
• Dying and death
• Mental deficiency
• Emotional disorder

You might journal or do worship sharing to explore the implications of mutuality, listening and love in these situations as the meeting brings them under its care. You may want to journal your experience first before you turn to the queries below.

How does the spirit of the care-giver or the nature of the care offered affect your feelings? How might reluctance to receive help affect community relationships? ... communion? Have you been the recipient of un-listening, intrusive, interfering or demeaning care? What did it feel like? What did you do? Has your meeting overlooked you in time of distress? If so, how did you feel about your commitment to the meeting? What did you do? Where have you turned?

Do you feel that giving care to others places you in a superior position? Can you accept help as easily as you give it? If not, reflect carefully on what gets in the way. What is your rationale for being unable or unwilling to receive loving help? What role does rugged individualism play? Does self-centeredness, rather than God-centeredness, enter in? ... a sense of superiority? ... of shame? ... of self-denigration?

Do we, in fact, all take care of each other, or has the responsibility simply fallen by the wayside? Has it been professionalized in a secular rather than a religious way? Do you feel members are responsive to one another's need for care? ... to receiving it? Have you participated in care giving? ... benefitted from any? Has it enhanced or expressed your sense of spiritual community? In what areas is your meeting particularly gifted in care giving? Who are the people who seem to be particularly gifted, led or called into this kind of activity? How are they nurtured or supported by the community? Do others remove some of the burden from their shoulders? Where is your meeting deficient in care-giving?

How does your meeting respond to death? Is it borne as a community? Or are the families left to themselves to practice the virtues of rugged individualism or ostensibly to protect their privacy? How are the needs and wishes of families ascertained? Are there people among you willing and able to listen to the dying and to the bereaved? Does your meeting encourage and assist members to keep their affairs in order and make decisions and arrangements—such as wills, living wills, simple burial or crematory arrangements—that will ease the burdens of their bereaved families?

Does your meeting have a "casserole ministry" for families that are in distress? Does it find other ways to ease things for those especially burdened by life at any given time: families with a new baby? ... parents of young children? ... working single parents? ... people caring for elderly parents or for seriously ill people? ... chronically ill people? ... people who have lost their sources of income?

Is your meeting, in fact, involved as a community in the discernment and decision making in preparation for marriage? Does it attempt to be part of the process of gaining clearness about the particular leadings, opportunities and challenges of the couple's relationship in God? Or does it rubberstamp the couple's request? Does it turn out as a community for the meeting for worship for marriage or leave it to the privacy of the families? Does it actually take the organization and celebration of the marriage under its care as a meeting? Does it isolate people to protect their privacy?

How does the meeting respond to troubled marriage or divorce: with conflict-avoidance? ... with humble listening to all parties? ... with support in finding professional help where needed? ... with encouragement to find unity even if it means separation? ... with help in finding assistance in negotiation outside our legal system that incites, supports and exacerbates an adversarial stance?

Are you open to being guided into care for others during your personal practice in prayer and worship? Have you felt yourself to be more tender to the needs of others, over time? Has your experience of a gathered meeting altered your sensitivity or your sense of responsibility for the needs and pains of others? Have you experienced a specific leading to care for another? Have you been the recipient of such care? In either case, how did it unfold? What were the consequences for the one receiving care and for the care-giver?

References and resources for mutual care giving or pastoral care

Howard Brinton.
Friends for 300 Years.
ch. 7.

Sandra Cronk.
Gospel Order.
PHP #297.

Geoffrey Hubbard.
Quaker by Convincement.
IV, ch. 5.

C.S. Lewis.
A Grief Observed.

Douglas Steere.
Where Words Come From.
p. 14.

Gladys H. Swift.
"Our TLC Support Group".
FJ, 5/95.

Frances Taber.
"Applying and Adapting the Tradition of Eldering for Today".
The Conservative Friend.
Fall 1996.

William Taber.
"A Fruit of Gospel Order".
QL, 4/89.

Jean Vanier.
Community and Growth.
Jean Vanier writes more profoundly and movingly than anyone I'm aware of about the difficulty and pain of living in loving, spiritual community with people different from ourselves. In *Community and Growth,* he shares some of his meditative reflections on his experience in the L'Arche communities he founded, in which people with handicaps and people supposedly without them undertake to live together in mutuality and equality. Vanier draws together psychology and spirituality in his exploration of the pain, work and issues of growing toward love.

Jean Vanier.
From Brokenness to Community.

Elizabeth Watson.
"Worship that Comes from Silence in the General Conference Tradition".
QW.
Explores some aspects of community in the course of discussing worship.

Chapter 5

Listening for—and Hearing—the Spirit among Us as the Ground of Community Life and Organization

The unity that comes of gathering as the basis of the meeting for worship with attention to business

Experiencing and valuing unity, union or communion together is the central revelation and fruit of listening—or attending—together to God. It has had profound consequences for every facet of Friends' faith and practice. The revelation of unity feeds the listening spirituality of Quaker life in ways that deepen both the processes of discernment and the conduct of relationships in formal as well as informal settings. Being gathered into unity has implications for the nature of personal and corporate relationships. Those implications are nowhere more thoroughgoing than in those meetings for worship where questions concerning the governance of the corporate body are brought into the Light for Divine Guidance. In this era of Quakerism we emphasize this dimension of our experience by calling such meetings, the meeting for worship with attention to business.

Friends' meeting for business is the corporate effort to turn over governance of ourselves to God, at a variety of levels. Most overtly, this happens during time spent in silent worship, holding a piece of business and our own responses to it in the Light, while we wait for Guidance. We may also move in and out of worship as we attempt to absorb information and to sense the spiritual implications of our inner and corporate responses to it. At the heart of the meeting for business is the experience of the gathered meeting. It underlies our listening, our intentions and our intentionality.

At times, Friends have felt graced by a time of gathering in which their course in relation to a piece of business has become clear and unified. At other times, it is sufficient to re-center and invoke memories of our experiences together as a gathered people. Sometimes we just need to be reminded of the centrality of that experience and its implications, when we seem to be slipping into more secular modes of evaluating questions and making decisions. On still other occasions, we need to remember the gentleness, peacefulness and love for one another that have arisen in such times.

Conduct, baptism and peacemaking

One of the places where Friends found the Bible expressed their experience of union—and the value they placed on unity—was in the Letter to the Ephesians, sometimes called the "Gospel of Peace".

> Treat one another charitably, in complete selflessness, gentleness and patience. Do all you can to preserve the unity of the Spirit through the peace that binds you together. There is one body and one Spirit—just as you were called into one hope when you were called. There is one Savior, one faith, one baptism, one God and Creator of all, who is over all, who works through all and is within all.
>
> *Ephesians 4:2-6. int*

This passage is probably the most succinct statement of—and exhortation to—the Pauline sense of the mystical nature of unity in spiritual community. It names behaviors, virtues and practices that, paradoxically, are the fruit of unity and are required to enter into unity in the Spirit—as well as to preserve it. This was one of the New Testament passages on church order that formed Friends' sense of how they were called to be together.

The behaviors mentioned in this passage, sometimes thought of as personal qualities or abstracted as virtues, have been valued by Friends in their life together. These ways of behaving are inextricably related to one another, to the experience of unity and to the experience of baptism as discussed in the chapter on worship.

Selflessness—or humility—*gentleness* and *patience*, invoked in the passage from Ephesians, are resurrected behaviors that follow on the death of willfulness and egocentricity in the Quaker baptismal experience. Humility, gentleness and patience are behaviors that cannot indefinitely be simulated or coerced from the self, on principle, without an outburst of their opposites. Yet—as with so much in the spiritual life— they are strengthened with practice in response to inner openings and nudges. They are one more part of the "already and not yet" of the spiritual life. They are crucial to life in spiritual community and to the conduct of business among Friends.

Misuse of the word "humility" has given it a bad name among many modern people. Humiliation is something that degrades a person either in his own estimation or in the estimation of others. Humiliation works contrary to humility, for it almost invariably focuses a person's attention on themselves and the wrongs done them. Both self-importance and self-denigration place the self at the center.

Humility means no more—and no less—than a way of being in the world that proceeds neither from an inflated sense of the self nor from a false denigration of self. Humility is a way of behaving that is focused on the situation at hand or on the other person, rather than on our own self-image. It is both listening prayerfully to the present moment and a simple, open response to what is, without imposition of ego. It is another "resurrected" behavior that is possible after the painful, dying experiences of baptism.

Patience requires giving over our own agendas for a situation and listening or being present to what is. It requires endless practice to be transparently present in this way, not champing at the bit to take charge of things, not grinding our teeth at the slowness or difference of others. It's another form of dying to ego-centered motivations and listening for, waiting on, responding to what arises in and with others, rather than trying to force outcomes.

Gentleness is another name for the tenderness for others that arises in a gathered meeting. It comes of truly seeing the other as a subject—rather than as an object—even as we ourselves are subjects. This seeing engenders loving behavior that is as respectful and careful with other children of God as is the treatment for which we ourselves long. Gentleness was often mentioned among eighteenth century Friends as a virtue.

Love for one another is another face of the experience of gathering. This love can be a basis of mutual support that is impossible to coerce from ourselves on the basis of mere knowledge that it is nice, or the right thing to do. Love, as a name for the Spirit herself, can empower and support the resurrected behaviors of humility, patience and gentleness.

Perhaps most significant for modern, liberal Friends is the invocation of *"the peace that binds you together."* In this context, it is important to point out that historically Friends have not understood peace only in the relation to outward, politically motivated wars—or as a calm demeanor or even as an undisturbed frame of mind. As in other matters, earlier Friends delved for the deepest, spiritual meanings of peace. They understood peace as the ongoing, reconciling work of God that integrates all disparate, dissonant people and creation into one harmonious, organic life together, moving them to relinquish enmity.

In the early church, one aspect of this reconciling work was seen in the drawing together of Jew and Gentile in a single, new body. Among early Friends, peace, reconciliation and harmony emerged as a dimension of the experience and vision of the meeting gathered together in the Fisherman's net, in the Life and Power of the Lord. The peace that binds us together is the love in which we support one another, or—viewed from another standpoint—our union in God. Peace was to be invoked in the life of the community: in personal disagreements as well as in the vexed issues of corporate business when people of good will and integrity see things differently.

The boundaries among these behaviors and qualities blur. Each supports and meshes with the others. All are part of the vision. All are essential to the fullness of Quaker life together and to the conduct of business among Friends. Obviously we fall short. Yet it has been an important part of Quaker practice to seek to live more fully into the measure of Light we are given to embody the vision of unity, love and peace. The meeting for business is one of the major testing grounds, arenas—or schools of the Spirit—where growth into the vision is fostered, challenged and given room to flourish.

Both Howard Brinton and Damon Hickey relate Quaker commitment to peace and peace-making to the reconciling search for unity in the meeting for business. Hickey challenges us to search our own innermost motivations, rather than those of others, as we find ourselves engaged in a difficult and emotional struggle to come to unity.

Discernment, gathering and unity

The mystical sense of the Spirit of Christ, as the head of the corporate body—over, through and within all—takes the search for corporate guidance out of the realm of purely human analysis, debate, persuasion or manipulation and into the realm of worship.

Without commitment to growth into transformed behavior, the conduct of business can become an exercise in secular techniques of persuasion, manipulation or power. Without confidence in the presence and availability of the guidance of God, it becomes an utterly human search for consensus. Unless we intentionally listen for the movement of the Spirit beneath and through the human interactions, it's just politics.

Michael Sheeran says Quakers build everything on the gathered meeting. In the spiritual exercise of the meeting for business, that often means invitations to re-enter the gathered experience, through re-centering in silence. In the silence we recollect or re-enter the experience of union: the Spiritual Reality that has brought and held us together pervades and encompasses the questions before the meeting, discernment and decision-making, and their outcome.

Many people have commented that not every matter that comes before the meeting for business requires the full weight of a gathered meeting or a spiritual discernment process. A lawyer, who is a member of my meeting, finds a helpful analog in provisions of the United States Constitution. It requires a simple majority to decide ordinary questions, whereas questions that go to the heart of the compact that holds the government together require a two-thirds majority. He makes a parallel distinction between matters that touch the heart of our spiritual life together and those that are more peripheral or routine, like Sheeran's example of painting the meeting mailbox. The closer the matter is to the heart of our life together, the greater the need for spiritual discernment.

Quaker folklore, however, is replete with stories of meetings spending years in discussions that evoked hard feelings, even resignations or residual bitterness requiring healing—on such apparently innocuous questions as carpeting the meeting house. We might be tempted to despair of the failure of spiritual responsibility that seems to be implied in such contentiousness.

Yet we are heirs of Old Testament prophets who required that we measure our actions carefully by the yardsticks of justice and mercy. We are heirs of Jesus who requires that we love one another. Most especially we are heirs of John Woolman who was both gifted and meticulous in tracing the invisible economic connections and ethical implications of ordinary actions and objects. So it is hard to anticipate which innocent-looking questions will plunge us unexpectedly into issues that touch on the very heart of our spiritual life together. A former clerk of my meeting refers to these questions as "exploding cigars".

An exemplary story

In our case, the question was air conditioning. Air conditioning used to seem effete or decadent to me when I lived in New England. In the drainage land between the Potomac and the Chesapeake, the quality of the summer air as well as its temperature are serious health issues. In summer my meeting moved the worship time from 11:00 to 9:30. Even so, before 10:00, under the roof of a converted garage, the trickle of sweat down my body was a definite part of awareness. On some August mornings, my head might be swimming before 10:30. Those who had the means, or fortunately placed family, often just left town. Many elderly and infirm people stopped attending meeting from June through September.

A proposal was made that the room be air conditioned—especially, but not exclusively, for the sake of our infirm members. They were, after all, excluded from worship for about a third of the year. Prolonged absences disrupted and eroded the community. Air conditioning, however, is a costly business with harmful effects on the environment. Swamp coolers are not a live alternative in a swamp. Furthermore, our meeting is in an affluent suburb. In the metropolis we adjoin, only a fraction of the numerous poor people have air conditioning. Poverty and crime vitiate efforts to live a decent life.

Over the course of two years, the meeting labored with the question of air conditioning. Several groupings of views emerged: 1) There were those who felt they could not, in love for those in fellowship with them, do other than make worship available by air conditioning the meeting room. 2) There were those who felt they could not, in conscience, spend a substantial amount of money on comfort for financially comfortable people while myriad forms of misery called for help such a short distance away. 3) There was a smaller group, that overlapped with the second, who felt strongly that they could not participate, in conscience, in the environmental insults inherent in the technology of air conditioning. 4) Still other Friends felt that it was not only ecologically but spiritually sound to accept the heat as it was, to accept it as the natural consequence of life in this particular climatic zone, to give over trying to impose technological solutions on self-created problems, to give over the willful control of nature or efforts to evade the consequences of our choices.

During the two years the issue was before the meeting, Friends experimented with alternative technological solutions that not only would mitigate the environmental effects of cooling but also would represent a smaller outlay of funds for the physical comfort of the meeting. Most Friends found these solutions inadequate to the challenges of the local climate. There was an uncomfortable impasse in the meeting that strained the sense of unity, occasionally brought out adversarial feelings and—among some on all sides—led to a feeling that "the others" were being obstructive and simply wanted their own way.

In the climactic meeting for business, members of each group reiterated their sense of the ethical issues. There was no movement. At length, a former clerk called for a time of worship in which to consider the impasse we were in. After a period of silence, a greatly valued member of meeting, known for her profound concern for social order, rose. She said she was deeply distressed that we—who are so close to one another racially, ethnically, economically, socially, and in the bonds of loving community— could not find a way to unite with one another in Love. She said that, if we could not find our way to loving unity, she would never again be comfortable with us in a demonstration or in a letter-writing exercise advising distant people, divided by historic conflicts exacerbated by racial, ethnic, economic, and social divisions, to settle their differences and live in peace.

There was a deep and prolonged silence. Then, one by one, those who had opposed air conditioning spoke—not to unite with the feeling about the rightness of air conditioning, but to stand aside, to set aside the differences that stood in the way of unity. Thus the meeting was united in its decision to air condition the meeting room. In subsequent months, the meeting went on to make a new commitment to sponsor a second low-cost housing development as Way should open, and to explore several ways of possibly being more useful to homeless people.

Some implications of the story

I give so much space to this story because I think it is exemplary. It does not present an idealized view of how we respond to the challenges and movements of the Spirit among us. This is a story of living, breathing, sweating people laboring to be faithful to God in the midst of human limitation. It shows the intersection of our experience of gathering and our efforts to arrive at decisions that accord with Divine Will. It also shows the meeting for business helping us to recognize and come to terms with those parts of our human nature that make it so difficult to give over our own wills. It is hard to give over cherished points of view that may be ego-centered or may simply not accord with where we are being corporately led at the moment. We seldom have to choose between good and evil. When we do, for most folks the choice is clear. It's listening for God between good and good that is so difficult for us.

There are many implications of the gathered experience and vision implicit in this story. Just a few seem important to mention here. It may be useful to you to search this story for others. It may be even more useful to reflect on the spiritual implications of some stories within your own experience. The listening practice for this section might be to carry the question in your heart whenever you attend meeting for business. Or all of the above.

Unity or sense of the meeting, distinguished from consensus and majority politics

First of all, there is the clear understanding among Friends that, except for aberrant circumstances, we will make no decision unless all of us feel united in it. In the case of our air conditioning, that obviously didn't mean everyone finally agreed about the relative weight of the ethical principles involved. The decision was a question of how our community was led at that time, rather than of deciding among principles.

The experience of gathering makes itself felt in the sense that we are deeply one. To exclude or disregard someone—or to have someone withhold themselves from the process—is destructive of the Oneness itself, as well as of our sense of Oneness. If it were anything but a very rare event, the spiritual ground of community as well as of the meeting for business would disintegrate. Some people who withhold themselves do so out of a mistaken sense that the goal of the process is avoiding conflict. Any withholding of oneself is a disservice to the meeting, in that it can create a false appearance of unity where unity does not actually exist. In fact, withholding oneself from the process practically guarantees that any unity reached will be false. Such a false unity will crumble sooner or later—or create strains that will emerge in later deliberations, possibly disruptively.

Similarly people who adopt an adversarial or manipulative stance also misunderstand the process of groping toward where unity lies in a particular instance. They see the search in terms of the kind of a political process in which acting out conflict—or trial by combat—is thought to be the way to truth. They assume this is a process in which truth is victorious, the false or less satisfactory is vanquished, and the winner takes all. The adversarial stance that divides us into parties to be coerced, manipulated or vanquished, and disregards the views of some, is not only betrayal of our underlying Oneness; it is destructive of it.

In his great work, *Democracy in America*, deTocqueville refers to majority rule as "the tyranny of the majority". Quakers are not a democracy, because there is no place for tyranny in a community that builds everything on being gathered in God's love. Both withholding oneself from the search for true unity and attempting to enforce majority rule on the community subvert the deepest sense of the ground and purpose of its being. In the rare instances when someone's views are set aside in a Quaker decision, it is most likely to be someone who has resisted—over a prolonged period—invitations to relinquish an adversarial or manipulative position *vis à vis* all or part of the community.

Friends will labor for years to find the way that stirs the resonant chord of Truth in everyone. Merely being agreeable or nice delays, rather than aids, this process. Neither is a confrontational, argumentative stance helpful. *Nothing will do but courageously and tenderly acknowledging and facing differences for as long as it takes.* We must face them in confidence that even the anger of faithful people—when lovingly held in the Light with the intention of allowing contentiousness, rancor or fear to dissolve—has something to tell us of Truth. We are supported in this exercise by our ultimate confidence in the availability of Divine Guidance to lead us to a right solution.

Suppression or failure to acknowledge anger and other feelings associated with difference or conflicting views can undermine both the discernment process and our opportunities for spiritual growth through them. This is not an endorsement of acting out anger in tantrums or hostile behavior. It is a reminder that these feelings, too, are part of "what is". To ignore them jeopardizes and falsifies our search for true unity. It may even be that our anger is a prophetic wrath that is the shadow side of authentic vision telling us that the vision has faltered or failed.

Arriving at unity as peace-making

The process of working toward unity through what divides us is nothing less than peace-making—in both the "already" and the "not yet" realms. In the "already" realm, peace-making is an enactment, an embodiment, a fulfillment of the spiritual reality of our humanly separate, disparate, often dissonant selves being bound together in peace. In the "not-yet" realm, it is just one of the ways in which the meeting is—as Sandra Cronk puts it—a School for Peace Making. As part of our dedication or consecration to proclaiming peace to the world, or exhorting the world to peace, we live through this monthly *practicum* in peace-making among ourselves. We seek, in the words of Ephesians, "[w]ith all humility and gentleness, and with patience, [to] support each other in love. ... [to t]ake every care to preserve the unity of the Spirit by the peace that binds [us] together." This was the deep experience and truth invoked by the person who spoke the prophetic word to my meeting. And its resonance carried us beyond impasse.

Impasse

Impasse is excruciatingly painful for us. Yet we must not overlook its importance in reaching unity. The pain of impasse is not only the pain of finding no way forward. It is the pain of having exhausted our human resources. We have done the best we could in terms of information and insight, sometimes in terms of seeking acceptable compromises. Yet nothing is working. We can make nothing happen. It becomes clear that the solution is—in more than one sense—beyond us.

The word "excruciating" is not irrelevant in traditional symbolism. The Latin root refers to the torment of crucifixion. Among early Friends, the Cross referred primarily to the pains into which we are led by trying to have our own ways, and to the pain filled process of relinquishing our wills. Impasse is excruciating because it is the cross to our own plans, agendas, solutions. It is the hard, bare place where we wait on some new thing we have not imagined, over which we have no control.

Authentic impasse may last for months or years. While nothing is happening on the surface, it may be a time when people are being brought inwardly to confront the true sources of their motivations and to seek for their cleansing. It may be a time for healing broken relationships within the meeting, for renewing bonds of love and peace that have become eroded. Where it is not simply a time for a hardening of adversarial positions, impasse can be extremely fruitful in the life of the meeting, in spite of the pain—or perhaps because of it, because of the way it breaks us open and focuses our attention on work that needs to be done.

When the inner work of the Spirit has truly been accomplished, the time will be right for some centered soul to carry the meeting to the place where the members can recognize that the issues are not what they thought they were. Sometimes the impasse is the consequence of two groups of people addressing very different dimensions of the problem, neither group seeing the question whole. In the case of the air conditioning story, the real issue was neither the care of infirm people, nor the care of the dispossessed, nor the care of the environment, although each is an important concentric ring of the unity in which we live.

In the first instance, we moved from agonized listening to hearing by invoking silence. For Friends, silence is an invitation to re-enter worship, perhaps to re-enter gathering.

At the very least, it is an invitation to remember the intentions that define us as a spiritual community. In the second instance, there was a further invitation to recall our fellowship in love and our concomitant commitment to peace- making—at home, as much as in more distant places.

Another dimension of our ground in unity was underscored, even while we worked toward it, by the fact that the pivotal suggestion did not come from the clerk's table. Everyone is of equal value in the search. Everyone is responsible to be sensing what is right at any moment. The prophetic word may come from any person present and given over to the search. Yet it is not insignificant that the words did come from people whose service—especially dedicated to listening, hearing and focusing on the exercise of the meeting for business—had sensitized them to the deepest implications of our labor. Articulation of the deepest movement of the Spirit among us, is also a kind of vocal ministry. Like vocal ministry in worship, it may arise in any of us; but it is not surprising when it arises in those who have dedicated themselves and prepared for the exercise.

In the following excerpt from Edward Burrough, a beloved Friend of the first genera-tion, notice the distinction he made between the way we are to work together and persuasion, argument, manipulation, capitulation, agreement or consensus:

> Being orderly come together, [you are] not to spend time with needless, unnecessary and fruitless discourses; but to proceed in the wisdom of God not in the way of the world, as a worldly assembly of men, by hot con-tests, by seeking to outspeak and over-reach one another in discourse as if it were controversy between party and party ... , or two sides violently striving for dominion, not deciding affairs by the greater vote. But in the wisdom, love and fellowship of God, in gravity, pa-tience, meekness, in unity and concord, submitting one to another in lowliness of heart, and in the holy Spirit of truth and righteousness, all things [are] to be carried on; by hearing, and determining every matter coming before you, in love, coolness, gentleness and dear unity;—I say,

as one only party, all for the truth of Christ, and for the carrying on the work of the Lord, and assisting one another in whatsoever ability God hath given; and to determine of things by a general mutual concord, in assenting together as one ... in the spirit of truth and equity, and by the authority thereof. In this way and spirit all things are to be amongst you, and without perverseness, in any self-separation, in discord and partiality; this way and spirit is wholly excepted, as not worthy to enter into the assembly of God's servants, in any case pertaining to the service of the Church of Christ; in which his Spirit of love and unity must rule.

LYM #354.

Queries

Have you experienced a gathered meeting for business? Was it an occasion when sacred experience seemed to enter into the resolution of difficulty? How did that come about? You might find it useful to journal about some outstanding or precious experiences of the conduct of business after the manner of Friends. Consider your personal part in the corporate spiritual practice in the meeting for business, whether it was inward or outward. What has it been in the past? To what might you be being called at this time?

Have you found yourself emotionally distressed over some matter of business before the meeting? Were you ever able to focus on your own role in creating or maintaining the difficulty rather than focusing exclusively on the behavior of others? ... to become less attached to your own view or will? ... to come to peace with the situation of difference or conflict in the end? If so, how did that come about? Were you changed by the experience in any way?

John Punshon asserts the importance of business meetings in schooling us in discernment and reconciliation. Have you and/or your meeting approached them in that spirit?

References and Resources for gathering and discernment in the conduct of business

Robert Barclay.
The Apology in Modern English.
Dean Freiday, ed.
Proposition 12.

Howard Brinton.
Guide to Quaker Practice.
PHP #20.
Structure, Meeting for Business, Business before Meeting.

Howard Brinton.
Friends for 300 Years.
ch. 6.

Howard Brinton.
The Quaker Doctrine of Inward Peace.
PHP #44.
The Philosophical Basis; Inward Peace as a Test ...

Thomas S. Brown.
When Friends Attend to Business.

Edward Burrough.
quoted in LYM #354.
BrYM 2.87.

Wilmer Cooper.
A Living Faith.
chs. 2, 6.

Sandra Cronk.
Peace Be with You: A Study of the Spiritual Basis of the Peace Testimony.
esp. pp. 24-26. The Meeting: the Place of Discernment. The Meeting as a School for Peacemakers; The Meeting: Discerner of God's Will.

Matthias C. Drake.
"Beyond Consensus: The Quaker Search for God's Leading for the Group".
CD. Also excerpted in *FJ,* 6/86.

Constance Fitzgerald.
"Impasse and Dark Night".
Tilden Edwards, ed.
Living with Apocalypse.

Robert Halliday.
Mind the Oneness: the foundation of good Quaker business method.

Damon D. Hickey.
Unforeseen Joy: Serving a Friends Meeting as Recording Clerk.
esp. pp. 5-6.

Rufus Jones.
"The Sense of the Meeting".
QR.

Thomas Kelly.
A Testament of Devotion.
1941 ed.
The Simplification of Life.

Paul A. Lacey.
Quakers and the Use of Power.
PHP #241.

London Yearly Meeting.
Christian faith and practice.
ch. 7, #349-354.

London Yearly Meeting.
Church government.
chs. 17, 20, 21.

Patricia Loring.
Spiritual Responsibility in the Meeting for Business.

Barry Morley.
Beyond Consensus: Salvaging Sense of the Meeting.
PHP #307.

John Punshon.
Encounter with Silence.
ch. 12.

George Selleck.
Principles of the Quaker Business Meeting.

Michael J. Sheeran.
Beyond Majority Rule: voteless decisions in the Religious Society of Friends.
Part II, esp. ch. IV, and esp. p. 81.

Douglas Steere.
"Some Dimensions of the Quaker Decision-Making Process".
FJ, 5/15/1982.

William Taber, Jr.
"The Friends Discernment Process: One View of Gospel Order".
CD.

William Taber, Jr.
"On Ministering to the Meeting for Business".
Address to PYM
Worship and Ministry Retreat,
3/25/87.

Lloyd Lee Wilson.
Essays on the Quaker Vision of Gospel Order.
esp. The Meeting for Business.

Mutual service embodied in committee structure

Historical overview

One more expression of the Oneness we have heard and felt in the gathered meeting is a mutuality of care for and service to one another. The most striking evidence of this particular aspect of Oneness in meeting life is the absence of a single person who carries the responsibility for care of the rest of the meeting. Outwardly, this absence can be seen as a logical conclusion of the Reformation's progressive stripping away of ecclesiastical authority—as well as stripping away people standing between the congregation and God or Christ. For Friends, it's one outward expression, in a negative form, of the positive inward reality that we are all one under the head-ship, leadership and guidance of the Inward Christ. The positive expression is that we share the care for each other, both formally and informally.

In this century, shared care has been expressed organizationally in meetings' structures of committees. In earlier times, the organization of meeting life was looser and less agenda-driven. The history of the formation of standing committees is meandering, sometimes local, often intimately connected with influences from the wider religious community or, later, from the secular world as Friends became more immersed in it.

That history is beyond the scope of this book, other than to point out a rough evolution from a looser structure to a more formalized one. At the present time, our committee structure is a kind of exo-skeleton for the life of the meeting. Within the exo-skeleton lies our life and Oneness in the Spirit. That Oneness is manifested in the participation of the membership in the jointed articulation of the shell. We may be aware of the Oneness or we may find other outward reasons for participation. Nonetheless, our participation manifests our love, by our willingness to serve one another in the tasks that keep the outward life of the meeting running. These include fellowship, housekeeping, finances, administration, education, and reaching out to the wider community, as well as pastoral care and care of the spiritual life.

After a period in which Friends experienced the temptations and hazards of entrenched and willful leadership, most meetings now rotate responsibilities. Part of our humility and love in our life together is manifest in willingness to serve in more mundane capacities as well as in those of more searching spiritual responsibility. All are necessary to the functioning of the organism.

Committee service and spiritual formation

Another function of the committee structure is the way in which it seasons—or forms—the members and the attenders considering membership. To serve on a committee is a commitment to the life and well-being of the meeting, whether or not it makes full use of our gifts or is invariably stimulating in its consideration of profound spiritual issues. As in the case of the meeting for business, many matters are routine and don't take us to spiritual depths. The spiritual commitment is precisely in the willingness to perform these unglamorous tasks, *in humility and love*, for the body of which we are part.

Another aspect of the seasoning or formative function of committee work is that it invariably brings us into contact with people we find difficult. Committee work can be a microcosm of our spiritual development or transformation in relation to other people. It challenges us to find ways of engaging with one another in love, in spite of boredom, exasperation or active dislike; to find and grow in the ways of proceeding with business without being manipulative or coercive; to be responsible in seeing through what we initiate; to let go of seeking to have our personal agendas, ego-needs or emotional needs satisfied by a captive audience; to grow in the ability to wait on those whose thought processes or discernment processes may move more slowly— possibly more deeply; to grow in our ability to wait on the Spirit, rather to be driven by a plan to manage the process.

Some metaphors and models for the life of mutual service

Biblical models and metaphors

Mark 9:33-37 and 10:35-45 speak about the humility and servanthood of leaders:

They returned home to Capernaum. Once they were inside the house, Jesus began to ask them, "What were you discussing on the way home?" At this they fell silent, for on the way they had been arguing about who among them was the most important. So Jesus sat down and called the twelve over and said, "If any of you wants to be first, you must be the last one of all and at the service of all."

Then Jesus brought a little child into their midst and, putting his arm around the child, said to them, "Whoever welcomes a child such as this for my sake welcomes me. And whoever welcomes me welcomes not me but the One who sent me."

Zebedee's children, James and John approached Jesus. "Teacher," they said, "we want you to grant our request."

"What is it?" Jesus asked.

They replied, "See to it that we sit next to you, one at your right and one at your left, when you come into your glory."

Jesus told them, "You do not know what you are asking. Can you drink the cup I will drink or be baptized in the same baptism as I?"

"We can," they replied. Jesus said in response, "From the cup I drink of, you will drink; the baptism I am immersed in, you will share. But as for sitting at my right or my left, that is not mine to give; it is for those for whom it has been reserved."

The other ten, on hearing this, became indignant at James and John. Jesus called them together and said, "You know how among the Gentiles those who exercise authority are domineering and arrogant; those 'great ones' know how to make their own importance felt. But it can't be like that with you. Anyone among you who aspires to greatness must serve the rest; whoever wants to rank first among you must serve the needs of all. The Promised One has come not to be served, but to serve—to give one life in ransom for the many."

John 13:2-15, 17 speaks to caring for one another in community, stressing the essentially mutual and non-hierarchical nature of our care. The passage is in some sense a dramatization of the stories in Mark.

They were at supper, and ... Jesus ... got up from the table, removed his outer garments and, taking a towel, wrapped it around his waist; he then poured water into a basin and began to wash the disciples' feet and to wipe them with the towel he was wearing.

He came to Simon Peter, who said to him, "Lord, are you going to wash my feet?" Jesus answered, "At the moment you do not know what I am doing, but later you will understand." "Never!" said Peter, "You shall never wash my feet." Jesus replied, "If I do not wash you, you can have no share with me." Simon Peter said, "Well then, Lord, not only my feet, but my hands and my head as well!" Jesus said, "No one who has had a bath needs washing, such a person is clean all over ... ."

When he had washed their feet and put on his outer garments again he went back to the table. "Do you understand," he said, "what I have done to you? You call me Master and Lord, and rightly; so I am. If I, then, the Lord and Master, have washed your feet, you must wash one another's feet. I have given you an example so that you may copy what I have done to you.

" ... blessed are you if you behave accordingly."

NJB

Washing the feet of people who went barefoot or shod in sandals in a hot, dusty country with little paving, plumbing or sanitation was an unpleasant service usually relegated to the least valued slaves in a household. Friends have viewed the reciprocity and equality implicit in Jesus' example with utmost seriousness. They eschewed service as payment in advance or apprenticeship for preferment or superior position. They've established non-hierarchical structures of mutual service and reciprocity that make us all responsible for one another. Such service is yet another manifestation of the unity in which we are gathered.

In the previous chapter I quoted the long passage from I Corinthians 12-14 in which Paul developed "the Body of Christ" analog or metaphor for the church grounded in mutual service. The letter is written to the most contentious of his churches, in which people were claiming ascendancy over one another on the basis of their contributions to the life of the assembly. The gifts named for the sake of the community are somewhat different from those we might name; but the human interactions are familiar. On one level, this passage may be read as yet another metaphorical exhortation to mutual service, respect and love. Paul's mystical sense of living "in Christ" gives an added dimension to his sense of the community as being somehow the outward, visible, physical body of the Spirit of Christ—a bit like the exo-skeleton I mentioned above.

The vision of the wholeness and integrity of one body guided by the Spirit, articulated in the passage from I Corinthians, is a backdrop for understanding the search for corporate guidance, as well as communal life.

The Quaker vision of Gospel Order

This vision, like Paul's vision, reveals community and community interactions as another sacrament in Quaker life. A sacrament is said to be an outward sign of an inward spiritual reality. In that sense, equality, reciprocity and loving mutual service in non-hierarchical relationships are the most visible manifestations of our inward experience of unity, gathered together in God's love.

A similar view of spiritual reality is implicit in the Quaker vision of community known as "Gospel Order": an ordering of common life that both permits and relies on the immediacy of Divine Guidance. Both Sandra Cronk and Lloyd Lee Wilson speak of this distinctive Quaker understanding of the basis of church government. The gospel referred to is not the four books of the Bible. Friends, characteristically, found the Gospel in the good news and power that lay behind those books. For Friends *the good news* has been that "Christ is come to teach his people himself". They experienced God immediately here, with us, as an Inward Teacher and Guide whose work was manifested most fully in the personality and work of Jesus of Nazareth. For Friends, *the power* has been the sense of Life and empowerment that comes of the presence of the Holy Spirit, the Spirit of Christ, within and among us as Inward Teacher and Guide.

Among earlier Friends, Gospel Order referred to the dynamic ordering of life together, when each person separately, and the community together, is brought under the guidance of the Spirit of God. Sandra Cronk contrasts it with church communities that have been acculturated to the values of the wider, individualistic, privatized society. The institutional contrast lies in having non-hierarchical structures that support equality and mutuality of service—rather than hierarchies of authority and participation in the work of the church. Insofar as they are faithful to God and tradition, even the hierarchies of monthly, quarterly and yearly meetings find their spiritual authority rises from the bottom up, rather than from the top down, as in secular structures and in most other church orders.

A deeper question concerns the way in which the structures mediate the authority of God in the community. In short, how do the structures of the community shape our listening to God? In a hierarchical community, listening for God is understood to take place most reliably at the top of the hierarchy, with the messages transmitted downward through the hierarchy, or codified in tradition or canonical scripture. Gospel Order requires each member of the community to be listening for—discerning—the Word of God for the community on an ongoing basis. We do that in times of personal retirement, in meeting for worship, in the conduct of business, in the interactions of community members with one another and in the relationship with the wider world. This is one aspect of what Friends have called "continuing revelation".

It may be sufficient for the present discussion to point out the strenuousness of such listening for Divine Guidance in everything. It requires a level of commitment in the entire membership that is required only of the few in a hierarchical structure. To share the burden of discernment equally requires that we share equally the responsibility for waiting on God. Where codification in scripture, creed, principles or values is eschewed, we cast ourselves upon the confidence that 1) Divine Guidance is in fact available to us in all things; and 2) all of us together, like an array of radio telescopes, will probably—but not necessarily—gather the fullness of the guidance better than any one of us alone. Robert Barclay's analogy is more elegant. It reads:

> Many lighted candles, when gathered together in a single place, greatly augment each other's light and make it shine more brilliantly. In the same way, when many are gathered together into the same life, there is more of the glory of God.
>
> *Barclay's Apology*

Even at those times and in those situations where it's been conceded that some people have been more prepared or more gifted in listening or discerning, we've tended to rely on the group of which they are part (Committees of Ministers and Elders, for example) rather than upon any one of them singly. When such groups have been found to be habitually working from something other than Divine Guidance and authority, their authority has been denied and taken back into the membership at large, or rotated among the membership. Genuine Spiritual Authority is derived from living close to the Spirit. Authoritarianism is grounded in structures of power or coercion that are contrary to Quaker tradition.

Another aspect of Gospel Order worth mentioning here is its fluidity. When authority is not located in particular individuals or codified in creeds, principles, values or traditions, we are more open to God creating a new thing in and though us at each moment. Being open to new possibilities is also strenuous and requires great flexibility in the membership. Lloyd Swift remarks on the flexibility of older Quakers borne of a lifetime of giving over personal leanings to bend to the leadings of God. Being open to new things also carries the risk that—if we fail to learn and reflect on our history—we will spend considerable time in each generation re-inventing the wheel or, worse yet, running again and again down the same blind alleys, into the same brick walls.

To live in Gospel Order requires being genuinely given over to God and to Divine Guidance, grounded in regular personal spiritual practice as well as in active participation in the life of the community. It also requires patience with the fact that not all of us are at the same point in our spiritual journeys or in our level of commitment. In short, it requires the patience of saints living in communities of people who are flawed but nonetheless mostly of good intent.

Queries

Are you more comfortable with the image of the Body of Christ or of Gospel Order for spiritual community? Do you feel your meeting life is more nearly governed by Gospel Order or acculturated to the wider society? What would be required for it to reclaim the fullness of early Friends' understanding of Gospel Order? How might you help or hinder that process?

If your yearly meeting has a book of discipline or faith and practice, it gives some descriptions of committees. Have you ever served on any of these? Was your service to the glory of God? ... for the building of spiritual community? If you haven't served, what prevents you? Might you be being led to it? Do you serve outside the meeting community? If so, does that affect your meeting service? If so, how?

How might your personal spiritual formation be supported by committee work? Are you open to the spiritual lessons of drudgery? ... of dealing with difficult people or situations? ... to the peculiar grace and joy of finding yourself guided in harmony with others?

Michael Sheeran and Sandra Cronk speak of Friends in the context of the hunger for community that exists in a very individualized, privatized society. Sheeran's suggestions for the cultivation of the spiritual ground of community include a greater care for the spiritual basis

of religious education and membership procedures, as
well as nurture of the spiritual experience of gathering.
Do you feel your meeting does any or all of these things?
Would you feel comfortable to have it do so? Do you
feel your meeting provides adequate religious education
to begin to form adults and children in spiritual community? What are its strengths and weaknesses?

References and Resources for a church of mutuality and gospel order

Robert Barclay.
*Apology in Modern
English.*
prop XI, p. 280.

Lewis Benson.
Catholic Quakerism.
ch. 3.

Howard Brinton.
Friends for 300 Years.
ch. 7.

Wilmer Cooper.
*A Living Faith:
A Historical Study of
Quaker Beliefs.*
ch. 6.

Sandra Cronk.
*Gospel Order: A Quaker
Understanding of Faithful
Church Community.*
PHP #297.

Douglas Gwyn.
"John 15 and its
Community".
QRT, spring 1980.

Thomas R. Kelly.
A Testament of Devotion.
The Blessed Community.

London Yearly Meeting.
*Christian faith and
practice.*
ch. 7.

Donald S. Nesti.
"Early Quaker
Ecclesiology".
QRT. vol. 18, #1.
(Autumn 1978).

Michael J. Sheeran.
*Beyond Majority Rule:
voteless decisions in the
Religious Society of Friends.*
esp. Conclusion, in particular,
pp. 111-114.

Lloyd B. Swift.
"On Discipline".
FJ, 3/89. pp. 6-7.

Lloyd Lee Wilson.
*Essays on the Quaker
Vision of Gospel Order.*
The Quaker Vision of Gospel
Order; Quakerism and the
New Creation; The Meeting as
Covenant Community.

Roger C. Wilson.
*Authority, Leadership
and Concern.*

Similarities to and differences from secular forms

Secularization through assimilation to similar forms

Worship

In the opening part of this volume, I mentioned some of the many secular forms and experiences that people bring to their interpretation, experience and activity in the meeting for worship. There is nothing wrong with any of them except that they do not go to the heart of Quaker worship. That failure in itself is not pernicious; but the behaviors that derive from it have the unhappy consequence of frequently inhibiting the deeper worship and gathering of the meeting as a whole, both inwardly and outwardly.

The differences are most patently manifest in the quality of vocal ministry. Yet the real difference lies in the interpretation of the meeting for worship, and in the interior activity that precedes the vocal ministry. In the nineteenth century, the solution was often sought in a form of expostulation, admonition or eldering, to inhibit what was felt to be inadequately grounded vocal ministry. The result was an externally-imposed discipline that nearly inhibited vocal ministry altogether. Some meetings, left without the outward nourishment and scaffolding for interior work that vocal ministry can provide, either withered away after years of total silence, or succumbed to the energetic evangelical preaching of the revivals that arose around them.

A true solution would seem to require drawing people into a deeper sense of the nature of inward religious exercise in meeting for worship. Drawing people into this exercise is difficult to do with no creed, liturgy or systematic theology. Obviously the simple invitation to experience God in the silence is insufficient for many people, without more guidance or assistance. For much of Quaker history there were catechisms. Without them, there is little in the Queries to assist the worshiper. Some yearly meetings, my own among them, have eliminated Advices which are—according to Britain Yearly Meeting—"a reminder of the insights of the Society" (1.01). Regular reading of Advices as a reminder of collective insights, both in meeting and for devotional reading, supplies much spiritual guidance. Some meetings draw on the Advices of several yearly meetings other than their own when they provide particularly apt expressions of "the insights of the Society". The journals of Quaker ministers, that were such important spiritual nourishment for many, are now mostly out of print.

Sheeran's suggestion that we proceed through more careful and intentional religious education, combined with more invitations into the gathered experience, seems to offer the best possibility of assisting a return to the traditional ground of Quaker spirituality. Support for exploring together not only our history and our forms but the deepest ground of our longings and experience is, of course, the purpose to which this book aspires.

It is, however, axiomatic that usually the people most in need of such educational experiences will be the last to attend them. They might be too busy with other pursuits. They might prefer other activities that inadvertently form their understandings of worship. They might feel they have been attending meeting long enough to have developed an adequate idea of what is going on. They may have some interpretations they do not wish to have challenged. Or they may be resisting being drawn into the uncertainties of a more profound interior life.

Membership

Such understandings may also surface in the process of applying for membership. We may need to be more careful in discerning them in the membership clearness process. We have been reluctant to do these things, lest, once again, we fall into external disciplines without Life—or appear insufficiently loving or hospitable to people who seek to join us. We need to reclaim the understanding that to discern is not to be judgmental but to become clear about what is—and is not—legitimately part of Friends' cherished path to and with God.

The remembrance of diminishment in numbers of the membership especially in older yearly meetings, almost to the vanishing point in the late nineteenth century and early twentieth century has made us fearful of not being liked. It is important to remember that dwindling membership was in many ways the consequence of a heavy-handed, outward discipline by rules and principles. Before and beneath the heavy-handed discipline was the failure of the spiritual experience. It was the spiritual experience that put early Quaker evangelists and later Quaker traveling ministers on long and difficult roads, afire with the concern to bring to others their message of the presence of God with us, within us, among us, and guiding us.

If we value the Light and Power to live a more abundant and loving life closer to God and to one another, we must find ways to assist one another to be more attentive to the Source from which they derive. If we do not, we may well become indistinguishable from the melange of new age or ethical culture groups in the wider society.

Business

There is similar concern for assimilation to secular models of the conduct of business among us. The foremost model is that of consensus or a negotiated settlement that bears many outward resemblances to that of the meeting for business' search for unity. Barry Morley has written eloquently of the differences between the laudable secular search for consensus and the spiritual sensitizing to what God requires of or offers to us in a given instance.

Our membership has become educated, more able to deduce underlying patterns of interaction from our traditional behaviors. It is also more aware of parallels to other patterns of social interaction. Unless the unique spiritual ground is kept in perspective, however, there is an intellectual tendency to identify similar secular and spiritual forms. The equation has been made both to make our way more easily understood to newcomers and to bring the blessings of Quaker "process" to people who are not attuned to its Ground.

We often undertake to communicate through "common denominators". When we do, it's hard to notice that spiritual discernment of the sense of the meeting is factored out of consensus. It's easy to lose sight of what's missing and its significance. By referring to Quaker "process" or Quaker "decision-making", we complete the reduction of our life together to components that are describable in sociological terms. As in the case of the meeting for worship, the process tends to become what we think it is. The spiritual component can drop out when we find it indescribable in terms of social sciences.

Yet, it has been a cherished part of our convictions as a religious body that we can, if we are willing, be drawn into a course of action that is not an accommodation of the ideas and desires of those present, but surpasses them, drawing them into harmony with Divine Will. In this spiritual process of submitting to Guidance, we go beyond negotiation, in which we give and take to find something we can all live with. We reach out for the new thing being offered us that is beyond our human desires and ideas. In order to enter this unity together, we reach out to receive the guidance of God that fulfills and surpasses our desires and ideas. We sacrifice nothing but our human willfulness.

We must consider whether we are really more comfortable with the human enterprise of "building consensus" than we are with the yieldedness of entering "listening worship" and "the sense of the meeting". We must decide whether we need to remain within the limits of humanism and intellectual soundness that are our own achievements, or if we can receive them more fully as fruits of faithfulness to the Spirit—for the purpose of supporting our life in and with the Spirit.

Committee structures

The issues in committees are at once more subtle and more pervasive than those in worship and the conduct of business. In this period, almost everyone has experience of committee work in other settings and for different purposes. The smaller size, lesser formality and relatively brief history of committees makes them more vulnerable to the tendency to assimilate to worldly patterns than are the larger meetings that have a few built-in correctives. One Conservative Friend is fond of saying, "The trouble with committees is that they feel they must commit something."

Implied is the sense that we have taken over self-justifying and self-perpetuating secular models of generating programs, mission statements, job descriptions, lists of functions and agendas—rather than waiting upon what the Light raises within us in the moment. These things are all good servants, but tyrannical masters. A good committee needs to be clear about what facet of our life together it is responsible for; but it must open to that facet with a fresh sense of listening for God's guidance. The problem is particularly troublesome for people who hope to be led by the Spirit.

Frequently the committees with the weightiest responsibilities become so agenda-driven and bogged down in carrying out routine functions that they never have time to consider—much less hold in the Light—the deeper implications of their care for the meeting. Where secular models are the touchstone, time spent on matters without tangible result is seen as wasted and unproductive.

Secularization through accommodation to values and techniques of management

Efficiency

The consideration of committee work brings us squarely to questions that are not so much a matter of structural form as of values, modes of activity, or techniques imported from business management and administration. The operating principles of business have pervaded a secular society that is focused on producing and consuming. Certainly Friends place no value on inefficiency, slowness and ineffectiveness. Most of us have probably sat through more than enough committee or business meetings in which time was frittered away to no good purpose, through lack of prior preparation or through self-indulgent inattentiveness, meandering and repetition. At such times, the urge to enforce some management techniques is well nigh irresistible.

Yet—as in the case of "exploding cigars"—the question of where to draw the line is not as simple as it might seem. Our ultimate purpose is not, after all, to produce a product at minimal cost, or to persuade anyone to buy anything. Even our personal time is not the ultimate value. If we permit our process to be driven by efficiency, speed, effectiveness and other good management practices, it is possible for a good clerk to so prepare business and control the process that it will go through with little pause. Yet it is often in the silent pauses, in the unexpected questions, in the glitches and the hitches and the impasses that we have found the Spirit has an opportunity to move. As in our prayer and worship life, it is possible to have such tight control of process that God never has a chance to get a word in edgewise.

Organization

A position may be so prepared in advance, with a wealth of supporting data, that no other positions have a chance to arise. At the same time that it raises certain questions, a questionnaire may preclude other questions from arising. A good clerk may limit possibilities at the very moment he is trying to be aware of them. The choice of which reports will be read and figuring out in advance who might speak to various positions may be as limiting as it is expediting. None of this necessarily presupposes an intention to manipulate—only ordinary human limitation and fallibility. The tension between preparedness and openness to the unexpected is just one of the many tensions in which we must live if we are to leave room for the Spirit to move.

To guard our openness to the unpredictable movements of the Spirit, our procedures need to leave room for the unexpected, space for something different, possibilities for a new thing. However, it is important that individuals in the group discipline themselves not to speak gratuitously, but only with promptings of the Spirit. If there is too much casual or even frivolous talking, then the clerk will feel obligated to institute procedures to by-pass the time wasting.

The price of relinquishing control over the outcome of committee or business meetings is usually a certain amount of wasted time, unproductiveness and meandering. Yet I'm struck by how often Friends remember such times of searching and exploration together—as long as they don't become self-indulgent or tendentious—as times of having been drawn close to each other as a community. I rarely hear such observations about meetings driven by efficiency. Rather, we tend to come away with a vague, uneasy sense that something was left out, overlooked or missing from our more efficient meetings. Indeed, a tightly organized agenda may well require leaving unconsidered some new perspective that has arisen spontaneously.

One is more apt to feel this omission or hear it lamented at large gatherings, such as the yearly meeting. But it can easily come in the meeting of a small, local committee with responsibility for a large amount of routine business as well as for care of deeper aspects of the meeting's life. Contributing factors are a responsibility to get through a large number of issues raised by the membership, within a time that usually has to be arbitrarily limited. Yearly meetings customarily schedule a set number of business sessions of fixed duration, often in a space rented at considerable cost for the occasion.

Some monthly meetings place a time limit on business sessions. Sheer physical limitation decrees how long flesh and bones can sit. Other considerations in our lives determine how much time we can "take away from" other relationships and obligations.

Effectiveness

The question of effectiveness seems to arise most often in connection with our witness to concern for merciful and just social order. Instead of attending to what the still, small voice within is prompting us to do, where the little breeze of the Spirit is wafting us, we are often tempted to engage in good management analysis of where our resources may be expended to greatest effect. As adherents of a listening spirituality, we first listen, as a matter of discernment, for whether or where the Spirit of God is calling us. Has an authentic concern been laid on someone or is it merely a good idea? Are we called by God to "get under the weight of it"? If so, how? Our good management techniques may then become servants of the sense of the meeting rather than usurping it.

Among spiritually grounded activists there is a saying, variously attributed, most often to Dorothy Day, that many use to recall themselves to the sense of where the action comes from: "We are called by God to be faithful, not necessarily to be effective."

Consonant with that reminder or mantra, I'm especially fond of a story related by a former member of the AFSC staff and quoted by Michael Sheeran. It tells of an occasion when the AFSC was requested by the UN to take on a task in the Gaza Strip, that was analyzed by everyone present as simply too large for the resources available. "No, with regrets" was the decision reached. Then, after a period of silent meditation and prayer, it was found there was complete unity to take on the task.

Corporate spiritual practices analogous to our private practice

Simplicity in the use of time and restriction of business

It may be helpful to ask what corporate spiritual practices, analogous to the personal practices discussed in the previous volume, might look like. In terms of committee work and the conduct of business, the coordinate practices of restriction of business and of simplifying or clearing out our time might speak to the condition of our corporate life. (The original sense of "speaking to one's condition" pointed to what needed to be purified and re-visioned.) It might be a useful personal and communal exercise to scrutinize what we do and how we do it, as a matter of spiritual discernment.

In some cases, we might need to take more time, rather than less, for committee and meeting business, in order to give each item enough room to show itself in its fullness, in ways that uplift Life and help to "bring in the kingdom", rather than just getting a decision made.

To address our business in this worshipful way, we may also need to limit how much or what kinds of business we undertake. It may be that we need to return to the Center to feel just what it is that has been laid upon us by the Spirit and what has been undertaken from our own eager, active and agile minds and wills. It may be that we need to become more careful to approach each undertaking in such a way that the Spirit will have room to move, to bring greater spaciousness and abundance into our lives and greater fullness to our tasks.

Meeting to meet

Each time I read of an early yearly meeting when Friends could not bear to part and remained together for longer than planned, I marvel and experience some longing.

> Could this have been because they had little agenda, rather than so much? Could it have been because they met to meet? ... to worship long and often? ... to feast on the "bread of life" in companionship with like-minded people? ... because their religious life was at the

center of their lives? ... because their world, and they themselves, were less clock-, calendar- and schedule-driven? ... because they rejoiced in having it that way and worked to have it happen? ... because they were less divided in themselves than we are about what was important in their lives?

I am caught in the prolifieration of agendas and organization as much as anyone. I have no solutions; but I do think we must begin to live with the questions, to carry them in our hearts, and to pray them. If we ask earnestly, one day we may be given some answers.

Queries

How much of our committee time is spent on routine tasks that need not occupy a full committee? In what ways, perhaps unconsciously, have we accepted the patterns of management structures and procedures from another milieu? How often does your committee or meeting undertake to decide questions that are interesting and even worthwhile, but have not arisen from a spiritual concern laid upon anyone in the meeting—or not laid on the meeting as a whole?

How might we encourage committee or business meetings to become times of refreshment, of a renewed worship in our sense of giving ourselves and affairs over to God, of being drawn into living, loving fellowship with one another—rather than a crowded, anxious, hurried burden on already burdened lives?

Resources and References for secularization and spiritual responsibility in the conduct of business

Britain Yearly Meeting.
Quaker faith and practice.
#1.01.

Brenda Clifft Heales &
Chris Cook.
Images and Silence.

Patricia Loring.
"Spiritual Responsibility
in the Meeting for
Business".

Barry Morley.
*Beyond Consensus:
Salvaging the Sense of the
Meeting.*
PHP #307.

Michael J. Sheeran.
*Beyond Majority Rule:
voteless decisions in the
Religious Society of Friends.*
esp. p. 83.

R. W. Tucker.
"Structural Incongruities
in Quaker Service".
QS.

Roger C. Wilson.
*Authority, Leadership and
Concern.*

Chapter 6

A Listening Relationship with God as the Patterning Principle of Wider Quaker Service

The hierarchy of structures for discernment

The previous chapters of this book have been concerned with structures that support discernment—or listening for God—in the monthly meeting. In this chapter I'll be focusing on the continuities and discontinuities between the monthly meeting structures for discernment and those that have evolved in the hierarchy of meetings and in the larger Quaker organizations among us.

One helpful vehicle for examining the structures of discernment is to track the course of a leading into ministry. When a leading touches a concern beyond the monthly meeting or affects the wider Religious Society of Friends, the discernment process extends through all the levels of the Quaker hierarchy, from clearness committee through yearly meeting. I hope to trace the trajectory of discernment from the personal, through the monthly meeting into the wider Quaker Society. The trajectory of this process of discernment may help us to explore questions of personal ministry that are arising among us again—as they haven't for some time. At the same time, it also opens up the nature and relationships of the various levels of Quaker organization.

I hope it will also reveal the constancy of the listening and discerning stance that underlies these very different-looking organizations. It should also reveal or highlight some of the practices and preconceptions among us that threaten to undermine our openness to Divine Leading even as we meet together to discern it.

Clearness

The individual heart is the prime recipient of God's word to us. Accordingly, the clearness committee is the most intimate structure for discernment in the meeting. Chapter 3 of this book speaks of its purpose and form. Readings in the bibliography describe them at greater length. The clearness committee is the starting point of the Quaker hierarchy of discernment. In it increasing numbers of Friends, over concentrically widening areas, are drawn into a sense of their unity or disunity.

First the individual with a sense of leading into ministry is assisted to personal clearness about both the nature and the origins of his leading. Then a committee of the monthly meeting is assisted to become clear about whether this ministry feels like an authentic leading of God for or within the meeting—and whether the person carrying it is the one suitable to carry it out. If so, the committee will explore all the pertinent factors and prepare a report and recommendations concerning the leading for the monthly meeting for business.

Depending on the weight and time value of the leading, the monthly meeting may let the matter lie over for at least one month, to give questions and information about the leading time to arise and percolate through the meeting. Our interior spirituality has made us quite aware that apparent leadings can easily be prompted by countless other motivations within us. Objections to leadings can also arise from sources other than discernment.

Friends have found that allowing ample time for questions of fact to be answered and grounds of objections to be sifted allows a leading to be seasoned. Seasoning may consist of consideration of ramifications not foreseen, or of counting costs in a realistic way. It can also consist in laboring with objections that seem poorly grounded, either to draw out their basis in Truth or to expose ego-centered agendas or needs. All this and much more goes into seasoning.

The process may take months or years. At the end, the meeting should find material, as well as spiritual, clarity as to the rightness of the leading. Seasoning should also help build a firm basis in either unity or disunity with the leading. Where unity or disunity remains unclear, usually some members of the meeting are withholding their genuine feelings from the process.

Meeting minutes and their implications

The role of a minute as a sense of God's leading for the meeting emerges with a special clarity in the instance of minutes that support leadings. In minuting its support of a leading, a meeting is not giving warm-hearted moral support to someone's personal desire. It is certainly not giving encouragement to a person to go out individualistically to do his or her own thing. It is not celebrating someone's specialness.

In minuting approval and support of a leading, we are recording a sense that some dimension of God's purpose has been laid on this person in particular, to be carried out with the support of the meeting. We do not minute our approval of the person or the task. We minute our sense that God has indeed laid a certain responsibility upon a certain person. We take the responsibility under our care.

In a sense, the person carrying the leading is secondary to the leading itself: the task to which God is drawing us forward as a meeting at this time. The person is the vessel or vehicle for the accomplishment of the leading. Each vessel is unique. His or her unique history, personal characteristics and gifts will, to some extent, determine the way in which the leading is carried out. We support the person to the degree our support will also enable God's purpose in the leading to go forward.

The question of the degree and kind of corporate support required is a communal dimension of Thomas Green's reminder that, in giving ourselves and our lives over to God's will, we give God a blank check. We don't first discern God's will, then decide whether we want to follow it. An activity or undertaking, discerned to be God's will, imposes a holy obligation upon us to determine what may be required of us individually and collectively to assist its performance.

Taking into prayer the amount of the meeting's resources of time, energy and finances that may be required to support the leading is a legitimate part of the process of discernment of whether the meeting is to undertake support of a leading. This challenge must not make us timid, however. A former clerk of Princeton once said, "Quakers are accustomed to being asked to do the impossible—and to finding ways to do it." Michael Sheeran's account of the AFSC's undertaking of an impossible task is an example of this Quaker truth.

Some leadings require little more of the meeting than an affirmation of their rightness to be carried out by the individual. Others demand involvement of a considerable amount of the meeting's resources and may require the meeting "getting under the weight" of the leading in terms of commitment of time, energy and funds.

Oversight of the leading on behalf of the meeting

Elders and discernment

Oversight of a leading is always required of a meeting that has minuted its finding of the leading's authenticity and has taken it under its care. By oversight, a meeting shoulders a share of the responsibility of seeing that God's will is carried out in this instance. This kind of oversight is partly a pastoral responsibility and partly a spiritual responsibility. As such, it requires the gifts of elders in discernment of the leading's spiritual dimensions and requirements and of whether it is being fulfilled or over-reached.

Another of the traditional elder's gifts required for oversight is the ability to continue sensing where the bearer of the leading is coming from. The meeting needs to take readings on whether the minister continues to be centered in Divine Purpose or is drawn into ego-centricity or over-involvement in the inevitable worldly dimensions of the leading.

In taking the leading under its care, the meeting assumes a careful oversight of the spiritual integrity of the leading and its bearer. To carry it out in faithfulness will require the services of experienced elders with tested gifts of discernment. These should be carefully chosen and appointed to a committee for oversight. To open such service to the membership at large is to risk oversight that is either excessively partial to the undertaking or the minister—or excessively critical of one or the other. The spiritual discernment function should be protected from the possibility of more political agendas.

Authority: to whom does the leading belong?

Spiritual Authority in leadings resides where it always does with Friends: in the Spirit of God, as discerned to the best of our ability. It is subject to all the problems of our human fallibility in this as in all our efforts. Our tests are, as always, corporate: the Light refracted through as many people as possible, prepared for the undertaking by prayer and relinquishment of their own agendas and wills. If the leading is of God, then it belongs to God and not to any one person or group of people. It belongs neither to the minister carrying the leading, the committee responsible for its oversight or even to the meeting itself. We are all responsible to God for rightly carrying out the leading. We each do our bit, according to our gifts and seasoning.

The committee for oversight will meet with and without the minister as often as feasible, given the leading. In support of its spiritual function, it will worship together, pray its questions and listen prayerfully for the Spirit moving in the minister's accounts of her or his work.

As the organ of the meeting's care, it will report to the meeting as often as appropriate in the circumstances. It may be annually, semi-annually, quarterly or monthly. A personal report by the minister of the leading may be part of some or all of the reports.

Where the leading does not carry within itself a specific time limit, it's part of the oversight committee's responsibility to discern on an ongoing basis whether shifts in the shape of the leading are faithful to it, whether there is still Life in the leading, or if it has become an empty form. When the minister feels clear of the leading or the oversight committee senses that the Spirit has departed from it, the committee will report to the meeting. The meeting as a whole will discern whether it is time to lay down the leading and its care.

The minister bears the primary level of spiritual responsibility for his or her leading. The oversight committee bears a level of spiritual authority intermediate and mediating between that of the minister and the meeting. The united meeting bears the ultimate level of spiritual responsibility to God in the matter. All are servants of the leading, servants, together, of God.

Community support of the leading

Spiritual support

The function of support, along with oversight, is part of the responsibility of the meeting's care of a leading. In some instances, it may be appropriate to appoint a separate committee, with differing gifts, to exercise the various supporting functions. In most instances it will be less clumsy to combine the oversight and support functions in a single committee. That committee, however, needs to be conscious of the range of, and distinctions among, its various functions.

The most significant overlap between the support and oversight functions will be helping to carry it and the minister in prayer. Oversight requires that the committee itself remain centered to exercise discernment. Support requires the minister be encouraged and helped to remain centered in prayer and Divine Guidance. As in other meeting committees, the temptation will be to focus on outward functions of support. The urgency of agendas can easily usurp both the focus of the committee meetings and of the work if we aren't watchful. It's important, from the outset, that the milieu in which the committee functions and the work of the minister are exercised—whether in social concern or spiritual nurture—be prayer. It may be the most critical kind of support of the leading a meeting can provide.

Practical support

Appropriate practical support, of course, will vary widely depending on the nature of the leading. The following list of kinds of practical support I've received will indicate some possibilities. A great many people in my fairly large meeting have assisted in one way or another. In addition to an oversight committee and a working group, a number of people have been coopted to contribute their special gifts.

In its initial form, my leading to nurture the spiritual life was exercised primarily as teaching adult religious education classes in my home meeting in Bethesda MD and in Sandy Spring (MD) Friends Meeting. One person printed and handed out leaflets, acted as a source of information for interested people, registered enrollments, and collected fees for classes. A coordinator also arranged for the availability of suitable space. On the evenings when classes were held the coordinator came early to arrange furniture.

When the classes were offered to more meetings, several people collaborated to produce a traveling triptych and a brochure. As the work expanded, a member of my oversight and support committee would sometimes drive me to a distant meeting where a workshop or retreat was held, and attend the event. This helped me be less fatigued both for the weekend and for my arrival home. The companion also helped keep me centered in the Source of the work. This kind of support is close to that of the elders who traditionally companioned the traveling vocal ministers.

As my teaching work has become increasingly focused on writing this series of books, the leading has been supported in much more varied and sophisticated ways by many people both within and outside Bethesda Friends—as mentioned in the "Celebrations" at the beginning of this volume. Groups assist with work on the text and the practical details of publication. The oversight and support committee continues in its primary function of oversight and support of the leading, including fund raising and seeking grant support to enable me to spend most of my time on the work.

These many hands contributing to the production of the books have broadened awareness and support of the leading both within Bethesda Friends Meeting and outside it. For another leading, different kinds and amounts of practical support would be required. The spiritual support would probably remain the same.

Financial support: supporting a leading versus hiring a minister

The final and most controversial kind of support of a leading is financial. Many modern, liberal Friends confuse the early Quaker openings that opposed both enforced tithes to a state church and hired, ordained clergy, with support of authenticated leadings into ministries of social concern or spiritual nurture. The postscript to the early letter of the ministers and elders of Balby, that is quoted as an epigraph to most books of faith and practice, cautions against taking any advice as a rule to walk by, in lieu of being guided by the Light to fulfill the Spirit (LYM, for example).

In practice, rather than principle, it's been understood that ministers, who are able to bear the cost of carrying out their approved leadings, will do so. From the early days of the Quaker movement, however, recognized ministers who were unable to bear the cost of carrying out their leadings, were supported by the Society wherever possible. Fox's letter on tithing speaks of the material support given to ministers in return for their spiritual support. His primary concern was that support be voluntary and given to people whose leading into ministry was discerned to be of God, rather than coerced by church or state as income for professionals. Most of the early ministers lived frugally, but were enabled by Friends to give themselves over completely to their ministry for long stretches of time, rather than to their previous occupations (*Rules of Discipline*; Jones).

From her home at Swarthmoor Hall, Margaret Fell administered a fund of both goods and money to support needy Quakers. The Kendall Fund was applied to the expenses of traveling ministers, as well as to relief of Friends whose property had been confiscated under one of the restrictive laws or destroyed in anti-Quaker rioting. In the classic period of traveling ministers, meetings not only contributed whatever was needed in kind to support the minuted minister along his or her way, but tended to the needs of the minister's family and livelihood at home when that was necessary and possible. A birthright Friend attests that Friends not only provided room and board for traveling ministers, but also offered cash, according to their means, to ministers to help them on their way.

When clear lines of oral transmission of Quaker tradition are becoming attenuated almost to the vanishing point, the term "hireling" is often used in any situation in which money changes hands. Business and institutional models of organization are so imprinted on our minds that it's hard to think in terms of simply supporting someone in their response to God's leading rather than paying a fee for service.

The use of the word, "minister", also complicates the concept for some people. Many have come to Friends from churches in which clergy are hired by the congregation or a hierarchically higher body to perform within a job description, for a fixed salary. For such people, ministry automatically implies a person who has been hired to perform functions prescribed by others.

For Friends the word, "minister", implies someone led by God to perform a service in a way unique to themselves. Approval of their ministry by the meeting implies that, within the limitations of approval and oversight, these people are trusted to discern for themselves how to carry out their charge from God.

As we've seen, the range of possibilities among us is as varied as the individuals called or led. At the present time, in my yearly meeting—in addition to my own work—ministers are being supported to assist a Native American council on education; to help rebuild churches destroyed in the South; and to develop peace teams to assist in places of violent conflict. We all have in common a sense of having been led by God to a service that has been authenticated in the unity of our monthly meetings.

Another commonality among us is the need for financial support to free us for the work to which we're called. It's only in the modern era that some Friends have felt that God would not call anyone to service who does not have the means to support the service. Exclusion of those who are not well off or in sufficient health to support themselves while they serve the Society would not have occurred to earlier Friends. God's leading might fall on anyone, regardless of outward circumstances. In fact, experience of need or incapacity might be the very opening into ministry through which God leads some people. Well-off members of earlier Friends' communities would make up from their abundance any lack that impeded service by other members of the body.

Today's ministers are even more apt to be in need of financial assistance than were ministers of other times. The wider society in which we must function no longer recognizes barter to the degree done in earlier times. Taxes, insurance and medical coverage are issues that do not yield to non-financial solutions.

There are fewer ways of supporting ourselves that are flexible in the use of time than there were in earlier times. Farming used to have at least a brief season of less intense activity. An artisan, like George Fox, might carry his employment with him on his travels or periodically close his shop without destroying his business. Fewer and fewer of us today elude the net of employment by large or multi-national corporations that set the times and circumstances of our employment as well as the job descriptions. If we are—like James Nayler—simply to walk away from the plow at the behest of God, we must—like James Nayler—be supported by those who sense the authenticity of our call.

As I write, my own yearly meeting is experimenting with ways of undertaking the care of financial arrangements for the diverse ministries within it, that its committees affirm as authentic. I'm sure there are other experiments afoot elsewhere as we all grope for ways of supporting individual ministries outside the large service organizations that have grown up among us this century.

Taking the leading outside a monthly, quarterly, or yearly meeting

Most of us try to work within the gestalt of our traditional discernment structures—starting with successive discernments in monthly meetings. Modern forms differ in detail from those of tradition; but we seek to remain in the posture of listening attentiveness to the will of God.

Our hierarchy of discernment differs sharply from that of top-down structures. Both the numbers of our membership involved in our discernment and the weight of authority carried by those discernments broaden from the base. Our base is not the usual bottom of a pyramid. It is, rather the center of a series of concentric rings of discernment. Our discernment gathers preparation, seasoning and weight as it gathers growing numbers of our membership into the process. Discernment and authority proceed laterally, rather than vertically in our "hierarchy". Quaker experience has found Barclay's image of the greater light thrown by a bank of candles is as apt for discernment as it is for worship and gathering.

Each level of the hierarchy is inclusive of the level before it. Everyone who belongs to a monthly meeting is automatically a member of the quarterly meeting of which that monthly meeting is a geographical part. Every member of a quarterly meeting is a member of the yearly meeting of which that quarterly meeting is a part. Inclusive membership is not merely a matter of being subject to the authority of the preceding level. Every member of a meeting is also rightly a participating member of all the discernment levels following it.

A former clerk of Baltimore Yearly Meeting has observed that our traditional lateral hierarchy can be misunderstood, or even subverted, by people who join us from other churches. If people assume authority comes from the top down in an organization, they may fail to participate in the wider circles of discernment in our structural hierarchy. They may perceive the wider levels of discernment and authority as "them", rather than a more inclusive "us". They can diminish the authority of our broader discernments by their failure to participate.

When members decline to attend the meetings of bodies in the hierarchy following theirs, they artificially create a separation of themselves from the discernment process and authority of those meetings. As Sheeran notes, those who withhold themselves from the discernment process, frequently deny authority to decisions ensuing from that discernment. The yearly meeting is the membership of all the monthly meetings within it and its authority, as well as its discernment processes, are undercut when people withhold themselves from participation.

The criterion for forwarding a leading into service has been roughly the same as that for determining whether it is appropriate to forward any piece of business, in which the monthly meeting has united, to the quarterly meeting—or to forward a piece of business in which the quarterly meeting has united, to the yearly meeting. If a piece of business is apt to affect, to be of concern to, or to require the practical or financial support of members of the higher body, it is right to forward it.

No piece of business or question of ministry should appear before a more inclusive body unless those bodies included in it have united in its discernment of its rightness. Such seasoning by the questions, objections and suggestions of successive circles of discernment can spare the larger bodies ill-prepared business, refining what is to be considered to a point of manageability.

Similarly, if the ministry of an individual is suitable to be carried out beyond the bounds of the quarterly meeting, the monthly meeting can recommend it to the quarterly meeting for discernment of its appropriateness. If the ministry is to be carried out beyond the boundaries of the yearly meeting, the quarterly meeting may discern whether it unites in forwarding its recommendation to the care of the yearly meeting. If the ministry is to be carried out beyond the boundaries of the yearly meeting, the yearly meeting will discern whether it unites in a traveling minute recommending the minister and ministry to the care and consideration of those in whose meeting the ministry is to be carried out.

This lengthy process can be frustrating to those accustomed to the methods of contemporary businesses and institutions. It can exasperate the desire to get on with what seems to be a perfectly good idea. Patience is a fruit of the Spirit and a hallmark of yieldedness to God. We do well to practice it in examining both leadings and objections to them. God's timing is more spacious than our own and less fraught with anxiety.

Friends have found that it's worth giving extra time to allow hidden objections or problems to surface, to allow strong feelings to soften, emotions to cool, reasons to give way to discernment. A minute, whether of business or of ministry, is almost invariably stronger for having passed through the refracted light of so many other Friends and gathered the solidity of so much unity behind it, before it is given the authority of unity by a quarterly or yearly meeting.

Resources for leadings discerned and supported by the meeting

Notice that, few though our resources on discernment are, there is even less guidance for meetings on the practice of supporting leadings or releasing Friends for ministry, whether ministry to Friends' spiritual life or ministry to the social order. Accounts of meetings' experiences in this area would be a helpful addition to the literature.

Rules of Discipline of the Yearly Meeting of Friends PYM. pp. 95-96.

Barclay's Apology in Modern English. Dean Freiday, ed. pp. 222-4.

Samuel Bownas. *A Description of the Qualifications Necessary to a Gospel Minister.*

John Calvi. "Released to Do Good Works". *FJ,* 11/1994. pp. 22-24.

Suzanne Farnham *et. al. Listening Hearts: Discerning Call in Community.*

Thomas H. Green. *Weeds Among the Wheat: Discernment, Where Prayer and Action Meet.*

Marty Grundy. "Discerning Ministry and Gifts: the Meeting's Responsibility".

T. Canby Jones, ed. *The Power of the Lord is Over All: The Pastoral Letters of George Fox.* #29, On Tithing.

Paul Lacey. *Leading and Being Led.* PHP #264.

Val Liveoak. "Liberating Friends for Volunteer Service". *FJ,* 3/1993.

Patricia Loring. *Spiritual Discernment: the context and goal of clearness committees.* PHP #305.

Patricia Loring. *Spiritual Responsibility in the Meeting for Business.*

Jan Hoffman.
*Clearness Committees
and their Use in Personal
Discernment.*

Parker Palmer.
"The Clearness
Committee: a Way of
Discernment".

Michael J. Sheeran.
*Beyond Majority Rule:
Voteless Decision Making
in the Society of Friends.*
p.83.

R. W. Tucker.
"Structural Incongruities
in Quaker Service".

Lloyd Lee Wilson.
*Essays on the Quaker
Vision of Gospel Order.*
esp. Parts 2 & 3.

Louise Wilson.
Inner Tenderings.
Quaker journal of a modern
Friends' minister.

John Woolman.
The Journal.

Structures and leadership consonant with the Quaker gestalt and Gospel Order

Being faithful to Gospel Order

We've seen that "Gospel Order" is not a set of rules or an institutional structure derived from the New Testament. Rather, Gospel Order refers to the loose, fluid life of the body ordered in such a way as to be responsive to Divine Promptings. I've used Paul's metaphor to describe Quaker structure or church order as an organic body of committees. I've also referred to the structure as an exo-skeleton for the Life within. Another metaphor would be a scaffolding for lives and life together, constantly under re-construction as we move toward spiritual maturity.

At our best, we've sought an order among us that is more organic than architectural: an order, pattern or gestalt that accommodates, encourages, supports, expresses and gives shape to the efforts—of each member and of the body as a whole—to live in openness and responsiveness to the immediate guidance of God. We've been confident that, if we listen for the guidance of God and heed it, we will be brought into mutuality of love and service. We've also referred to that order as "Gospel Order", "right relationship" or "the good order among us".

In Gospel Order we meet for no other purpose than to meet with one another, to wait on the word of the Lord, rather than to fulfill some preconceived agenda. We meet in confidence that we will encounter God directly. Our encounter may be within ourselves or with and between one another. Our listening contains the confidence that, if we listen, in God's own time we will hear what we're meant to hear. Paraphrasing the Bible: when we hear, we obey. Our discipleship lies in a sense that we listen not merely to hear our personal options. If the voice we hear is that of the Divine, our commitment is to obey.

The hierarchy of meetings

Above I followed the progress of leadings into service, or ministry, through the hierarchy of meetings. That progress is as much an introduction to our peculiar hierarchy as it is an exposition of the traditional course of Quaker ministry and its underlying spirituality. Our hierarchy of structures developed in order to provide a scaffolding for Life among us, beyond the monthly meeting—in the past and present. Throughout our history, it has functioned, paradoxically, in support of broadening, non-hierarchical, Quaker spiritual discernment and mutual service. Our hierarchy of meetings gathers progressively more people, rather than fewer, into the discernment process.

As in the case of the monthly meeting, over time outside forces have helped shape our broader meetings for discernment. In some areas outside models have been helpful. In others our underlying organic pattern or gestalt is at risk of subversion by adopted patterns that obstruct listening for Divine Guidance in all things. As we seek ways to go forward in faithfulness, we need always to keep our eyes on what has lain at the heart of Quaker faith and practice. It will provide criteria for what may be fruitfully and faithfully integrated with our traditional structures and what will be best left to others.

Monthly meeting

The character of the monthly meeting (North American style) has been covered in the previous chapters. I'll add only that this style is not the only pattern among Friends. Mainly, but not only, in Britain several meetings for worship that meet weekly join together once a month to conduct business. In Britain Yearly Meeting, those weekly worshiping meetings are called preparative meetings. In the US and elsewhere, the term "preparative meeting" is usually reserved for recent, weekly meetings for worship that have not yet attained the status of "monthly meetings" that conduct their own meetings for business. I'll move directly to sketch quarterly and yearly meetings as I've experienced them in the United States.

Quarterly meeting

Of all the hierarchical levels, the quarterly meeting has undergone the most change. Its structure and functions are less clearly defined than those of the monthly and yearly meetings. In some areas, the quarterly meeting is the place to season business in preparation for yearly meeting. In other places, minutes proceed directly from monthly meetings to yearly meeting, without further seasoning. This can result in an excessive amount of business on the floor of the yearly meeting. Without discernment in the quarter, business is not well prepared for consideration, and the wider membership is not sufficiently aware of it and its ramifications to make a discernment. It can happen that, without business to attend to, attendance at quarterly meeting falls off dramatically. In at least one case I know of, the quarterly meeting has been reduced to a scarcely attended half-yearly meeting, with minutes kept only spasmodically and not circulated.

Whether quarterly meetings do or do not continue to attend to business, they are also an occasion for Friends from a geographical region to come together for fellowship more regularly and intimately than they might otherwise. A program by some Quaker organization, a yearly meeting committee or someone feeling under the weight of a concern may be arranged for part of the day. Fellowship with Friends is extended beyond the confines of one monthly meeting. Wider concerns are shared, new ideas encountered. New meeting houses are visited and different ways of proceeding are seen. It can be a rare opportunity for urban and rural Friends to meet and share the differences their demographic situations make to their meetings. It is a wholesome stretch of one's sense of fellowship beyond the monthly meeting.

Yearly meetings

London Yearly Meeting and its *Church government* stress discernment, love and unity in the conduct of business just as they are at the center of monthly meeting conduct of business. At the yearly meeting level, it requires even more care to stay centered on them, given the greater concentration of information in committee structures than is found at the local level.

Attendance at yearly meeting is emotionally intense because we see and become engaged with dear F/friends sometimes not seen since the previous year. Ideally yearly meeting also provides an intense involvement with matters that have been sifted, seasoned and concentrated through the discernment process at all the previous levels within the yearly meeting.

It is both exhilarating and exhausting to absorb so much concentrated information in a short space of time, and to hold it in the depths of prayer and worship for discernment of Divine Guidance. We may experience even more profound bonds of love than usual with others who undergo this exercise with us—or we may be even more shattered if, for any reason, we fail to experience unity in matters before us.

We require preparation of our souls as well as of business before engaging in this annual, concentrated exercise of discernment of issues that affect the entire body of the yearly meeting. Some yearly meetings offer a time of spiritual retreat just prior to the opening of yearly meeting. In this way, at least a core group will have engaged in extended centering before the meeting for worship with attention to business begins. The quantity of information and the intensity of attention require frequent reminders throughout the sessions of the Ground of our discernment, guidance and being.

Still wider organizations: FGC, FUM and EFI

Friends General Conference (FGC), Friends United Meeting (FUM), and Evangelical Friends International (EFI) have functioned as organizations of yearly meetings to address matters of wider, mutual concern and to nurture their members in ways the yearly meetings may be unable to—especially in areas of sparse population and few meetings. Like monthly meeting membership in yearly meetings, membership in a constituent yearly meeting confers membership in FGC, FUM, or EFI.

Although my monthly and yearly meetings hold membership in both FGC and FUM, I am more familiar with the functions and activities of FGC than those of FUM or EFI. FGC has tended to gather together those yearly meetings that have remained unprogrammed or non-pastoral, and were labelled Hicksite at the time of the separations in the nineteenth century. It now includes the yearly meetings that have reunited the various branches (Orthodox, Hicksite, Gurneyite, and Wilburite), plus some of the newer unprogrammed yearly meetings formed in the twentieth century.

EFI and FUM have tended to function on behalf of those yearly meetings that gather up programmed meetings, with paid pastors. Five yearly meetings that are mostly non-pastoral have joint FGC and FUM affiliation.

FUM has no authority over the constituent yearly meetings, and its yearly meetings' authority over local meetings varies from one yearly meeting to another. FUM's ultimate decision-making forum is the Triennial sessions, which anyone may attend and at which any Friend may speak. But there is a greater culture of deference to perceived authority of staff and officers in both FUM and EFI than in FGC. EFI has only delegated powers. It is the servant of the constituent yearly meetings, doing assigned functions. The individual yearly meetings retain autonomy and authority.

FGC neither makes policy for its constituent meetings nor does it have a hierarchical place *vis à vis* the yearly meetings. While the membership of FGC's program committees is largely self-selected from among those serving on the large Central Committee, many of the representatives to the Central Committee are appointed by the consitituent yearly meetings. Central Committee approves the budget each year, and has recently engaged in discerning a long term planning process that identified goals and objectives. Within those guidelines, program committees are pretty free to develop their own programs without much interference from Central Committee or staff.

Beneath differences, the common center of discernment and authority is perceptible in all three organizations. None has structurally conferred authority over constituent yearly meetings. All three are variations on the model of widening, increasingly inclusive, concentric rings of discernment and authority. Quaker discernment and authority gain weight as our lateral hierarchy involves more of our members.

Friends World Committee for Consultation (FWCC)

Although it is not a policy-making body, Friends World Committee for Consultation is the only body that tries to include all Friends. As such, it is the widest level of organzation among us. Its primary focus is bringing Friends together in face-to-face encounters. It also encourages consultation and communication among Friends; and it publishes newsletters, translations between English and Spanish, internet web pages, directories and brochures.

Its discernment is of its mission and is made internally. The organization, however, underscores the fact that our hierarchy is lateral, rather than vertical, each level embracing more and more Friends in a wider and wider fellowship.

Organizations that act on behalf of Quaker testimonies and concerns

Friends Committee on National Legislation (FCNL)

The Friends Committee on National Legislation (FCNL), is the Quaker organization that lobbies Congress from the basis of our testimonies. In the view of several of the writers in Chuck Fager's collection of essays, *Quaker Service at the Crossroads*, and a number of other people, FCNL comes closest of any of the large Quaker organizations to governance by a Quaker discernment that seeks to be grounded in the larger Quaker constituency. With humility, the staff has asserted that, if it comes close to that grounding, it is because the unique character of its mission permits it to elicit discerned guidance concerning its congressional agenda from monthly meetings on a biennial basis, in response to congressional agendas and presidential budgets.

American Friends Service Committee (AFSC)

The American Friends Service Committee is usually regarded as the Quaker service organization in the United States. Since its founding in 1917, the AFSC has evolved considerably in its organizational structure, in its responsiveness to Friends' meetings and in the nature of its staffing. Those matters have been the subject of much discussion and criticism in recent years.

The partisan, sometimes unQuakerly re-examination of the relationship of the Society and the AFSC is painful for those on all sides. It has, however, evoked considerable creative thought and analysis concerning critical issues of discernment and governance among us. It has also gathered up most of the questions that are raised regarding large-scale Quaker organizations, whether they are yearly meetings, schools or other groups. The issues, as they surround the AFSC, may bless us all in the end. Exercises that began with examination of and reflection on AFSC governance may help guide us to spiritual clarity about appropriate governance in all our large, contemporary Quaker organizations.

Governance of large Quaker organizations

It's a worthwhile challenge to blend governance that is faithful to the traditional Quaker experience of the presence and guidance of God with organization on a scale that can respond to contemporary needs. Among other issues, we may come to grips with pressures for cost-effectiveness that we encounter when dealing with extremely large sums of money. In some cases, an added complication is that much of it comes from non-Quaker sources that share our goals—but perhaps not our vision of Divine Governance from the individual outward. We may also reflect on whether and how a hired staff—no matter how profoundly grounded spiritually—may discern our concerns for us and act on them for us, with our financial and moral support.

For much of the twentieth century, Friends have assumed that Quaker forms were utterly compatible with democratic forms such as building consensus, and with sound business practices. Now we're almost at the end of a century of stripping our forms to their sociologically definable characteristics. With some perspective on the evolution of business practices, many of us have begun to feel discomfort with the result. We begin to question whether continuing to follow the example of business or government is consistent with our spirituality and ethics.

The end of this century has been the era Doug Gwyn refers to when he quotes studies on "third-stage capitalism". Many large businesses were growing into multi-national corporations with more power than most nations, alienated from human realities they control, and with little regard for anything but their bottom-line. Mid-century saw the beginning of "the military/industrial complex" against which our little-regarded President Dwight Eisenhower warned us on his departure from office (Gwyn). There were also present in embryo many other complexes that currently control significant aspects of our lives and society, notably the medical/pharmaceutical/technical/insurance complex.

There has not been much writing that explores the effect of continuing our twentieth-century tendency to adapt business practices to our purposes, and our practices to those of business. Douglas Gwyn's study is the most detailed of which I'm aware. Otherwise, R. W. Tucker's much older essay relates his remarks about the AFSC to the usages of twentieth-century Friends in general. His is the strongest encouragement I know to re-examine our practices for their spiritual implications (Gwyn; Tucker).

Tension with incorporation of secular structures and values

Michael Sheeran examines analogous questions in the early evolution of governance in London Yearly Meeting and its Meeting for Sufferings, and in Philadelphia Yearly Meeting more recently. By applying sociological theory, he pinpoints some of the tensions between the Quaker theological impetus to looser structure, and social pressures for tighter, more centralized structure (Sheeran).

The pressure for tighter organization is even more pervasive among modern Friends in all our organizations above the level of quarterly meeting. In some instances, the pressure for tighter structure has even seeped down to the level of the monthly meeting and its committees. On the cusp of the twentieth and twenty-first centuries, such pressure may be the greatest challenge we encounter to the adaptability of our "formless forms".

A two-edged effect of a gift for institutional organization is a tendency to formulate procedures that may be universally applied in similar circumstances. The attempt to anticipate as many contingencies as possible and to refine prepared responses to them shows our human discomfort with the unknown and lack of control. Such anticipation can preclude the gift of some new thing arising among us—can quench the Spirit.

Closely related are pressures for long-range financial planning and cost-effectiveness. Like a closely-written manual of procedure, long-range planning and commitment of funds can preclude the possibility of response to some unanticipated movement of the Spirit. Pressure for cost-effectiveness can preclude our participation in activities to which we're moved by the Spirit, if they do not guarantee a measurable result, but promise only faithfulness to the prompting. John Woolman's trip to Wyalusing has taught us the importance of yieldedness to the promptings of Love and Truth, even when there is no nameable result.

The challenge to the Quaker gestalt is most evident in the extent to which we take on secular procedures without examining their implicit assumptions. Conversely it is also evident in the extent to which we fail to be alert to tendencies both in ourselves and in others, to manipulate and maneuvre in a political manner.

Our gestalt is protected by keeping intentionally and explicitly to forms that open us to God. Observing such forms keeps open the possibility of our encounter with God. Sheeran has pointed out that Friends' open waiting, along with our frequent failure to actually discern where the words are coming from, are factors that leave us vulnerable to political tactics that undercut encounter with God. In the final analysis, the actual locus of our Ultimate Concern will determine our sense of what is happening in worship and how we attend to business in the context of worship.

Leadership and being led: authority, power and empowerment

In ministry to our spiritual lives, one advice traditional since the time of John Woolman has been to seek "where the words come from". In our outward concerns, whether within or outside the Society, the question we must carry is, "Where does the action come from?" Our most pressing concern in the monthly meeting, the yearly meeting or one of the larger Quaker organizations must be care for the spiritual grounding of the action, rather than for a particular outcome.

If we truly open ourselves to attend to God, we may trust that the outcome will be God's will. We can give God a blank check. If we truly give ourselves over to the guidance of God, part of the blank check will be relinquishment of long-term planning of projects, in favor of waiting on the unexpected, new things that God wants to bring forth among and through us.

For Friends there can be only one answer to where the words, the action, the leadership, authority and power come from. Our Society is founded on the experience that we can receive these from the Holy Spirit if we are willing. Our tradition also acknowledges implicitly that only words, action and leadership that proceed from the Holy Spirit have both authentic authority and the power that empowers us to do the Truth, rather than coerce others to do our bidding.

In this frame of mind we look for the prophets that God will raise up among us. Our leaders will be those who have given themselves over to being truly led by God-with-us. The words of God they speak will be answered and verified by that of God in us. The power of God in them will empower us to do what is required of us. If we truly attend to the Spirit of Truth as it is manifested in others as well as ourselves, we can trust the authority of those authentically raised to leadership among us. We will discern true leaders rather than suspecting of egotism everyone who raises his head above a single level, confusing spiritual authority with authoritarianism, and under-mining action that comes from clear leading. We will be blessed with the prophetic or charismatic leaders and guides we need and deserve.

We will also be blessed with another kind of leader, whose humility arises not from encounter with God within himself but from encounter with God within the corpo-rate body. The servant of God manifested through the corporate body may be a monthly meeting secretary or the executive secretary of a yearly meeting. These folks are often regarded simply as administrators—and they need considerable administative ability. In another religious body they might be regarded as functionaries. They may very well have a job description. Yet, to the extent they also possess a gift of discern-ment, these functionaries can act as servants of Christ who is embodied in the body of the meeting. They will be as charismatic as a prophet to the degree they have a gift of listening for the will of God. Divine Will is rarely expressed only in the formulations of the meeting. Perhaps even more often it is expressed in the interactions, the prob-lems and crises, the impasses, dynamics and yearnings within the membership. R. W. Tucker points out that a person may be led to be a "functionary". Following this path of servanthood is a calling in itself.

The important thing is to be more attentive in all things to intimations of the Holy One than to the stirrings of our own desires. We can trust that, if we attend to God, our needs will be cared for better than we can care for them ourselves. Historically, Friends have felt that the only true leader is the Spirit of Christ. In modern terms that is frequently translated to say that our true, human leaders are those who yield them-selves to being authentically led by the Holy Spirit—and are careful in discerning that leading.

Queries

Do you participate in your monthly meeting's meeting for business? Were you aware that membership at the monthly meeting level automatically made you a member of the quarterly and yearly meetings?

Have you ever attended any meeting other than your own? Are you familiar with any other meeting than the one you presently attend? If so, what differences have you observed? To what do you attribute them?

If your monthly meeting is part of a quarterly or half-yearly meeting, have you ever attended it? Do you attend regularly? Which of the functions in this section does it serve? What are its most and least attractive aspects?

Have you ever attended your yearly meeting? If so, journal some of your outstanding impressions and recollections.

Are you one of those who feels it's time to adopt structures more like those of modern businesses and institutions, in the interest of meeting the needs of the Society and society with more efficiency? Are you inclined to cling to ancient forms, regardless of inefficiencies? In either case, why? Can analyses such as these be helpful—or do they just exacerbate conflicts best left alone?

Do you think we can act together in large bodies, in the modern world, with pressures for efficiency, loving care of employees, long-term planning, cost-effectiveness and rapid response to crisis, without being conformed to its assumptions about what is important in decision-making and action? Try sketching an organizational structure to do this.

How might we preserve structures that are spacious enough to open us to governance by the will of God? How can the loose structures that facilitate discernment be enabled to survive the importation of practices from large-scale organizations? In what ways might we continue to practice our listening spirituality in a corporate setting? How can we avoid our organizations becoming so tight that they squeeze out the spaces in which the Spirit moves?

Reading and journaling exercise on yearly meetings

The reference below to *Church government* of London Yearly Meeting gives a thumbnail sketch of the history of London Yearly Meeting, now known as Britain Yearly Meeting. In fact, New England Yearly Meeting is the oldest of the yearly meetings. However, this is the best, brief history I know. It points out a few salient features of the evolution of yearly meetings among Friends: from something that was much more nearly a meeting—although restricted to ministering Friends—to today's open gathering of as much of the membership as can be persuaded to attend. What do you see as the strengths and weaknesses of the two kinds of yearly meetings?

Notice the chronological relationship between London's first Women's Yearly Meeting and the recognition of rights and personhood of women in the wider society. Also be aware that women's monthly and quarterly meetings for business had been in existence since the seventeenth century, although the scope of their business was more restricted than that of men's meetings.

Note, too, the change in the nature of the business conducted by yearly meetings, the range of its concerns in the wider society and—again—the chronological relationship between Friends' concerns and those of the wider society.

References and resources for Quaker structures and leadership consonant with the Quaker gestalt and Gospel Order

William Braithwaite.
Spiritual Guidance in the Experience of the Society of Friends.

Howard Brinton.
Friends for 300 Years.
chs. 9-10.

Wilmer Cooper.
A Living Faith.
esp. pp. 159-164.

Chuck Fager.
Without Apology.
A sketch of a theology for liberal Friends.

Chuck Fager, ed.
Quaker Service at the Crossroads.
A collection of essays both critiquing and defending historical changes in governance and service within the AFSC.

Paul Lacey.
On Leading and Being Led.
PHP #264.

Paul Lacey.
Quakers and the Use of Power.
PHP #241.

London Yearly Meeting.
Church government.
1968. ch. 20, #781-784.

William Penn.
The Rise and Progress of the People Called Quakers.
p. 38.

Michael Sheeran.
Beyond Majority Rule.
ch. 2, The Growth of Central Decision Making, 1666-1736. esp. p. 83; ch. 5, Quaker Leadership. esp. pp. 99-106.

R. W. Tucker.
"Structural Incongruities in Quaker Service".
QS.
In my opinion, the most broadly grounded and helpful essay in the volume; the only one of the group to explicitly relate his remarks to general problems among twentieth century Friends beyond the AFSC; the most significant overall contribution.

Roger C. Wilson.
Authority, Leadership and Concern.
Teasing out dimensions of the the three areas in the title, from experiences in Quaker service organizations in Britain during the Second World War.

Continuity and change in Quakerism

Modern thought

A twentieth century value, rather than structure, that encroaches on our prayerful listening is the rationalism and reductionism, that have been the intellectual fashion in the wider culture for most of the century. As respect for the sciences and their methods has grown, the tendency has been to regard them as the only ways of knowing. Truths established by outward observation and measuring are regarded by many as the only valid truth. Intuitions of unmeasurable truth are regarded as wholly subjective and without validity outside one's self.

It's ironic that this restriction of thought should become pervasive in the common culture just as the work done on quantum mechanics and the uncertainty principal, in the early part of the twentieth century, has become generally accepted as valid in particle physics. With scientific acceptance of this once-cutting-edge theory, has come a scientific acceptance of mystery and of dynamisms that may remain unknowable by human reason. An underlying or Ultimate Reality has become thinkable for physicists, just as laypeople have become accustomed to excluding such possibilities.

The two layers of thought in our culture will move on. It's impossible for me to anticipate where scientific thought is going. I am, however, certain that educated thought will catch up with the present scientific thought, in time. Until then, the reductionism of earlier scientific thought makes it harder for some people among us to trust in the existence of a radically other, unknowable God moving not only within but among us. A concern for scientifically provable truth, rather than Truth in the sense of Spiritual Reality, makes many cling to psychological reductionisms that characterize all intimations of Divinity as private, subjective drives or imagery.

Many of us find Buddhist meditation practices helpful in centering, in becoming more aware and in shifting consciousness. Those practices also are connected with a spirituality that rejects interpretations, even conceptualizations, as illusory constructs of the human mind. Our Quaker gestalt has a constellation of conceptualizations and interpretations that gives coherence and meaning to our life together as Friends. It's doubtful we could properly claim to stand in a Quaker line of succession, rather than the Buddhist line, were we to gently but firmly put them aside as Buddhist practice suggests.

Having put aside interpretation in favor of bare awareness, Buddhism is a non-theist religion. That is, there is in it no explicit sense of the existence or nature of God. Similarly other reductionisms in the area of religion also are, or point to, a non-theistic understanding of the universe: metaphysics rather than religion.

Quakerism, on the other hand, is founded on a trust—or faith—that the Presence and Guidance of God is available to every person: within and among us. Such explicit affirmation of God is a form of theism. As I've affirmed implicitly throughout these books, Quakerism is a theistic religion. Its tradition is theistic. To expect us to join in non-theistic belief, rather than to embrace our own faith tradition is to become something other than Quaker. To insist that Friends eliminate the cornerstone of their spiritual experience in the interests of conformity to current thought is to reverse the sense of Romans 12:2, that has been advice treasured by Friends. Such lack of trust—or faith—in the existence of anything beyond the supposedly closed systems of ourselves is another impediment to our ability to listen together for the Spirit moving among us.

Inevitable historical change

That we have always been somewhat responsive to the currents of ideas and theology in the wider culture is evident from a careful reading of our history in John Punshon's *Portrait in Gray*, as well as George Fox's account of his early search for Truth through the smorgasbord of possibilities in Civil War England. In *The Covenant Crucified: Quakerism and the Rise of Capitalism*, Douglas Gwyn has traced with great care—just within the lifetime of George Fox—the shift of Quaker viewpoint, practice and implicit theology from that of a covenant community, toward that of a contractual community shaped by the rise of capitalism and liberalism.

Knowing what it is, in addition to God, that has been at work in our history does not exempt us from the influences and pressures of the surrounding culture; but it can help us become more aware of which aspects of our tradition are of the culture and which are of the essence of our gestalt as a patterned relationship with God. Recognition of the cultural and historical dimensions of our tradition can act as a lens through which to examine our tradition in the present, our options and proposed innovations. It can free us from blind enslavement to cultural norms and inform our choices as a religious body.

We need to examine the extent to which, and the ways in which, our contemporary rationalism and liberalism are faithful to the requirements of listening obedience to the Spirit of God—and how they fall short. We need to re-visit Lewis Benson's vision of what our Religious Society would be like were it faithful to the vision George Fox had. We also need to revisit Howard Brinton's vision of Quakerism as a balanced fusion of various elements accreted over the centuries. We must look again at Wilmer Cooper's vision of "an emerging Quaker spirituality" that "can accommodate and utilize the diversity, commitment, loyalty, and enthusiasm of all Friends". Cooper proposed a symbiosis of differing Quaker organisms or gestalts.

Revisions that add richness by additions

In the process of change, it's possible we'll integrate within our gestalt some insights and practices that have come from other "listening" traditions. It's important, however, to be careful that we attempt to assimilate only those insights and practices that truly fit. Sometimes we can only test the "fit" experientially, by trying to integrate the insight or practice to see how well it works; what changes must be made in order to integrate it; whether those changes are Life-giving for lives within our gestalt—or tend to dis-integrate it.

Many of us have felt enriched by Native American traditions that accept the natural order as a vehicle of the Spirit. They help us feel the sacredness of all life and of the earth at a time when our environmental circumstances have made us aware of the lack of such a consistent sense of the sacred in our own tradition. It would be a mistake, however to think we can incorporate, into our own gestalt, the gestalts of several various, complex Native American traditions with long histories in other cultural and environmental circumstances. To simply take from them a few elements, out of context, is to miss and to devalue their unique wholeness.

Similarly, many of us have benefited from the meditation practices of both Hinduism and Buddhism, insofar as both traditions value listening, attention, awareness and transformed consciousness. To equate either tradition with our own, or to think we can import them into our own, again would be to miss and to devalue the unique wholeness of their gestalts—and the subtle but significant differences of their intentionalities from our own.

If our own gestalt loses its distinctive pattern now, it will probably be a result of our desire to be kind and accommodating to strangers among us; from an openness that refuses to discern what is consonant with our unique gestalt and what is different; from a fear that discriminating what belongs uniquely to ourselves is to be judgmental of others; from lack of encouragement to live close to the Source. Our membership might not dwindle; but the depth of what we have to offer might.

We may have arrived at a place where we must choose between maintaining a coherent religious tradition, or gestalt, and becoming assimilated, as a body, to a patternless pot-pourri of the religious or secular understandings brought to us from peoples' previous experiments. Clearly, I do not wish for us to be governed by the letter of whatever was among us in the seventeenth, eighteenth, nineteenth—or even twentieth—centuries. Yet, if we value immediacy and the Light and Power to live a more abundant and loving life, closer to God and to one another, we must be more attentive to the Source from which they derive, lest we become indistinguishable from the melange of new age and other groups in the wider society.

The same discerning faithfulness is also required in all the dimensions of Quaker life where change and cultural drift are underway. In Chapter 5, I've spoken of this issue in relation to the adoption of practices from the wider culture when preparing our business for the monthly meeting. In Chapter 4, I spoke of it in connection with distinguishing an authentic leading of God from some general principles and values that can be derived from our testimonies. If we are careful and discerning, we may remain faithful to what lies at the heart of the Quaker tradition, even if we do not observe all the forms of earlier times. We may distinguish efficient, compassionate or merely novel activity from what assists our listening attentiveness and our expression of God's loving us into unity.

We can't choose to stop the clock at any particular period of Quaker history, whether it's seventeenth century evangelism precisely as "the valiant sixty" undertook it, eigh-teenth century detachment from the wider society, nineteenth century movements back toward main stream Christianity, or twentieth century liberal emphases on universalism and the social gospel—or the effort to make pacifism the unifying ele-ment in Quakerism (Smith).

Post-modernism

We are obviously at a transition point for this historical period. We must be aware that, historically, we stand poised in the tension between modern and post-modern approaches. Modernist—or liberal—approaches have lost touch with the integrative power of tradition with its attendant coherence, stability and ability to give meaning to our experiences and lives. Out of the generosity and tolerance, that are two meanings of liberality, we have moved into and beyond a cultural and spiritual relativism. Many of us have not only granted the validity of other religious paths but have gone on to mingle and confuse them with our own path. The result does not leave us with many paths up the mountain, but rather wandering in the woods at its foot.

In the period of modernist thought, we've come close to losing the distinctive framework of our own path. In enthusiasm for the riches of other paths, we come close to denying the distinctiveness of others as well as of our own. In a gestalt or organic whole, the parts evolve in relation with one another, with a distinctive fit that they won't have without extensive adaptation within another gestalt. Without a clearly defined path or tradition, we lack the necessary support for all the dimensions and experiences of our spiritual lives. We lose the power to integrate and find meaning in our experiences as a whole.

Post-modernists, on the other hand, often overtly reject an integrative world view as oppressive and totalitarian, in favor of unfettered pluralism and difference (Rothenburg). There are certainly post-modernists among us with their attendant individualism and resistance to spiritual authority as mediated by the body of the meeting.

The preceding chapters, however, should have made clear that post-modernist rejection of mutual care and responsibility as well as of living within the tension between individual and corporate authority destroy the traditional gestalt of Quakerism. It's not clear that eliminating these elements would leave us with any continuity with Quaker tradition beyond the name. Such rejection even raises the question whether the resulting version of Quakerism could even be called a religion. Religion, by definition, binds people with the Divine as well as with one another.

We must be fully conscious as we confront the options open to us. We must neither blindly accept or reject what is new. We mustn't approach the new as a smorgasbord.

Rather we must approach it as elements that may or may not be integrated organically into our gestalt. The question of whether Quakerism will retain its distinctive gestalt runs through just about every meeting I've encountered, although it rarely surfaces in a single issue.

Wholeness

The wholeness of our gestalt, greater than the sum of its parts, may be eroded or destroyed if we resort to a kind of universalism that reduces our faith to the lowest common theological denominator that may be extracted from plural traditions—or to a utilitarianism that reduces our practice to what can be assimilated to good group dynamics or decision-making practice in the wider society. Such reductions deprive us of many elements in our tradition that can brim with meaning when experienced in their fullness.

Such reductions may also prune away some of the rich variety of the many paths to God that share the same constellating practice of listening and responsiveness, hearing and obeying. In eliminating the variety, these subtractions can close off many doors to God that provide precious openings. Worst of all, they may create a new rigidity or even idolatry of "only one legitimate way" to Mystery that reveals itself in a variety of unexpected ways. The risks of idolatry in a homogenous religion are very great indeed (McFague).

There are equivalent risks in adding elements willy-nilly from other religious traditions where they have become laden with meaning by their constellation in their own gestalt. It's possible that they cannot be integrated in any meaningful way with the Quaker gestalt. In the new context they may stand awkwardly alone without their own overlayers of interlocking and supporting metaphor and myth. They not only lose the wholeness and meaning they have in their original traditions. They may also, by their very unassimilability, destroy the wholeness of the gestalt on which they are imposed.

We retain earlier forms insofar as they still have Life in them, insofar as they help keep us focused on the Divine and expressive of the loving Oneness we share in God. We may strip away what has proved to be merely cultural over time—but only after that judgment has been painstakingly discerned and carefully seasoned at all levels of our discernment process. We don't modernize for modernity's sake—or even for the sake of our survival as an institution. Faithfulness to God takes precedence over our institutional preservation.

Our worth and meaning as an institution consists precisely in being faithful to listening for the Divine in our lives and to expressing, in our relationships and activities, the Oneness that we have experienced or in which we trust. In changing historical and cultural circumstances our continuity and faithfulness lie not in preserving antique—or lifeless—forms of any kind, but in what has been referred to as a dependency of mind, expectant waiting, holy obedience and faithfulness to God.

The continuity that will steady us in the midst of change comes of allowing our contemporary gestalt to be patterned by the same intentionality and directionality of being that patterned earlier versions of the gestalt in the seventeenth, eighteenth, nineteenth and earlier twentieth centuries. The resulting ministries may have looked somewhat different in earlier times because they were facilitating the listening and expression of unity for people in different historical and cultural circumstances. We can barely guess what outward forms they may take in the twenty-first century. We can only hope they will continue to be patterned by listening for God.

Spiritual validity and institutional failure

A major formative element in the post-modernist mileu we inhabit is Freudianism. Freud's influential book, *The Future of an Illusion,* is a stunning indictment of the failures of institutional religion. It's equally stunning that Freud displays no sense of any living spirit within the flawed structural form of church and dogma. It's hard to know whether this is due to overwhelming experience of institutional failure, lack of interior experience, reductionism of interior experience to psychological drives—or all of the above. In any case, he presents a lucid exposition of the way in which the failures of flawed institutions may lead not only to condemnation of the institution but to lack of trust in the reality of the interior spiritual experience the church is meant to support.

Many of the refugees from other churches who come to us have been hurt by institutional failures. Sometimes the very reticence of Quakers concerning interior experience leads those seeking a new spiritual home to believe there is nothing coherent or shared going on in the silence. Perhaps our peculiar risk of institutional failure is less the pain we inflict by our words and behaviors than the failure to communicate what lies within the minimalist scaffolding of our institutional structures. If we fail, it will be less because of the evils of our structures than because of their hollowness.

Holding out the vision of implicit Quakerism in the midst of existential reality

At the end of this treatment of the heart of corporate or communal Quaker practice, it's only reasonable to touch on how different it may look from the meeting life most of us actually experience. The assumptions differ from those that many of us make about the underlying reasons and rationale for our being in a Friends Meeting.

I've been giving an account of what I've come to think of not only as the "Quaker gestalt", but as "implicit Quakerism". The gestalt is a pattern implicit in the midst of the existential and historical realities of Quakerism as we experience it. Much of the pain of our experience as Friends lies in the gulf we frequently experience between the possibilities implicit for us in Quakerism and the all too human realities we experience as we live it out with others as flawed as ourselves. Conversely, the joys we experience in the context of Quakerism are most often the moments when the implicit possibilities of Quakerism and our existential experience intersect in a lived reality, when we find ourselves actually living it, experiencing it together. It's in such times that we renew our faith in its potential and our commitment to faithfulness.

Having a clear sense of what we're reaching toward helps us in our efforts to be faithful. It helps to be able to hold the vision of a life together lived in attentiveness and responsiveness to the movements of the Spirit, in a loving mutuality with one another that reflects and expresses our Oneness in Divine Love. It also helps to be tender with ourselves and with one another when we fall short or miss the mark because we, ourselves, are not yet perfect or spiritually mature. We'll probably never live in a spiritual community or church in which all the members have come to that condition.

Some of our pains come of the failures of ourselves and others to live into the possibility of implicit Quakerism. Other pains and failures are inherent in the very patterns of implicit Quakerism itself: the defects of virtues, the long shadow cast by a high aspiration. Some pains are ours by virtue of being part of a tradition shaped in the Radical Reformation in England. The hungering and thirsting for righteousness implicit in the progressive purifications of that Reformation threw a shadow of judgmentalism that sometimes casts out love and gentleness in relationships.

Our tradition was born in the century of England's great revolution and civil war, of enormous political, social, economic and religious change. One of the last of the increasingly radical social and religious groups to be formed in that milieu, standing in opposition to the received order, the Quaker movement shaped the pattern we have inherited. From its inception, Quakerism has been counter-cultural in the root sense of the word. It stands over against both the prevailing culture and the inescapable existential realities of whatever times in which we find ourselves. Quakerism is counter-cultural in speaking prophetic words to the wider society. We speak of the gulf between the society's institutions, structures, assumptions, values and ways of living and those we've glimpsed when we hold things in the Light and experience being gathered—together with our community, humanity and all of creation—in the Love of God.

Perhaps the most difficult part of working with the idea of a Quaker gestalt is that the form may become, as George Fox said of those of other churches, empty or dead—no longer a container for God's Life, Light, Power, Love—or even an invitation to open to them. The second risk is that—having seen the emptiness or lack of true, spiritual functionality in our forms—we will abandon not only empty forms but the spirituality, or way of relating to the Divine, that shaped both our forms and our living sense of what used to fill them.

Queries

As a people who claim to stand outside modern culture, to reject it as the ultimate authority and even to critique it prophetically, we must take care where our words, notions and actions are coming from. Do they have the integrity, coherence, and ability to confer meaning on our lives that have been the hallmark of our gestalt? Are they the fruit of attentive listening for the movement of the Holy Spirit? Do they embody the fruit of the Spirit? (Galatians 5:22-23) When we choose them, do we "Choose Life!"—as God enjoined the Israelites in Deuteronomy 30:19 when he invited them to love him and join their wills to his? Or are we setting off on our own utterly existential human lives?

How can we covenant our lives with one another, to participate in the Great Life in which we are held? In what ways, after the manner of the society around us, do we choose lives alienated from one another, from the Divine, from Ultimate Meaning—and even from our innermost selves? How can we guard against choosing lives streamlined for efficiency and effectiveness in the service of production and consuming? How can we maintain the center of the Religious Society of Friends as an organic whole? Will we shiver to bits, clinging to our assorted rigidities and notions, disappearing into the uncommitted, alienated, willful larger society around us?

How many people move on from your meeting, in their spiritual search, after a period of a few months or a year or two? Is there a common pattern?

References and resources

Wilmer Cooper.
A Living Faith.
p. 159.

George Fox.
The Journal.
Nickalls, ed. pp. 2-3.

Sigmund Freud.
The Future of an Illusion.

Douglas Gwyn.
*The Covenant Crucified:
Quakerism and the Rise
of Capitalism.*
A historical study, from the
perspective of Marxist socio-
economic analysis, of some
factors at work in the development of Quaker self-understanding and organizational
structures, in the socio-
economic upheaval of seventeenth century England.

Patricia Loring.
*The Hidden Center
and Outward Scaffolding
of Quaker Spiritual
Community.*

Sally McFague.
*Metaphorical Theology:
Models of God in Religious
Language.*

John Punshon.
*Portrait in Gray: A Short
History of the Quakers.*

Donald Rothenburg.
"Ken Wilbur and the
Future of Transpersonal
Inquiry: An Introduction
to the Conversation",
in *Ken Wilbur in Dialogue.*
Rothenburg and Kelly, eds.
pp. 1-2.

Allen Smith.
"The Renewal Movement:
The Peace Testimony and
Modern Quakerism",
in *Quaker History* (Fall 1996).
pp. 1-23.

Lloyd Lee Wilson.
*Essays on the Quaker
Vision of Gospel Order.*
The Meeting as Covenant
Community. esp. pp. 65-70.

Chapter 7

Coming Together for Mutual Support as a Listening Community

The nature of Quaker counter-culturalism or marginality

Each reformation of the church or of monastic orders has been a call to turn away from assimilation into the wider social order of its time. Within the Christian church, it has been a call to return to the simplicity of the gospel, to the good news of God's loving relationship with humanity. For Quakers the good news of the gospel was that "Christ is come to teach his people himself." They understood that the promise in John to send a Paraclete, the Spirit of Truth had been fulfilled; that the Spirit of God is within and among us to teach, guide and change us (John 14:16-17, 25-26; 15:26; 16:7-8).

Quakerism was subversive from the outset. Its central theological insight, the claim that there was "that of God in every person", was subversive of the institutional establishment of ministry and subversive of the authority of the established church. Many Quakers were jailed in life-threatening conditions for such blasphemy.

That theological insight implied ministry by spiritually experienced, but otherwise not necessarily educated, people who attended to God within and directed others to do so. In the words of Penn, "They were changed [people] themselves before they went about to change others." It was subversive of the established order that they found their unity as a church or people in their interior experience, rather than in a shared formulation of creed, dogma or liturgy.

Friends' subversiveness continued in their outward lives. They identified with the Old Testament prophets who cried, "Woe to them that are at ease in Zion, ... " (Amos 6:1 KJV). They cried shame on the comfort of those who were well off in virtue of having conformed to the values of contemporary society. They challenged the values and orientation of the respectable citizens of England. Friends, thereby, voluntarily placed themselves on the margins of their society.

This marginality or liminality of Friends was defined by standing outside institutions (such as the church) of their time, as well as outside many of the common grounds of fellowship (Fox).

Friends found their true fellowship in their oneness in the Love of God. Their discipleship was marked by willingness to suffer for the Truth they had found. Friends were united by more than their opposition to the prevailing society. More important, they shared a countervailing vision of a peaceable kingdom governed by the inward Christ and manifest in the virtues of the early church. Their vision illuminated the structures of Untruth around them.

Friends' suffering response when their adjurations to peace, justice and religious freedom met with violence was a counter-cultural testimony in action. Early Friends fell back upon the suffering of Jesus and his example of meeting force with love, refusing to participate in a culture of violence, even to defend themselves. Fox and others fought the Lamb's War, by putting on the line their words, their possessions, their bodies and their lives. The nature of Friends' resistance witnesses to a Spiritual Reality counter to the reality of a society that has defended itself against its own members and children with guard dogs, fire hoses and even bullets.

Friends' twofold witness is by the example of love within their beloved community and by a prophetic stance over against the prevailing culture. Today, the prophetic stance is seldom that of a Jeremiah. Instead, we aspire to Woolman's capacity to love the sinners and respect the integrity of their motives, gently drawing them forward into Truth. The first one Woolman changed was always himself.

Some earlier ways of supporting one another in a life with priorities counter to the wider culture

Everything that has gone before in this book stresses a way of life—both interior and exterior—that imposes expectations, demands, priorities and uses of resources different from those of the culture surrounding us. It's a strenuous discipline to remain in an attitude of listening for the Spirit, rather than to slip into easy conformity to the patterned ways, styles and assumptions of the wider culture. We need all the support and reinforcement we can get.

In earlier times, Quakers—having recognized how easy it was to slip into their neighbors' ways of thinking, behaving and spending time—had erected a "hedge" between themselves and "the world". The hedge consisted of a number of distinctive or "peculiar" practices that overtly distinguished Quakers from other people. In the beginning many of these practices were shared by the Amish, Mennonites and Brethren whom William Penn had invited to his colony of Pennsylvania, precisely because of the plain ways they shared with Friends. Over time, there has been a culture drift among all these people toward assimilation with the wider culture. Of all the plain people, the Amish have remained most faithful to their original practices, although there are numerous small differences in assimilation among various church districts. Many Mennonites have also retained some of their original practices.

In the twentieth century, Quakers have all but abandoned the "hedge" of plainness that outwardly distinguished them from the world. The hedge consisted of such distinguishing characteristics as plain speech, plain dress, simple living and rigorous truth telling that was closely connected with taciturn speech, and refusal either to swear oaths or to bargain in business.

Plain speech

Plain speech, "theeing" one another, had been part of the Quaker prophetic witness to equality and humility in the wider world. In the more highly inflected English of the seventeenth century the singular, "thee" or "thou", was the word used to address children, intimates and one's inferiors. One's superiors were addressed with the plural, "you" or "ye." Part of the original Quaker witness to equality was to address everyone, without regard for rank or status, by the intimate, singular form—even when Friends were jailed for such disrespect. "Thee" was an implicit assertion that all were equal children, humble before God.

In the intense restriction and persecution after the Restoration, most of the earliest generation of Quaker ministers died of abuse or disease in seriously unhealthy jail conditions. By the beginning of the eighteenth century, Quakerism was drawing in on itself in exhausted acknowledgement of its inability to prevail against the rising capitalist culture and liberal attitudes (Gwyn). The hedge was born in this indrawing. "Thee" became a prophetic address to everyone regardless of status. Along with use of the title, "Friend", and the refusal to use any other titles, "thee" also began to be a sign of intimacy within the counter-cultural, outsider movement that became Friends.

In this century, "thee" is used—with its related verb forms—mainly intimately between Quaker spouses and families, especially but not exclusively, in the Conservative Yearly Meetings and among a few, older Philadelphia Friends. It remains an intimate acknowledgement of their mutual belonging to this outsider group. The intention is very different from original usage; but it marks an important need to acknowledge, affirm and support our intentional differences from the wider culture, as other ways of making that affirmation have fallen away.

It's a telling cultural note that modern English has also adopted a single form of address for all persons; but it is the plural, "you", formerly reserved for superiors. We live in a culture in which everyone aspires to ever higher status, rather than humility.

In losing plain language as we've assimilated to the wider culture, we've lost one reminder of our differing intentionality. Some people try to revive the usages for the sake of the testimony. We might do better to consider what might be an equivalent way of testifying to equality that will speak with as much clarity to today's culture as plain speech did to a culture in which "thee" carried immediately obvious and socially inferior class connotations.

Plain dress

Like plain speech, plain dress was part of the hedge that separated Friends from members of the wider culture. One had only to look at a Quaker to know that this was a peculiar person who did not aspire to be fashionable or attractive according to the ways of the world. Not only was the demeanor of others affected by this difference; a Quaker's own demeanor was affected by the knowledge that he or she automatically reflected, and reflected upon, the Society and its testimonies. There was no carelessness in the dress. It was tidy but deliberately out-of-date in fashion, modest in design and muted in color: often gray for women, black for men. It called attention to itself in no way other than by contrast with the modishness, immodesty or desire to be noticed evinced in fashionable clothing.

Among men, clothing was tailored so as to avoid any suggestion either of foppish desire to be noticed or of lapels, epaulets or other suggestions of military dress. No cravats or ties. A single color, black, assured no desire to stand out from one's fellows in appearance. A hat that remained placed firmly on the head, doffed only to God, showed that social deference to no human was a hallmark of Quaker testimony.

In its own way, plain dress was a testimony to equality among the Society. No one sought to stand out, be noticed or valued by reason of style, color, expense of cut or jewelry. Hair was mostly hidden by bonnets and hats. There was solidarity to be found in the uniformity. There was also witness to the culture at large that it was possible to be decently dressed without resort to great expenditure of resources, wastefully discarded at the behest of an industry or used to attempt to gain social advantage or vain admiration of appearance. The childrens' book, *Thee Hannah*, tells a story illustrating the way that plain dress also stood for certain kinds of integrity and other witnesses in the community (deAngeli).

In fact, the childrens' stories of Marguerite deAngeli and Brinton Turkle are among the best and simplest illustrations both of the Quaker culture of the "classic period" and of the inner dimensions of Quaker spirituality to which that culture was witness. They illustrate lessons learned by children of that culture as they grew into the inward meanings of the peculiar customs of their parents and the significance of those customs as witness in the world. Such parts of the hedge as plain speech and plain dress, along with numerous others I won't attempt to detail, were outward and visible signs and testimonies to the inner truths Quakers came to, as they grew into their listening spirituality. In that sense, they were sacraments of Quaker life. They not only witnessed to the world but established Friends, themselves, more deeply in the life to which they were committed.

Marrying in, marrying out and disownment

Another part of the hedge, often deplored by modern Friends, was the custom of marrying within the Society and frequent disownment of someone who "married out". In early Quaker communities where Friends lived, worked and worshiped together in enclaves, marriage within the Society was natural and almost inevitable. Potential partners may have been known from childhood and affections were formed naturally. Outsiders were rarely encountered on occasions that might foster wholesome intimacy.

As Friends became more dispersed in the wider community in the nineteenth century, outside contacts became more frequent. Attachments might more easily be formed with people whose orientation to life differed and consequently lacked common witness, goals or values. In these situations "marrying in" became an important way of holding the community together in its counter-cultural orientation and witness. Families were important to Friends as the primary place of spiritual formation in Quakerism. They were the places in which Quakerism was taught, practiced, carried on and witnessed to. They were the first level of the School of Love. Living, as most modern Friends do, in families that are not discernably different from those of anyone else would have been unthinkable to earlier Friends.

At its best, control over marriage probably helped deter a number of inappropriate ties. At its worst, efforts at control over marriage were indeed a violation of personal inclination that might have deleterious effects on a subsequent marriage or even the entire subsequent life of a young person. It might violate a personal leading among Quaker young people. I think of Elizabeth Haddon, the founder of Haddonfield, who is supposed to have said, "I have a charge to love thee, John", to her prospective husband by way of proposal (Bacon, 1974). Who, indeed, would want to interfere with a marriage that is truly the union of two souls brought together by God for their own good and probably the good of others?

Nonetheless, I'm aware of stresses and strains today among Friends who frequently are torn between inward drawings to become more closely interwoven with the community and claims on them of a spouse or family that has a different directionality and a different sense of how First Days or evenings or time, energy and money in general are to be spent—and in what company. We would not go back to the days of forbidding or disowning marriages outside the faith. Yet, as we become more aware of the demands of our counter-cultural faith, we become more aware of the divisive tendencies of very different orientations to life and expectations between partners. The strains and fissions may be experienced either primarily with the community or within the marriage. In either case, there's a risk of breaking something that has been whole or promised to become more whole over a lifetime.

In the era of the hedge, the community's choice was to preserve its integrity by "owning" only marriages within the hedge. The choice was not only for the sake of preserving the community's integrity of witness, but also to avoid pressures on the marriage. When one partner was challenged both to live a counter-cultural life with the community and to live into—or at least accept—the different expectations of the spouse, either the counter-cultural tradition or the spouse was often abandoned in the resulting stress. People who were disowned for going against Friends' order by marrying a nonFriend, or marrying outside the care of the meeting, could acknowledge and condemn their disregard of right order. If Friends felt it was sincere, they would be restored to membership.

Disownment was acknowledgement that one could not both live into the counter-cultural demands of Quaker life and witness and conform to the life of the surrounding culture. In some sense the old disownments were an acknowledgement that a union grounded in two separate traditions would always be a compromise between the two and the partners could never be fully united.

What do we have in place of the "hedge"?

In either giving up or clinging to the "hedge" as a quaint bit of Quaker antiquarianism, we have lost many of the inner meanings and the outward witness of which it was a sign. We have also lost the support and reinforcement that the implicit affirmations of the hedge gave us. This has happened at a time when we've also become even more dispersed within an increasingly mobile, alienated and pervasive outer culture.

Few of us live these days in the same neighborhoods with other Friends or see one another outside meeting. We live, work, raise our children and spend our days enveloped in media promulgating the common culture. We seek interests and entertainments in diverse ways apart from Friends. We come together mainly for silent worship, not always even for committee work or meeting for business. How then do we maintain our spiritual and counter-cultural identity as Friends? More importantly how do we come into touch and remain in touch with our sense of the inner realities and outer practices to which we have committed ourselves?

Many men are obliged to don suits and ties and do so without demur if the job is financially important to them. For the most part, Friends dress more casually than their fellow citizens and take that for simplicity. Such dress, however, does not usually serve to mark us off in any way from the consumer culture. Casual dress has become an option in a culture that has made even casualness a fashion statement, stamped with capitalist rank and price tag. In fact, casual dress or sloppiness was not the hallmark of plain dress. Especially in meeting for worship, respect for the occasion and the Divine was implicit in a style of dress, without show. Even for us, today, casualness has little meaning.

One Conservative Friend's weighty father decided toward the end of his life that denim work clothes were the last remaining valid simple dress, in solidarity with working folk and testifying against needless expense and vanity. In this day of designer jeans and T-shirts, even that testimony may be undercut or coopted by consumer values if one pays attention to form rather than to underlying significance.

Women among us are apt to choose casual comfort that may or may not be a fashion statement, but will probably *not* be a mark of deference to the Divine in worship. Or they may choose the quasi-nun-like propriety of plain suits and dresses without orna-ment or jewelry ... or a universalizing celebration of ethnic cultures and handiwork in dress and jewelry that may be exuberantly colorful, stylish and ornamented.

Some feel they are witnessing to preservation of the environment by wearing clothing made of natural fibers. Others feel they are witnessing to equality by wearing cheaper polyester clothing that is available to people of modest means. There is no uniform recognition among Friends either to witness or to the significance of how they are seeing one another clad.

The reason for choice is as apt to be comfort as anything else. I find dress in meeting in the western part of the United States to be markedly more casual than that of the urban East. I have no sense that dress is anywhere, any longer, a prophetic statement, a bond among us or a sacrament of what we have inwardly experienced. If this is true in meeting for worship, it's even more true outside meeting where many who eschew three-piece suits, jewelry or makeup within meeting, cheerfully don it outside meeting. We are comfortable to merge with the wider, consumer society outside meeting rather than to attempt any—possibly idiosyncratic or socially unacceptable—witness against it. Mainly we dress according to personal taste within local style.

As I mentioned above, hardly anyone uses "thee" anymore. Many other witnesses have been subverted by the wider culture or legal system. Our witness against oath-taking —or two standards of truth-telling—has been reduced to checking boxes on forms that say, "I affirm" or "I swear".

When Thomas Elwood refused to doff his hat to his father, it was a major commit-ment that cost him dearly socially. When William Penn first appeared in plain dress and failed to doff his hat or engage in elaborate ritual courtesies with friends of his own social class, it was a turning point in his life and relationships. We no longer have anything to mark a turning point in our lives or set us apart from that against which we are called to make prophetic witness. By and large, our rites of passage are so inward and hidden that they are easily trivialized, set aside, forgotten or concealed like embarrassing secrets (LYM; Ellwood).

Sharing our social witness

Much will be said in Volume III about concern for the social order and prophetic witness among Friends. Here, however, I want to speak of the fellowship, the mutual love, that can come of sharing together in a witness. That witness may be a demonstration of support, non-support or opinion concerning some social matter. The witness may also consist of working together on projects such as building or rehabilitating homes for the dispossessed; rebuilding churches for those robbed of their places of worship by people possessed by racial, ethnic or sectarian hatreds; or sanctuary support offered to refugees who haven't been given the authentic benefit of our country's laws and the Geneva Convention (Corbett).

Knowing ourselves to be part of one another in our embodiment of, witness to and acting out of the Great Love in which we are One, can be a very special kind of fellowship. It usually involves a sense of empowerment: not only seeking to empower others, but the empowerment that can come to us as we are joined together and energized by the movement of the Holy Spirit among us. In a massive society like our own, in which even our governmental representatives draw most of their financial support from multinational corporations, it is easy to feel powerless. Openings of the Spirit concerning where justice and mercy lie may feel very fragile as long as they remain interior and individual. It's hard to know how we may witness to the leadings of Love, much less hope to make any change in a massively powerful governmental/industrial/scientific/military establishment.

Apart from garden-variety crowd enthusiasm and excitement, there can also be true enthusiasm (in-Spiriting) where two or more are gathered together in the Name, in the Spirit, in the Love of God that moves them to witness. Always remembering the emotional crowd fervor of the Nuremburg Rallies, we must be careful to discern from which parts of ourselves our enthusiasms proceed. With grace, however, we may experience the true in-Spiriting and empowerment that draws us together in a community that is covenanted in God rather than merely "built by human hands".

Political demonstrations are more open to fervors of human psychological origins than are projects. In demonstrations we are also usually drawn together with a "mixed multitude" of people whose motives and behaviors may be neither the same as our own nor derive from the same Source. We must be discerning as to which are truly compatible with our own. As we listen together, however, we may know both our fellowship in the Eternal and in the leading to manifest it in the temporal. On down-to-earth levels, we may also share lunches, personal histories and reflections relevant to the occasion. These, too, may help us to be bonded in Love and mutual concern for the order of the society in which we are embedded.

Projects are generally more calm, less emotional affairs than demonstrations. They may last for a day or for a longer period. We share the burden of the work to which we have been individually called. We experience the pleasures and demands of cooperation. We learn each other's styles and rhythms of work and can begin wordlessly to enter into a kind of choreography of movement that is an outward symbol or sacrament of the one movement of the heart in which we are joined. If we are together for days, we share food, fatigue, rest, conversation and idiosyncratic daily routines that help reinforce the inward Oneness in which we are joined.

Queries

What practices or behaviors differentiate your life from that of your non-Quaker friends and neighbors? On what occasions do you opt for another activity than meeting? How often last year? On what occasions do you opt for another activity than a Friends' committee meeting? ... for your yearly meeting? ... for FGC?

In what ways have you personally witnessed to your disapproval or protest of a social condition or government action in the past year? In what ways has your meeting as a corporate body witnessed its disapproval or protest? Have you ever found yourself engaged in a witness with people whose motives and behaviors were very different from your own? What did you do?

Journal about some occasion when you felt your behavior and action exemplified clearly the spiritual ground of your witness. Draw out the reasons in detail. How might you prepare for such witness in the future? Is God calling you to any new, small or large, witnesses now?

Clearness for marriage

In relation to marriage, there is a tentative, hopeful development in a growing shift in our use of clearness committees. For most of our history, committees for clearness for marriage have functioned primarily as committees for clearance of the business dimensions of the union. The committee ascertained any facts pertinent to the proposed marriage that might affect the discernment of the meeting for business as to the appropriateness of the marriage. Their considerations might have included the question of previous entanglements and of financial arrangements for the children of a former, deceased spouse. If there were no serious impediments, the committees tended simply to endorse the couple's decision to marry.

In this century the clearness committee has evolved as a more intimate body for discernment itself. There have been numerous conscious and semi-conscious experiments with its use to discern the rightness of marriages proposed to be taken "under the care of the meeting". Traditionally the meeting's care has included assistance in times of illness, financial setbacks, departure of one spouse from "Truth", serious disagreements or divorce between spouses or problems with children.

With the increase of the divorce rate, even among Friends, it's been felt that extra care must be taken before the meeting offers itself for self-giving care of a marriage, lest the marriage prove to have been planted in the shallow soil of romantic passion, not equal to the sometimes scorching climate of marriage. The meeting is wary of finding itself caring for something the partners have not cared for very much themselves.

No clear-cut way of conducting such committees for clearness on marriage has evolved among us, allowing us to respond to the guidance of the Spirit in particular instances. The primary feature is to get out of the sentimental mode of sympathy with, celebration and rubber-stamping of the sweetness of a couple desiring to be united in marriage. The best aid to the discernment of the source of the leading into marriage lies in addressing the harder questions of what the marriage might imply over years of events impossible to anticipate. Many marriage clearness committees have found New England Yearly Meeting's *Living with Oneself and Others* a helpful resource.

Some hard questions worth probing at depth arise in issues around the modes in which the two partners habitually handle money; care of and provision for children of previous marriages; expectations about having or not having children and about child-rearing, education and expenditures for children; feelings about the care of possibly handicapped children, or about a spouse who could become handicapped; about the life-style anticipated, the bread labor, household responsibilities and other contributions of each partner.

The length and nature of the relationship should be probed. Have they been together long enough for "the first careless rapture" of sexual attraction to have settled down, to have weathered together some crisis in one or both lives? What is the habitual mode in which each responds to crisis? How does the other truly feel about that mode? Does each partner feel able to live with the other's characteristic response to crisis repeatedly for a lifetime? Do both truly accept that the other may never change or be conveniently re-formed to more congenial modes of approach to life and difficulties?

There are many more such questions, some peculiar to the particular union in question. There are no "correct" answers. The answers to such questions provide the climate in which discernment can take place. The clearness committee is presumably a body chosen not for their enthusiasm for marriage but for their gift of discernment, possibly with particular reference to or concern for the integrity of marriage.

Insofar as the clearness committee truly does possess the gift of discernment, the members will be able to hear and ask the questions that underlie the petition before them. Probing difficult topics before approving marriage under the care of the meeting may help marriage to be taken less lightly. It may help those who propose to marry across Quaker and some other religious traditions to see and meet the difficulties they face. Beyond blind confidence that "love conquers all", there are questions such as where they will worship and in what faith their children will be raised. Even more difficult questions concern their underlying orientation *vis à vis* the dominant culture.

One couple, recently married in my meeting, stated the fundamental shift for which they had been waiting. Both relinquished the question of whether the other was the perfect partner for them. They took up instead the question of whether each was willing to get up each morning for the rest of their lives and try again with the other. A clearness committee would ideally help thoroughly turn over the ground in search of the answer. Such a concern for the integrity of marriage is truly counter-cultural in a society that is pervaded with sexual stimulation, romantic ideas about marriage, minimal encouragement or assistance to see the family as a School for Peace-making and maximum encouragement for moving on to a new sexual excitement when the marriage is difficult or dull.

Meeting to share the physical maintenance of our communal space

One often overlooked communal opportunity for fellowship, bonding and sharing about our faith and aspirations are the work days that meetings have appointed to maintain the meeting's physical property. In most meetings, to this day, times are appointed periodically to share in routine maintenance: dusting and polishing benches in the meeting room and other furniture elsewhere, dusting books in the library, cleaning and tidying the kitchen and other areas, and seasonal yard work such as shoveling walks and clearing driveways in winter, leaf-raking in the fall, weeding among plantings, cleaning up litter from storms.

Rarely does any one person stay for the entire day. It is, rather, an occasion when people come and go for an hour or two or a half day as possible, accomplishing some specific task or offering themselves to an ongoing project. Sometimes children are invited into some of the tasks, have special tasks reserved for them or simply play together on the meeting grounds as the adults work. Sometimes snacks are brought to share either at a formal break or simply set out to be eaten as needed. Brown bag lunches are often part of the work day. Pot lucks are held less often, perhaps because they would create another layer of clean-up in the kitchen.

These work times are usually presented and accepted, or shirked, as opportunities to share in the mutual responsibility for property. Sometimes the burden is chiefly borne by those who have a gift or taste for tidying, cleaning or outdoor work—or a special love for the meeting house and its grounds. Among a number of urban meetings today the members feel themselves too pressed for time in a number of other activities to give themselves to these work days. Some feel that, their gifts lying in more sophisticated areas of activity, their time and energies would be better spent elsewhere.

Some meetings are held in rented property, where they are neither required nor permitted to do such work. Other meetings, especially in urban areas where the membership has numerous commitments and activities outside the meeting that make demands on time and energy, feel it's better to contract for the work to be done by professionals and dispense with work days altogether. In some places the work day has, in fact, disappeared.

I've noted in several places where there is no shared manual work—sometimes even disdain of such work as appropriate meeting activity—that there is often also a complaint of lack of sense of community in the meeting. Lack of sense of community may have a number of concomitant determinants, especially in an urban setting. The diffusion of energy in the variety of activities available in urban places is connected with lack of availability for committee work, study groups and pot lucks as well as for manual labor on behalf of the meeting.

In all these cases, there is not only a loss of the willing hands and minds required to do the work of the meeting. Maybe the most profound level of loss is the contribution that working together makes to fellowship, to solidarity, to mutuality in love within the meeting. Meeting together "to know one another in that which is eternal" is reinforced by meeting together to know one another in, through and over that which is mundane—in order that, in fact, we may be one, depending on our intentionality.

I've had searching conversations about spiritual matters with people—occasionally people I've barely had a chance to know—across the meeting room as we each slowly and carefully polished our respective benches. I've had a chance to meet children in an informal way, or to talk with people about their families, joys and concerns while raking leaves or weeding side-by-side. We speak more naturally and openly in the intimacy of shared work.

We come away from work days with a clearer sense of, and respect for, the personal burdens others carry in faithfulness, of the small and large human milestones and triumphs in the lives of families, of relationships with children, grandchildren and parents who may be outside the meeting. All this knowledge feeds back into our prayer for one another in meeting for worship as well as the outward support or celebration we may feel moved to offer in one another's lives. It is yet another of the traditional ways of being woven together in love that we risk losing as we accept contractual relationships for labor in the meeting.

Pot luck work

A special case of working together manually for the care of the meeting is the task of setting up and cleaning up for pot lucks. Little needs to be said of the actual work. The arrangements vary with the facilities available in each meeting place. It's a rare meeting house that doesn't have some sort of kitchen facility built into it, if only an alcove in a small meeting house.

I want to celebrate the fellowship of working in concert to set up tables, hot water urns and offerings; the clearing away. Most especially I recall the sharing in dishwasher-less washing-up and drying lines in small kitchens. The exchange of news, getting acquainted, conversation and sometimes song-fests are among some of my most cherished memories of intimacy with Friends in meetings where I haven't been able to visit for years.

Meeting to share food, news, conversation and faith with people of like mind and commitment

Most of the occasions that bring us together to affirm or explore our life together as members of a peculiar group are centered on eating. Consuming food together has been a major way of bonding in most cultures and many religious groups from earliest times.

Shared meals were one of the features of the early church. They, and their roots in the Jewish Passover meal, probably played a part in the evolution of the Eucharist meal or Commemorative Communion sharing of bread and wine in most Christian churches. Friends, typically, have internalized the sense of the gift of communion or sharing in the Bread of Life in the sense of gathering in their meetings for worship. They have, however, retained a sense of the importance of regular, shared meals of which all partake and to which as many as are able contribute.

Pot lucks

The classic shared meal among Friends usually takes place after at least one meeting for worship per month. The meal joins people together in that which is temporal, after the joint experience of that which is eternal. As in all meals, it is the company and the fellowship shared that are the most important elements. Especially where the meetings tend to be silent and the vocal ministry comes from a profound depth of spiritual experience, there can be a need to know the mundane concerns on one another's hearts. What are the causes people have for rejoicing or mourning, hope and fear? What is happening with parents, children, grandchildren? When we know these things we can share in lives, offer support where needed or simply be present for one another in prayer and love.

Pot lucks reinforce the sense of community: that ours is not a spirituality in which we worship separately and leave separately. Rather we worship as a community and spend time together as a community, coming to know one another in that which is temporal as we do in that which is eternal. We take time to listen to one another's concerns and opinions not only on matters within the meeting but on matters in the wider community and the world. It's a time to enjoy and rejoice in the discovery of samenesses and differences. It's a time for our children to learn to know each other by playing with one another in a Quaker setting that emphasizes non-adversarial or non-competitive play. All this is often more easily done in a smaller meeting. In a large urban area people are often drawn into a variety of non-Quaker activities on weekends. Urban meetings often scatter soon after the rise or at an appointed hour—reinforcing urban difficulties in knowing one another.

Pot luck dishes tend to embody the testimony to simplicity, adverting to the desire not to make a display, to consume costly resources or to vie for attention. There is also a testimony to equality in mindfulness of those who cannot eat rich foods and those who have very little to eat at all, eating low on the food chain in recognition of our relation and responsibility to stewardship of the Creation. Among modern Friends, often there is also a tendency to offer dishes made of especially wholesome foods: whole grains and legumes, fresh vegetables and fruits, home-baked bread. These dishes may be prepared with generosity and loving care, and may be quite delicious.

Occasionally we run short. More often it's "loaves and fishes", with the appearance of more food than can be consumed by those present. Usually a variety of foods turn up, although I remember fondly one astonishing pot luck in Princeton (NJ) Meeting that turned out to consist almost entirely of desserts. Mathematicians present amused themselves by computing the probability of the event.

Princeton also experimented for some time with occasional pot luck breakfasts with singing before meeting. They proved easier for single people to attend than for those with children. The clean-up was sometimes a scramble; but the renewal of ties was felt to be worth it.

In many meetings, the monthly pot luck is held after worship on the day of meeting for business. Such pot lucks not only supply sustenance for the conduct of business ahead. They also embody the inward communion of meeting for worship in the outward community of the shared meal and help us remember our life together.

Other meetings move directly from the meeting for worship into the meeting for business. They feel the condition of worship arrived at in the preceeding hour is the most appropriate grounding for the conduct of business. In these cases, the pot luck is usually served up immediately after the meeting for business as a restorative of nourishment and relationships in that which is temporal—especially if the business session has been an exercising one.

Both of these practices make for one First Day a month that is given over to our life together as Friends. When we linger together to worship, break bread, converse with one another and conduct business, we reinforce our life together. To separate these activities, as some large meetings do to permit people to participate in more non-Quaker activities in the day, is one more mark of the fragmentation of our lives as Quakers, the devaluation of our time spent together in a life increasingly assimilated to the wider culture.

Friendly Eights

Friendly Eights is a form of meeting with many variations among Friends. It appears in some form or another everywhere I've been. Friendly Eights offers an opportunity for a smaller group of people to meet once a month, usually over a meal, for a more concentrated opportunity to know one another.

Sometimes a committee undertakes to randomly re-sort the participants each month so everyone has a chance to spend an evening with everyone else. The responsibility of host is transferred each time in every instance I've seen. Sometimes the same group meets together for an entire academic year or for half the academic year. This allows more in-depth acquaintance to take place. Sometimes groups are focused around a project they've undertaken within or outside the meeting: reading a book together, rehabilitating a house as part of a larger project, building a playground. Sometimes they are focused around an activity like walking or some kind of field trip. Sometimes children are included, more often not. Special Friendly Eights groups may be formed of families with children, focusing on inclusion of children and suitable activities or outings. People without children may or may not elect to be included.

Most frequently a meal is the centerpiece of the meeting. The meal may be pot luck or include only a dessert and beverage provided by the hosts. In only one meeting have I encountered the custom of an entire, elaborate meal provided and prepared by the hosts with no one to share the burden. Most often the host or hostess coordinates the dishes brought by guests. The conversation may be general, with the purpose being deepening acquaintance among the membership.

In some meetings, general conversation during the meal is followed by worship sharing on one or more topics supplied by a committee with care of the spiritual life of the meeting. Sometimes those topics are arranged to facilitate the acquaintance of people present, using something like the Claremont Dialogue (Claremont Friends Meeting). More often the topics are addressed in a worship sharing mode. The topics are designed to open spiritual beliefs and experiences that might not be exposed in ordinary conversation.

This last type of Friendly Eights offers both the opportunity over dinner to become more sociably acquainted and the opportunity afterward for the group to become more focused on the deeper level of spiritual fellowship. The unities and differences offer fruitful occasion for tenderness and more attentive listening to one another where we differ.

Weekend get-togethers

Another way of coming to know one another in that which is temporal is the weekend get-together, not to be mistaken for the week-end retreat. My home meeting in Bethesda, MD excels at this kind of occasion. The Yearly Meeting Camp at Catoctin is taken for the weekend just before camping season begins. There are a few indoor spaces; but most people are accommodated in screened shelters with floors, roofs and bunks. There are rough, communal bathing and lavatory facilities. The camp has trails up the mountain side and a pond with a few canoes. Quite deliberately, little is programmed in the way of activity. It's a rare opportunity for an urban meeting to waste time together with no agenda. People sit around the pond in groups of shifting composition, chat and watch the children. Those who love making breakfasts make them. Conversations started at breakfast can go on as long as desired. There's no schedule for this highly-scheduled group of people.

As the get-together is usually held in strawberry season, some go off to pick strawberries. Others hull them as they sit around and talk. Often the teen-agers make shortcake. Almost everyone eats shocking amounts of strawberries. There may or may not be singing. At least once a square-dance caller was brought in. People come and stay or go as their lives permit. Some come only on First Day for worship and the final meal and clean up. Others come for Saturday or for the entire week end.

Photos and memories are taken away. New friends are discovered. And a level of relaxation rare for urban Friends is often achieved. In its own way, this unprogrammed get-together leaves room for the Spirit to move in encounters between and among people, creating new relationships, healing old ones, reminding us of the joy and pleasure to be found in one another's company. It's an excellent way for relatively new families to be gathered and received into the community.

The Meeting Retreat

The Meeting Retreat is almost invariably programmed, although the program may include some unscheduled time for optional naps, yoga, tai chi, hiking or quiet conversation within the confines of a limited space that acts as the container for the spiritual work. The Meeting Retreat is directed to the nurture of the individuals' spiritual lives or to the nurture of the spiritual life of the meeting. The occasion may be planned by a meeting committee or by a retreat leader invited from outside the meeting to permit all members to participate without having responsibility for the activity. The committee will, however, have to give the outside leader guidance as to what focus is most consonant with the life of the meeting at this time, as well the scheduling requirements of the facility that is to be used.

Quaker retreats are less apt than others to have much lecturing. They are usually a combination of some presentation by the leader, opportunity for meditative reflection by the participants, and opportunities to listen and to be heard in one of the modes discussed in chapter 7 of Volume I.

Occasionally there will be some major issue in the meeting that needs to be addressed in such a retreat. The most fruitful retreats, however, are those that simply nurture the inward life and weave the membership more closely together in love and in understanding of their relationship to God through Quaker tradition and practice. Often a great deal of silence will work as well as much talking. Occasionally a meeting will plan a reflection day or a retreat that is totally silent like one long meeting for worship, except for a final worship sharing about the experience. Friends may return from such various retreats with fresh commitment to personal or corporate practice and relationships. The participants may act as leavening in the meeting for those who were unable to attend.

Not infrequently, meetings attempt to combine the retreat with a get-together. Having everyone together apart from the usual setting makes it very tempting to try to do absolutely everything: have a relaxed, family time; program something for the children; and have a spiritually nurturing program for the adults.

Unfortunately, this kind of program is seldom as satisfying as choosing between the get-together or the retreat. When children are included in a retreat setting, the parents' attention is necessarily divided. Sometimes the children are distressed to be arbitrarily excluded from their parents' presence at exercises that don't lend themselves readily to nurturing both children and adults. Adults frequently find it difficult to shift gears or levels of consciousness from the meditatively quieting activities of the retreat to more sociable activities suitable to a get-together. The retreat, in turn, can seem like an interruption of the freedom of the get-together.

Some meetings may be able to plan one of each every year. Other meetings may plan them on alternate years.

Meeting to celebrate, to grieve, to heal

Some meetings have a time after the meeting for worship that is dedicated to "joys and sorrows", in which occasions for celebration, grieving, healing or prayer may be announced. Thus we may become aware of what is going on in one another's lives, the better to pray, to care for and support one another.

Sometimes the simple announcement and subsequent after-meeting conversation are inadequate. We may need time to come together specifically to give thanks or rejoice, to grieve or mourn or to pray for healing. These meetings may be appointed to bring forward the rejoicing, mourning, or need for healing in several or all lives. The occasion may partake of qualities of both a meeting for worship and a worship sharing. A profound entering into the sense of the presence of God is usually the setting or frame for whatever utterances are given. Prayers, remembrances, thanksgiving or comfort may be offered in the unintrusive, non-conversational way of worship sharing (see Volume I, pp. 168-178).

Ad Hoc Small Groups

I'll mention briefly the value—especially in large meetings—of small, *ad hoc* groups with special concerns or special ties. Apart from study groups, to be covered in the next chapter, most tend to be groups for particular kinds of mutual pastoral care. For instance, as I write, Bethesda Meeting has groups for "Quakers with non-Quaker Partners", "Mid-Life Transition", and "Care-givers". There is also a "Grandparents' Group" that meets occasionally for mutual support in grandparenting in a society that more and more frequently seems to require the incomes of both parents. The special nurture and support that may be received in such a group may not necessarily contribute to our sense of being a counter-cultural community in a society that espouses different values. They do bond people to one another and the community in ways that may open them to such work in other settings.

Summary and conclusions

These are some of the major, human ways that modern Friends seek to bond with one another in spiritual community to affirm and reinforce their spiritual stance over against a society rooted in something other than unity in the Love of God. As may be seen, the ways of modern Friends focus primarily on fellowship within the community. This is very important in a culture that fragments relationships and even our contacts with one another. However, the forms of our fellowship that overtly reinforce the sense of the ground of our community in a listening spirituality are in a distinct minority. Most of our modes of fellowship owe more to the purely human "community-building" techniques that evolved in the seventh decade of this century, a decade through which most of the present generation of Friends has lived. Many of us were actively formed socially through that period. It is a discipline to yield the techniques of that time to the less organized nudges and movements of the Spirit.

None of these ways of exploring or emphasizing our bonds in love necessarily helps when we return to the maelstrom of life and work in a society grounded in utterly different assumptions, behaviors and sense of reality. The memories do, however, bring us back to awareness that we are part of a community that seeks alternatives to the busyness, materialism, commercialism and competitive *foci* of modern society. That awareness may help to keep us open to the deeper work of the Spirit repatterning our lives that are lived in the outward context of the prevailing consumer culture.

> I urge you, my dear friends, as strangers and nomads to keep yourselves free from the disordered natural inclinations that attack the soul. Always behave honorably among the gentiles ...
>
> *I Peter 2:11-12a NJB*

People who use such terms [as strangers and nomads] about themselves make it quite plain that they are in search of a homeland.

Hebrews 11:14 NJB

So you are no longer aliens or foreign visitors; you are fellow citizens with the holy people of God and part of God's household.

Ephesians 2:19

Queries

How do we help and strengthen one another to cope with life in two worlds?

What can be our very late twentieth century/turn of the century reminders to ourselves and one another of our outsider status in a society dedicated to consuming in all its forms?

How do we declare in and on our persons our commitment to listening for God's guidance in all the affairs of life?

How do we bear *quiet but visible, daily witness* to our intentional marginality in a culture of greed, violence, death and numb indifference to the pain of humanity and the ecosystem?

References and Resources for fellowship among Friends, and Quaker marginality

Living with Oneself and Others.

Margaret Hope Bacon.
The Quaker Struggle for the Rights of Women.
pp. 4-5.

Howard Brinton.
Quaker Journals: Varieties of Religious Experience Among Friends.
esp. chs. 7-11.

Claremont Friends Meeting.
"A Meeting's Creative Experience".
FJ, 7/63.

Claremont Friends Meeting.
"Fellowship in Depth and Creative Renewal through Creative Listening: Suggestions for Leaders of Group Dialogues".

Jim Corbett.
The Sanctuary Church.
PHP #270. esp. pp. 24-38.

Marguerite deAngeli.
Thee Hannah.

Thomas Ellwood.
"Now Was All My Former Life Ripped Up,"
in West, ed. *QR.*

Amelia Mott Gummere.
The Quaker: A Study in Costume.

Leslie Hill. *Marriage: A Spiritual Leading for Lesbian, Gay, and Straight Couples.*
PHP #308.

Doris Janzen Longacre.
More With Less Cookbook.
Commissioned by the Mennonite Central Committee, in response to world food needs.

London Yearly Meeting.
Christian faith and practice.
esp. ch. 1 in general; #35-36, Penn in particular.

Patricia Loring.
"Bill Stillwell's Legacy: a retreat based on corporate silence".
FJ, 12/86.

John Sykes.
The Quakers: A New Look at Their Place in Society.

Frederick B. Tolles.
Meeting House and Counting House: The Quaker Merchants of Philadelphia, 1682-1783.

Brinton Turkle.
Obadiah, the Bold.

Brinton Turkle.
The Adventures of Obadiah.

Brinton Turkle.
Thy Friend, Obadiah.

Brinton Turkle.
Rachel and Obadiah.

Jessamyn West, ed.
The Quaker Reader.

Chapter 8

Listening for and Naming Your Experience in Tradition: Programs of Study

Listening spirituality, spiritual formation and spiritual transformation

Most of the contents of these first two volumes of *Listening Spirituality* would qualify as spiritual formation rather than study. By spiritual formation, I refer to practices or disciplines of the heart that seek to open it to the transformative power and love of the Spirit of God. A person's formation is a kind of personal shape, personality or stance in relation to the world that we take on within a particular religious tradition. These books take their title from the fact that both Quakerism in general and individual Quakers take on a prayerfully listening stance toward life, the world, one another and their inner promptings, as they grow into the practices of Quakerism. As we mature spiritually, we listen or attend to all things as potential revelations of the presence or guidance of God.

As we grow in our responsiveness to what we hear, we are increasingly detached from layers of socially-conditioned personality that alienate us from our deepest interior selves. Layers of the outward social scaffolding of our selves—built up during our childhood, adolescence and young adulthood—are stripped away as we come into listening maturity and into our ineffable, true selves in God. Socially inflicted distortions, brokennesses, and the overlays they create in our souls, are smoothed or scraped away as we grow more fully into the image of God in which we are created. This spiritual growth or maturing is our spiritual transformation. It used to be called perfection (as process rather than product) among Friends. The ways spiritual maturity is cultivated vary from religious tradition to tradition. Among Friends, our confidence has been placed in the widest possible prayerful openness and attentiveness for intimations of the Divine that has been called here "listening".

The importance of study as a spiritual discipline

In the present generation of Friends, study seems to be emerging as a major institutional way we are supported in our stance of listening for God in all things. In the absence of the outward reminders of the "hedge" of traditional Quakerism, we seek reminders for ourselves of what our listening tradition has been and meant.

Study will not identify us to strangers as people of an alternative culture. Thus it will not supply the public statement of our intentionality and the valuable interactions and feedback from others that plain dress, plain speech and other earlier Quaker customs evoked. The closest we come to a public statement of our personal identities as Friends is sharing the common cultural penchant for bumper-stickers and T-shirts stating our views cleverly or provocatively. In that, too, we may be assimilated to the cultural pervasiveness and reduced impact of such statements. We may become part of a culture of alienation, plastered with a variety of assertions of identity and ego—rather than standing outside the common culture.

Study may, however, sharpen our personal clarity about why we are doing the things we are doing, and in the way we are doing them. It may make us aware of the kernel of listening within an outwardly undemonstrative practice. It may make us more aware of how our peculiar ways have evolved in order to support listening and express what we hear as we listen. Study may make us more aware of the historical dialogue with the surrounding culture throughout Christian as well as Quaker history. It may strengthen us with examples of how others have behaved in similar situations in the past. It may make us more acutely aware of where our personal, human lives intersect with the Divine Life. It can make us aware of how different dimensions of our tradition mesh with one another to make a coherent whole, rather than a pastiche of unrelated items.

Developing a common language

On the most elementary level, study can help us understand our practice by naming both our interior experiences and the various manifestations of our gestalt. By helping us to name and constellate our experience as a group, it can facilitate a community of discourse among us as well as contribute to our sense of spiritual community.

In the absence of study, we often find individual members going their own way, cobbling together their own religions from congenial bits and pieces of faith and practice they've found here and there. This common practice fragments spiritual community. Or, in the absence of study, many project onto the silences of Quakerism the patterns of the latest book they've read or favorite aspects of previous spiritual groups they've attended.

Probably all churches take in one another's refugees. We certainly have many among us who are in flight from some other church experience. Often painful or distasteful experiences in other groups have led to strong aversions. Unity may be confused with externally imposed conformity. People who have been demeaned in situations involving masculine metaphors for the Divine, Christian language in general and rigid interpretations of spiritual experience, often request or demand that others respect their hurts by refraining from the use of language or bahaviors that remind them of their painful experiences elsewhere. This often leads to what one Phoenix (AZ) Friend refers to as a "don't ask, don't tell" policy concerning spiritual experience or belief among liberal Friends. At the very least, this practice inhibits the free growth of authentic mutual understanding that underlies and holds together spiritual community. It can also lead to isolation, alienation and outright division within meetings.

In such a situation, it is mis-expressed love or tolerance to refrain from naming or referring to our most precious inner experiences or to refrain from discussing our personal sense of the nature of Ultimate Reality. By this restraint, we deprive ourselves of the important basis of spiritual community that might bind up the very wounds being brought to us. We make do with pseudocommunity (see chapter 2, and Peck) rather than opening ourselves to the pain and work of authentic spiritual community. Authentic spiritual community acknowledges the wounds and brokenness of human experience and seeks Divine Assistance. It also acknowledges that there will inevitably be differences between us, some of which may never be resolved in unanimity. It is confident of the availability of Divine Assistance to bind up our wounds and bring us into wholeness.

Wounds deserve to be treated with reverence and gentleness. We may also, however, expect that part of the healing process will be for the wounded to learn to be as reverent with the spiritual experiences and labels of others as they expect others to be with their own. In our present theological pluralism, we must find ways that will enable us to trust one another with our precious experiences. We must be able to trust that others will listen beyond and beneath words for the authenticity of our experiences; past painful differences for underlying Love that unites us; past names and symbols for Truth itself; past rigid formulations for the profound dynamism of the Spirit moving among us. As long as we "don't ask and don't tell", we can never truly live into the Communion of Love to which God calls us. Something of great value will always be withheld from people we don't trust and with whom we, therefore, cannot be fully woven together in Love.

Growth in our willingness and capacity to "listen one another's souls into disclosure and discovery" (Steere) is a major way we can open to the ability truly to hear one another. Such listening enables us truly to be bound together, to support one another on the diverse paths that carry us away from the norms of culture into the mysterious, unknown paths of God, to be truly present for one another no matter what.

We must remember to do this without—or restraining—any intention to heal, fix, straighten out or convert others to our own point of view. Then we must take what we hear to the most profound level. We must try to hear whatever samenesses lie beneath the differences, the most profound possible meaning of what the other is saying rather than the most trivial or confused.

One of the most pernicious tendencies in cross-traditional conversation is the tendency of speakers to present their own favored tradition at its most profound level and compare it with the most foolish, trivial or unjust level of some other tradition. Some people compare the most rarefied practices of Buddhism or Hinduism with the most superstitious or violent Christian practice. Many Christians present their most elevated contemplative or ethical practices in contrast with the most unjust or superstitious practice of other religions. Many Quakers are fond of comparing the most

Spirit-led potentialities of Quakerism with the most mechanical or superstitious practices of other Christian faiths.

All who do these things, whatever their tradition, are guilty of the self-satisfied sin of pride of the Pharisee in Luke who prays, giving thanks that he is more righteous than other men. We are here to learn from one another, to listen one another into new depths of understanding what—as Elise Boulding says—we were born knowing (Luke 18:9-14; Boulding). In prayerful listening to one another, we may also be brought past our own superficial formulations into more profound levels and wider dimensions of our own experience.

Only through opening ourselves to one another's languages can we come to hear the authenticity and Truth of the Underlying Ground of what they have experienced. Only when we have heard where the authenticity lies can we discover our samenesses, rather than being riveted by and trapped in our differences, caught in the demand that everyone be just like us. We will never all be just like any one thing. We have not only been differentiated by our experience. We were born different as part of the infinite array of human possiblities. The glory and miracle of it is that we may be woven by the Holy Spirit into loving wholes inclusive of our differences—if we are willing to have that Love guide us.

Shared language and metaphor is one of the ways we may be woven together in a brilliant tapestry of differences. We can only come to shared language and metaphors if we are willing to hear the Life in one another's experience through the language in which it is couched. In the process, we may indeed discover that we are parts of different church gestalts. Even that need not prevent us from seeing beyond the particularities of individual gestalts or traditions to our underlying oneness in the Ground and Creator of All Being.

Entering the common tradition

As we learn our Quaker language, we learn the ways in which the spiritual insights it expresses and the practices it supports are interwoven and constellated in the great configuration, the wholeness I've referred to as a gestalt, patterned by listening. We learn our tradition is not simply a smorgasbord of independent possibilities, practices and ideas. The elements of the gestalt reflect and support one another to make a unified whole in which each part has its own function in relation to listening, much as in a great organism.

Some traditional metaphors or expressions point to one dimension of spiritual reality or relationship, while others point to another. None alone can express the entire Truth, which is one reason Quakers have eschewed a creed or dogma. Even taken together, our great associative chains of metaphors for the Divine or Divine Activity, or our gestalt of practices, do not express all there is to express of Truth. Taken together, however, they come closer and point more clearly to Truth than does any single fragment.

No one aspect of Quaker practice takes precedence over another. With grace, the three aspects of our practice unite in a seamless whole. First, individual practices nurture our personal inward relationship with God. Second, the practices described in this volume nurture our corporate relationship with God, expressed in our relationships with one another in meeting. The third type of practice moves us out into the alienation and pain of the world, bearing the fruit of our interior life with God and of the hard lessons of living with one another. With grace we open ourselves to the Divine in all these ways and express the transformative Love and Unity that can well up in and among us.

To support one another in the transformative inward relationship with the Divine and the transformative outward relationships with one another, we need the assistance of shared language and shared tradition. We need language to communicate the rich overlays and nuances of meanings in our shared interior experience. We need the tradition to remind ourselves of practices that have supported Quaker relationships with the Living God over centuries and to remind ourselves of the behaviors in which such a close relationship has ensued. We need to remember what others have suffered and endured to be faithful to the inward relationship with God and what the fruits of their experience have been for others and for ourselves. We need to know that others have traveled this road and parallel roads, that we aren't alone, that there are blazes on the trail, tear-stains of both pain and joy.

When we know the same stories and share interpretations of our experiences in terms of those who have gone before us, we can uphold one another in difficult times and share our thanksgiving and praise in times of wonder. Sharing a tradition through study can be a powerful force for knitting us together, for making a living hedge of ourselves as a spiritual community.

We need also to be cognizant of times when the community strayed from the heart or gestalt of the tradition, either wittingly or unwittingly. Especially we need to know the conseqences straying has had on relationships and on the shape of the practice and community. We need to know wherein the practices of various periods in our history differ from one another, so that we can discern what practices have accreted to Quaker-ism from other traditions or gestalts. Borrowings from other traditions out of context can draw us away from our own underlying gestalt of listening for the movement of the Spirit within ourselves and all things. Such borrowings also do violence to the wholeness of the tradition from which they are taken.

We also need to acknowledge practices that have accreted from other tradition, that have actually served to reinforce our underlying, listening stance in periods when we were wavering in our understanding or faithfulness. We need knowledge of our tradition in order to remain faithful to its unique interior commitment, as a people, to discern the presence and guidance of God inwardly and in all things.

References and resources for common language and tradition

Elise Boulding.
Born Remembering.
PHP #200.

Cecil Hinshaw.
Apology for Perfection.
PHP #138.

David Holden.
Friends Divided.

Sally McFague.
Metaphorical Theology.

Sally McFague.
Models of God.

John Miller.
"On Faith".
QRT #86 (Dec. 1995).

M. Scott Peck.
The Different Drum.

Douglas Steere.
Where Words Come From.
p. 14.

Lloyd Lee Wilson.
*Essays on the Quaker
Vision of Gospel Order.*
esp. The Quaker Vision of
Gospel Order; Quakerism and
the New Creation.

Listening for and naming your experience within tradition

The practice of study (personal or communal)

The discipline of study—when it is not wholly academic or divorced from experience—may be closely related to the discipline of devotional reading. Either discipline may be pursued separately; but, not infrequently, they open into one another. Devotional reading may foster a desire to know something of the historical or other intellectual underpinnings of what one is reading about. Reading about the historical or intellectual underpinnings of Quakerism or some other aspect of the tradition may move us into a devotional frame of mind *vis à vis* the ways of God in the world.

Study as activity

Study may include a variety of kinds of experience. Visiting places where significant events of Quaker, Christian or Biblical history occurred—particularly with guides to give us details and nuances that are the fruit of their own study—may greatly assist our understanding of the formative experiences of early members of the Quaker movement. The geography and settings can add vividness, solidity and reality to our very interior spirituality.

We may also be studying, in some sense, when we attend lectures, talks, videos or slide shows concerning some dimension of Quaker history, faith or practice. Some are down-home and informal, given out of the study or experience of members of our local meetings: a panel of people who have been conscientious objectors, a tour of northwest England with slides and explanations of the significance of events that took place there, a lecture that is the fruit of years of study of some Quaker writer, or the significance of certain biblical passages or expressions for Friends.

Field trips may also widen our view of Quakerism and our part in it. Visiting centers where Quaker study, decision-making, action or routine maintenance goes on today may enhance our understanding of ourselves as a people of wide-ranging connections and concerns. It helps broaden our sometimes cozy and parochial sense of ourselves as members in a single monthly meeting. It may encourage our growth into wider responsibilities among Friends.

We also study when we deepen our participation in various Quaker organizations. These may be organizations that maintain communication, connections and responsibility for actions taken within the Religious Society of Friends; that take responsibility for discerning and expressing current Quaker spiritual concerns in the national and international political arenas; or those that undertake to address situations of reconciliation or redress of social injustice they perceive within the social structures and communities around us. Participation will require us to come to grips with historical, structural and organizational details of social situations and possible ways of addressing them. We can become aware of the ways in which the Quaker gestalt meshes with the need for wholeness, rather than brokenness, within the situation.

Study as reading

Study is as much a mode of reading as it is a mode of dealing with the subject matter itself. When I discussed devotional or meditative reading in Volume 1, I took pains to distinguish it from the rapid, analytical reading in which we're schooled from an early age. The purpose of such reading is to find, organize and retain the main intellectual structure. This usually separates or alienates us from the material, as subject is separated from an object. Devotional or meditative reading is slower and more participative, meant to draw us into union with the experiences described rather than over against them.

Study is closer to the analytical reading of our schooling. It is, however, useful to our spiritual lives if we remain aware of the tension between our analytical reading and our meditative reading—and the need for both. It helps to practice being able to switch modes of reading as well as modes of consciousness from the analytical to the participative as the occasion calls for it. If the subject matter of our study is the outer skin of our spiritual life, then we cannot afford to let our study become divorced from the Life beneath the skin.

As we read analytically, we must remain alive to the vital dynamisms, the pulsing flesh-and-blood realities of which the words and intellectual constructs are a distillation or reduction. We read in this way for intellectual analysis of the causalities and dynamics of our history, of our institutional structures, and of the thought world or gestalt of our individual and corporate spiritual relationships with God. We never let the subject of our study become an intellectual construct independent, severed and adrift from its mooring in the life of the Spirit. We never let our study stray too far from our awareness of the existential reality of our life in and with the Living God—an existential reality lived out within the history, structures and practices of Quakerism.

Formation and study

The existential reality of our experience of God acts as a check upon the truth of statements made in our study about the nature and ways of God. It's also a touchstone for our relationship with God within the formal patterns of individual and corporate Quaker practice. We read our history within the Biblical tradition, within the checkered history of the Christian church (of which we are a relatively recent offshoot) and within Quakerism itself for how the Divine has been revealed, how humans have responded and how human response has been patterned.

The stories told—and the way they are told—within any given gestalt tend both to be patterned themselves and to pattern the responses of the hearers. So does the language used for Divinity, for human response, and for the patterns of behavior we may observe among seasoned Friends in "study as activity". To study our history and tradition of faith and practice is to open ourselves to being patterned or formed in the Quaker gestalt of listening and gathering. Study, both as activity and as reading, is an important part of our spiritual formation as Quakers.

Formation requires learning on all levels. We engage in "study as activity" that shapes us through interactions with and observations of seasoned Friends. We read participatorially to allow the subject matter to enter into us and stir resonances with our experience. We study analytically to learn the shape of Quaker experience and that which has shaped it. We are formed spiritually as the fruit of all this work comes together. Rather than objectifying our learnings as a system or set of laws or prescriptions of behavior, we absorb our learnings by integrating them with our interior experience and our behaviors. The study and learning are for the sake of reshaping our subjective self, life and behavior, rather than to acquire an objective body of knowledge. We are formed as Quakers by being drawn subjectively into participation in its patterns of thought and action, faith and practice.

Yearly meeting programs of study and formation

I will discuss two major yearly meeting programs of study and formation among Friends. Most others are variants of one or the other of these two. Both programs were put together in the 1980's by graduates of Earlham School of Religion who were at the time serving as Executive Secretaries of Yearly Meetings: Samuel Caldwell of Philadelphia Yearly Meeting and Thomas Jeavons of Baltimore Yearly Meeting.

Both programs require a year-long commitment on the part of their participants—a level of commitment not easily given among Friends. The two programs exhibit differences of emphasis in the area I'm talking about. The Philadelphia Yearly Meeting Program emphasizes the dimension of study. Its name is "The Quaker Studies Program". The Baltimore Yearly Meeting Program emphasizes the dimension of spiritual practice. It's called "The Spiritual Formation Program". Both include much of the same range of materials.

A yearly meeting program emphasizing the study of tradition

The Quaker Studies Program of Philadelphia Yearly Meeting

Philadelphia is the repository of tradition going back to the Quaker colony of William Penn, although it encompasses meetings in southern New Jersey, Delaware, and the eastern shore of Maryland as well as the eastern half of Pennsylvania. As one of the wealthier Yearly Meetings in the United States, it supports the only professional staff of significant size among the unprogrammed yearly meetings. It's drawn many graduates of Earlham School of Religion's programs in ministry, as well as other people with seminary training in Bible Study and Church History. The lenses through which these people have studied have not always been formed by Quakerism. The staff of Pendle Hill is also within its boundaries, as is that of the recently established School of the Spirit.

A program in Philadelphia Yearly Meeting, therefore, can draw upon a number of teachers with training in traditional areas of seminary study such as Bible Study and Church History. The program consists primarily of programs designed and taught by people who are well-qualified academically. The academic year is divided into three eight-to-ten-week segments: Bible Study, Christian Thought, and Quakerism, with a one-day retreat/work shop to explore dimensions of the spiritual life at the end of each term. There are four to six weeks between terms. All participants in the program within the yearly meeting in a given year are brought together for initial week-end orienting and closing retreats.

The reflection days tend to be the occasions when spiritual disciplines, such as journaling and spiritual friendship are addressed. Prayer has been addressed in a separate program, the Prayer Course. Spiritual practices, opening us to the transformative work of God, have therefore been the least emphasized link of this program in the past.

The Program's strength has been in the ability and experience of the teaching staff that developed and led the programs of study. Three college- or graduate-level eight-to-ten-week courses for thirty people from one or more meetings at a time have been offered to hundreds of people in PYM over the years. The substantive readings and expert lectures have given considerable background in Quaker tradition to members and attenders in most meetings of PYM, as well as in many meetings of Yearly Meetings that have taken on the PYM curriculum.

The Program is seen as a framework for spiritual and personal growth. The insights consequent on the cognitive knowledge assimilated within the classes have been the opening for many into a deeper interior relationship with the Divine as well as providing an interpretive framework for that relationship. These connections are often made by means of queries for reflection on the resonance of the readings with one's own spiritual experience. Spiritual growth is also supported by the assignment of a "spiritual friend" from the class, with whom to explore the personal meanings revealed by the study.

A yearly meeting program emphasizing spiritual practices:

The Spiritual Formation Program of Baltimore Yearly Meeting

Baltimore Yearly Meeting's Spiritual Formation Program took shape in a different demographic situation from that of Philadelphia Yearly Meeting. Baltimore Yearly Meeting encompasses all of Virginia, Maryland west of the Chesapeake, and most of the mid-section of Pennsylvania. Baltimore Yearly Meeting has stayed close to the tradition of low-cost programs staffed by volunteers from the monthly meetings. At its inception, the program relied heavily on teaching by Thom Jeavons himself.

Baltimore Yearly Meeting's program differs from the Philadelphia Yearly Meeting program, however, in its emphasis on spiritual authority, accountability and disciplines or practices. This emphasis laid the groundwork for an integration of the interior, experiential dimension of Quakerism and reliance on groups modeled on Methodist Classes in which "prayer, instruction, mutual confession and support" were offered to one another by a mixture of experienced and inexperienced members (John Wesley, quoted in Dougherty).

The individuality of the programs of prayer practices and lack of necessity for trained leadership for the accountability groups allowed the Spiritual Formation Program to function without relying on trained teachers for program or instruction.

In time, a group of facilitators experienced within the Spiritual Formation Program grew up. They were able to guide members of monthly meetings through the process of choosing personal spiritual practices, forming spiritual friendship groups, then guiding the groups into appropriate mutually supportive practice. Baltimore Yearly Meeting's strong point as a formation program has been its emphasis on experiential meditation and prayer practices and on companioning one another in what evolved from accountability groups on a Methodist pattern toward spiritual friendship groups or discernment groups.

The program of spiritual disciplines, supported by accountability or spiritual friendship groups, was only half the Spiritual Formation Program. The program had intellectual content as well as experiential focus and support. Each month a book that has been important to Friends was read by an entire monthly meeting group. A single, long meeting of the entire group was appointed for discussing the book and for hearing it discussed by a person, listed with the Yearly Meeting, to whom the book had been of special significance and who had had occasion to make a study of it and was willing to facilitate the group.

The opening weekend retreat, for all the people within the yearly meeting who have committed themselves to participate in the program for the year, includes not only introduction to prayer practices but time for monthly meeting groups to meet together to become acquainted and to select, from the yearly meeting's list, the books they will read together over the year.

Comparisons and contrasts

The weakness of Baltimore Yearly Meeting's Program, in my estimation, consists in the smorgasbord approach to the readings for the year. The list of choices includes mainly first-rate offerings; but it requires sophistication to put together from it a program of readings that would be as comprehensive, coherent and cogent as the range of reading covered by the Philadelphia Yearly Meeting Quaker Studies Program.

It is possible for a group to bypass Bible readings altogether, thereby missing a major dimension of historical Quaker self-understanding. There is little on offer that would place Quakerism within the history of the Christian Church, to help understand the underlying basis of either Quaker protest against the church practice of its day or the depth of history and meaning behind some Quaker insights. Similarly, specifically Quaker readings are focused primarily in the zone of the inner life—important, but only one dimension of Quaker faith and practice.

In stating these qualifications, I'm setting out the ways in which I see the Philadelphia Yearly Meeting and the Baltimore Yearly Meeting programs as complementary in their emphases. The Philadelphia Yearly Meeting program excels in providing the dimension of study. It gives a solid basis for interpretation of personal, interior experience within the Quaker reading of the Judeo-Christian tradition as well as creating openings for deepening that experience. Relative to the Baltimore Yearly Meeting program, however, it gives little explicit guidance or grounding for intentionally opening one's self to the Divine.

The Baltimore Yearly Meeting program, on the other hand, is rich in assistance to the devotional life both in interior practice and in readings in devotional works that focus and assist the opening to God in one's life. It is, however, reciprocally poor in locating that experience within the Quaker tradition and its antecedents. Where it offers some modern interpretations as possible readings, they are often in a vacuum of understanding of the tradition being protested or modified, or of the reasons why.

Among modern Friends, the Quaker interpretation of Christianity is so often taken as having been identical with other interpretations of Christianity that it's of special importance to emphasize the differences. Some modern protests against Christian tradition have their roots in the very issues and questions that constituted the original seventeenth century Quaker movement. Time can be wasted discarding things that

Friends discarded at their inception, rather than looking at how, in fact, Friends did read the Christian message.

Each of these yearly meeting programs builds on the strengths available within the particular yearly meeting. There is no question that the Baltimore Yearly Meeting model lends itself more readily to the situation of most yearly meetings, because the breadth of territory within its borders is too great to be covered easily by teachers traveling on weekends. Philadelphia has enabled some others to follow their pattern by providing study guides developed by some of their teachers. The study guides, however, do not always remain in print.

The first two curriculae for the Philadelphia Yearly Meeting model have been available through FGC. I'm told by users they work quite well without an "expert" leader, as long as the group and the leader are intentional and committed (Reichardt; Dodson).

There is a need for someone to put together a coherent program of readings for the study component of a spiritual formation program, lest study assume a cafeteria form that does not provide an orderly interpretative framework for the inner life. This does not require that there be a single interpretation offered. Study of the Bible, of Christian thought, and of the relatively brief history of Quakerism provide a ceaselessly shifting array of interpretations in dialogue, if not dialectic, with one another, each new one endeavoring to respond to or correct some perceived defect, error or insufficiency in what has gone before.

The Sandy Spring option

Within Baltimore Yearly Meeting, Sandy Spring Meeting is one of the two largest meetings, home of the Yearly Meeting offices, a large retirement community and a Friends School. Friends' House retirement community alone provides a tremendous resource to the meeting community because it houses many people who have given their lives in Quaker service and others who choose to live out their retirement years in a Quaker setting.

Sandy Spring Friends determined that their meeting was sufficiently large and rich in resources to develop their own version of the Yearly Meeting Spiritual Formation

Program. In the development, it was decided to make a special effort to draw in as many as possible of those who found it difficult to make a commitment to the full Baltimore Yearly Meeting program. In Sandy Spring, the spiritual discipline/spiritual friendship portion of the program and the reading/discussion portions of the program may be taken together as in the Baltimore Yearly Meeting Program—or they may be taken separately.

The spiritual discipline/spiritual friendship portion of the program is organized in very much the same way as that of the yearly meeting. It requires a year-long commitment to small groups in which mutual support for spiritual practices and ongoing discernment of the presence of God in one's life are the focus, most often in a worship sharing mode. The participants meet as a whole for an opening retreat. Most small groups meet monthly, but some meet more frequently. Groups may be organized on the basis of proximity to one another, on the basis of age or life situations, or on the intensity of commitment to the spiritual life.

The reading/discussion groups are more loosely organized. No year-long commitment to the reading program is required. A list of books to be read is published, with the name of the person who will give a talk and lead a discussion of the book on a particular First Day of the month. The richness of experience of the population at Friends' House—as well as the large meeting population in general—provides a great variety of choices of books, discussion leaders and points of view.

People may read the book and attend as moved, without previous attendance at other book discussions. This plan means that the community of discourse for the content of the books chosen is not constant, making it all but impossible to build understanding on previous reading and discussions. It does, however, open the possibility of participation to the widest possible range of the meeting community at one time or another. Sandy Spring has provided at least a taste of the Spiritual Formation Program to the greatest possible number of its membership. It has happened that, as people have a taste, their appetite for more is whetted and their attendance may increase from year to year.

The lack of commitment of individuals at any one time—especially in the reading/discussion program—makes it difficult to assert that coherent formation in Quakerism can take place in the midst of fragmentary and inconsistent attendance at various random or idiosyncratically chosen discussion groups. However, the Spirit of God is powerful and often works within whatever small openings we give it, especially given enough small openings over time.

Those who are committed to attend the spiritual discipline/spiritual friendship groups do have an opportunity to be opened to ongoing transformation by the Spirit in their practice, although the opportunity for interpretation in a traditional Quaker context is limited, depending on the Quaker experience of one's group members. As I asserted earlier in this volume, commitment is a critical part of growth in a spiritual community, often requiring strenuous effort against the fragmenting tendencies of the wider culture in which we live.

Components of a formation program combining practice and study

Supporting personal spiritual practice

Support for personal spiritual practice is crucial in any formation program. Without underlying spiritual practice, adult religious education can become a dry, intellectual exercise. We risk reducing our faith to externals, when the heart of Quakerism has been precisely in the internal connection with the Light, Life, Power and Love which is God.

Whatever outward dimensions of Quaker faith, practice, history or tradition we undertake to study in our programs, it's important that we include an element of support for individuals to make connections beween theory and practice, between Quaker life as it has been thought about and lived, and the life of the individual Quaker today. We need to encourage people to be more discerning of the movements of the Spirit within and the ways they resemble and differ from the experiences of Friends who confronted the issues of faith in different cultural and historical circumstances. Information *about* Quakerism needs to be kept within the context of the listening hearts of those taking it in.

The usual vehicle for making the necessary connections is group sharing in a prayerful setting rather than lively discussion groups. Discussion groups can be helpful; but too often they make it easy to reduce Quakerism to an object of discussion, rather than an experience lived by the people present. To create a prayerful setting with silent space around the utterances of participants helps us to take in their inner life at its deepest level and helps us to find the resonances within our own depths.

Worship sharing is one favorite mode of facilitating interaction that leaves room for the Spirit of God to move among us. It's good if the group isn't too large. In Chapter 7 of Volume 1 there are other suggestions of ways to come together to share the Life we find among us, connecting us with Friends who have gone before. We may form spiritual friendship groups that are a little like small, ongoing worship-sharing groups with the express intention of supporting one another's inner life. We may form spiritual discernment groups to help one another sense and articulate on a regular basis "how the Lord has been dealing with us" either in day-to-day life or over time, in relation to particular themes in our study.

The more closely the group is connected with study, the more helpful it is for a leader to spend some prayerful time in advance formulating questions that may draw forth the connections between the written material and lived life.

References and resources for spiritual friendship/discernment groups

Rose Mary Dougherty.
Group Spiritual Direction.
esp. p. 11.
This comprehensive book also has an excellent topical bibliography.

Patricia Loring.
Spiritual Discernment: the context and goal of clearness committees.
PHP #305.

Religious Education Committee of FGC.
Opening Doors to Quaker Worship.
Part 5: Opening Doors Through a Lifetime. Section 2, pp. 132-136.

Bible Study

Organized Bible study is relatively simple in a yearly meeting that has available well-trained students of the Bible who are able and willing to travel into different parts of the yearly meeting. (The size of the yearly meeting and the distribution of the Quaker population are factors here.) There are several ways it might be undertaken. One of the virtues of the original Quaker Studies Program was that it encouraged its gifted and experienced teachers to develop their own programs consonant with their experience and sense of what was needed within the overall Quaker Studies Program.

A favorite approach has been a survey of the Bible from the standpoint of the development of the text and stories over time. It is also possible to approach it from the standpoint of the development of the understanding of God over time; of the development of the Judeo-Christian ethical sense over time; of the developments in theology and ethics that led to the Christian message. Any, all or a combination of the above are possible with judicious selection of books or texts from the Bible.

Any, all or a combination will assist the understanding of words, ideas, viewpoints and actions of earlier Friends that might otherwise remain opaque to modern understanding. Early Quaker behavior that seems unreasonable or bizarre to modern Friends or historians, not only makes sense but takes on profound meaning as Friends' self-understanding is seen against the background of Biblical stories, prophetic tradition and teachings. Early Friends' behavior can search and question us for ways that are appropriate today to give expression to the truths they found in Biblical stories, prophecies and teachings.

An approach I've employed is to use the Bible in connection with a study of Quakerism in general or of some favorite Quaker themes. Overt guidance, prophetic commands, or metaphors for inward experience can be traced to Biblical origins that enhance the meanings and nuances of earlier Quaker thought and action. Earlier Friends, like the Church Fathers and medieval monastics, relied on a complex, interwoven tapestry of metaphors, no one of which was adequate for understanding Ultimate Reality. Together, however, they supplement one another—not to completion but to greater adequacy—in guiding us in our relationship with multifaceted Spiritual Reality.

My favorite book for this kind of study is Canby Jones' edition of Fox's letters, *The Power of the Lord is Over All,* examined with the Biblical texts. The Biblical material and Fox's complex development of themes and messages illuminate each other. In the letters, in spite of editing that has removed repetitions, it's possible sometimes to hear the cadence of early vocal ministry as it flows or rolls from image to image. It's possible to use other editions of the letters or other Quaker writers to develop classic Quaker understandings of faith, practice, spiritual community and ethical behavior.

Another, more immediate approach to developing this feel for the complex metaphorical juxtaposition of stories, images and words in Friends' use of the Bible can come of commitment to the discipline of using a lectionary for Bible readings for at least one three-year cycle. Lectionaries were used in the churches in which most of the first generation of Friends came to maturity—and in which some of the present generation have been reared as well.

The lectionaries were a grand cycle of Bible texts that included most of the Bible over a period of three years. Each day there was a text from the Old Testament, a text from a Gospel, a text from one of the Epistles and two Psalms. The texts were usually related, echoing one another in imagery, or addressing similar themes from very different perspectives. The relationships of the texts are especially striking in the great liturgical seasons of the church: Advent, Christmas, Lent, Eastertide and Pentecost. Through repetitive reading and juxtaposition of words or images, an interlocking complex of metaphors and cross-references were built up that served to interpret inward experience richly and variously by using single words or names. Before they became Friends, early Quakers absorbed this rich metaphorical language. To read early Friends without a grasp of this language is to miss the rich complexity of their thought and imagery.

Different churches have their own lectionaries. The particular one used is of less importance than becoming steeped in the related meanings found in diverse images from differing times and circumstances in Biblical history. It's possible to find lectionaries with the selections for each day printed in them. Some are elegantly bound, others quite simple. In the resource list below I name a small, paperback edition that includes only the listing of the selections for each day to be read in the Bible of your choice. For some possible Bible translations, see Volume I, pp. 28-29.

This is a practice that doesn't require a trained teacher of Bible or a student of Quakerism for guidance. It lends itself well to small group meetings to share discoveries of metaphor and theological and ethical themes. In time, this group study may flow quite naturally into an exploration of Quaker meanings and thought. Such Biblically dependent texts as Fox's letters, Michael Graves' collection of sermon texts or numerous other Quaker writers may be useful. Britain Yearly Meeting's *Christian faith and practice* is a fruitful source for finding Biblical metaphor as an ordinary means of Quaker expression.

Other methods of Bible study that don't require a trained teacher of Bible or Quakerism, may be found in the Spears' study guide, and in Dorothy Reichardt's version of Bible study in the Philadelphia Yearly Meeting program.

Resources for a 6-8 week study program in Bible study
The first three titles listed below are more thorough. They're suitable as resources in a meeting library or for upper-level courses of Bible study.

The Interpreters' Bible.
Choose a single book of the Bible to work with or over several years work your way through the set. This twelve volume series has an introduction, two texts (KJV & RSV), exegesis & exposition for each book of the bible, plus general articles on Old and New Testaments. There are sections by the Quaker Bible scholars, Henry J. Cadbury and Alexander Purdy. A revision of the original version from the 1950's is currently being reissued at the rate of two volumes a year, from beginning to end. Much of what is contained in the 1950's version is only now finding its way into popular writing on the Bible.

The Anchor Bible.
This gives much more extensive scholarly treatment of each book. The quality of the treatments varies considerably from volume to volume. I've been greatly helped by Raymond Brown's three volumes on the Gospel According to John and the Letters of John. I've also found helpful Marcus Barth's two volume study of Ephesians, sometimes called "the gospel of peace". Careful study of this one brief book amounts almost to a study of the early church and the Pauline letters.

Carol A. Newsom and Sharon H. Ringe, eds.
The Women's Bible Commentary.
A collection of essays on each book of the Bible by female, but not necessarily feminist, scholars. They draw out gender-sensitive issues in each book, their implications for the relationship between church history and church order, and the historical times and social order in which they functioned. They reflect on the questions they raise for living into non-exclusive relationships with God in our own time.

Marcus Borg.
Meeting Jesus Again for the First Time.
For an increasing number of Friends, especially those who have become disaffected from the Christianity of their childhoods, this work has been found helpful. The author, a Biblical scholar at a secular institution, relates his personal story of disaffection in youth. The book traces the emergence of a portrait of Jesus that has enabled him to return to a mature religious faith that is consonant with his scholarship.

Chuck Fager, ed.
Reclaiming a Resource: Papers from the Friends Bible Conference.
Twenty-five suggestions for Bible study by the presenters at the conference, in addition to the plenary address.

Chuck Fager.
A Respondent Spark.
A manual on the Bible with descriptions of the various translations and paraphrases.

Michael P. Graves.
"Mapping the Metaphors in George Fox's Sermons".
in Michael Mullet, ed. *New Light on George Fox, 1624-1691, A Collection of Essays.*

Michael P. Graves.
"The Rhetoric of the Inward Light: An Examination of Extant Sermons Delivered by Early Quakers. 1671-1700".
an unpublished dissertation.

T. Canby Jones, ed.
The Power of the Lord is Over All: The Pastoral letters of George Fox.

W. Douglas Mills.
A Daily Lectionary: Scripture readings for every Day Based on the new Common Lectionary.
A listing without texts.

Mary Morrison.
A Fresh Look at the Gospels.
PHP #219.

Mary Morrison.
Approaching the Gospels Together: A Leaders' Guide for Group Gospel Study.
Two works by the popular Pendle Hill teacher.

Michael Mullet, ed.
New Light on George Fox, 1624-1691, A Collection of Essays.

Dorothy Reichardt.
Finding our Way in the Bible.
Study Guide for the Bible portion of PYM's program. 8 2-hour sessions, can be expanded; 71 pages, loose-leaf.

Cecil Sharman.
No More But My Love: Letters of George Fox.
More severely edited than the Jones edition, also less costly.

Joanne and Larry Spears.
Friendly Bible Study.
A very successful and popular method of Bible study that does not require trained leadership.

History of Christian Church and Thought

Church history, like most Bible study programs, requires teachers able not only to outline the history of the church, its ideas and controversies but to bring forward most clearly those lines of thought which either anticipated or evolved toward Quaker thought. There is a sense in which developments in church history—or in the history of Christian thought—are both new and revelatory. At the same time, they are foreshadowed, or have arisen again and again in church history, and have even been present before Christianity.

People who have studied church history in seminaries of other traditions need to be capable of culling the events, ideas and turning points that led to or shed light on current Quaker thought. It's also important to realize when Friends are laboring to re-invent a wheel, especially if previous testing has found the wheel to be square. It's perhaps even more important to know when a perfectly fine, round wheel has been embedded in the tradition for centuries under a name that is subject to current prejudice.

It's important to know the historical situations and theological questions that were being addressed by particular formulations, forms of worship or solutions. It's also important to see that the questions of each generation are usually responses to solutions the previous generation had evolved to its own questions about the solutions of the generation prior to *it*. Revelation or openings take place within these very human—sometimes intellectual, sometimes political—contexts.

The history of Christian thought is also a long dialogue between theology and the succeeding systems of western philosophical ideas. These include ways of thinking about God, about appropriate worship, and about conduct in the world. When and where there have been crises or breaks in the intellectual or spiritual tradition—as we are experiencing now—it's important to see how the breaks have arisen. It's important to see how the solutions have been shaped by social and political circumstances to yield new insights into old revelations. To know where ideas have come from sometimes removes their mystery or mystique. It helps us also to know how we may articulate the message of our tradition afresh for each new generation. The message doesn't change to suit fashion; it finds new terms to express old insights that continue to be valid. Thus they may be understood afresh.

In our generation, it is a distinct challenge to find terms for our own tradition that are appropriately expressive as we meet deeper understandings of Native American and Asian spiritual traditions. We also need to meet new understandings of a unified reality that are arising in quantum mechanics, just as traditional western philosophy seems to have deconstructed reality into particles with no relation to, or explanatory power for, reality as we experience it. We are challenged ethically by many movements for social change as well as by experiments such as Marxism that seem to have deconstructed as thoroughly as modern philosophy. We are left with a triumphant capitalist system posing its own serious ethical issues that are no longer challenged by a coherent ethical alternative.

Friends are fond of behaving as though Quakerism were a full-blown divine revelation from the head of George Fox, perhaps with the aid of one or two other folks. There is no question something unique came to light and came together in the life and in the times of George Fox. We may understand ourselves and our heritage better, however, if we comprehend the extraordinary social, political and religious changes of the century in which Quakerism arose. In addition, it is helpful to know the historical circumstances that prepared for them in the previous centuries in English and continental European history and thought.

An Adult Religious Education Program in the history of Christian thought for Friends should trace strands in the history of Christian thought, spirituality, and church practice that foreshadow and prepare the ground for Quakerism. Important elements are the general Biblical, specifically prophetic, and the mystical traditions. Others include the shifting emphases on communal and personal spirituality and discipline. Finally, we need to look at questions of authority and accountability which gave rise to periodic re-formations of church government along with the new questions they provoked, in turn.

Resources for a short study program in Christian history and thought

For this subject, unlike the other topics for a Study and Formation Program, there is a paucity of brief, first-level overviews available. As I write, PYM's study guide is out of print. The following list is an offering of relatively short works on various periods of Christian history and thought. They may be excerpted by a careful leader to provide an overview that contains major strands in Christian tradition that are either ancestral to Quakerism or against which Friends have rebelled. Here, more than anywhere, we need good teachers and/or study guides that are suitable for Friends.

The first two works listed below are more thorough. They're suitable for second- or third-level courses or for reference works for a meeting library. Unlike the other lists in this book, the remainder of the following resources are arranged in historical order of their subject matter, rather than alphabetically by author. They are chosen less as historical records than as illustrations of the crystallization of particular spiritualities in the patterns of life of salient communities that have arisen in the history of Christianity.

Overviews

Jaroslav Pelikan.
The Christian Tradition: The History of the Development of Doctrine.
A reference work in five volumes, it covers:
1) The Emergence of the Catholic Tradition (100-600);
2) The Spirit of Eastern Christendom (600-1700);
3) The Growth of Medieval Theology (600-1300);
4) Reformation Church and Dogma (1300-1700);
5) Christian Doctrine and Modern Culture (since 1700).

Paul Tillich.
A History of Christian Thought.
A long and thorough study by one of the seminal theologians of the twentieth century. It is meticulous in its connection of theological trends with philosophical thought throughout Christian history. At least a second-level book.

Shirley Dodson.
Christian Thought.
Her version of the Christian Study portion of PYM's program, currently out-of-print, but may be found in meeting libraries.

Biblical Prophets, esp. Amos, Micah, selections from Jeremiah and 2nd and 3rd Isaiah.
These prophets, in particular, give the basis for a strand in church history that protests formalism in religion and injustice in society, as disobedience to Divine Will.

Very Early Church History: *crucifixion, peace, prophetic witness.*

Betty Radice, ed.
Early Christian Writings:
The Apostolic Fathers.
A brief selection of formative writings, mainly letters, from authority figures in the early church. Selections may be made from it to illustrate the self-view of early Christians as prophetic, and peaceful, suffering crucifixion for witness, not seeking, exercising or acceding to earthly power.

Roland Bainton.
Early Christianity.
This Quaker scholar's studies in Church History are invariably accessible and helpful, although some are beginning to go out of print. His viewpoint is less apt than that of some scholars to ignore Christian tendencies later enfolded in Quakerism.

Roland Bainton.
Christian Attitudes
Toward War and Peace:
A Historical Survey and
Critical Evaluation.
esp. ch. 5, The Pacifism of the Early Church.

C. John Cadoux.
The Early Christian
Attitude Toward War: A
Contribution to the History
of Christian Ethics.
esp. Introduction pp. 1-17; Summary and Conclusions pp. 244-265.

Thomas Merton.
The Wisdom of the Desert.
The introductory essay, together with the anecdotes and sayings of the fourth century "desert fathers", provides an introduction to the radically austere and mystical "desert spirituality". This movement arose when some members of the church began to withdraw from the larger society as the church became socially respectable, assimilated and even coopted, under Constantine. The retreat into the desert contained the seeds for the monastic tradition. It also suggests subsequent movements of radical critique of—and separation from—secular society, as in the Anabaptist movements and in second generation Quakerism.

The Medieval Monastic Tradition

Joan Chittister.
Wisdom Distilled from the
Daily.
In a way that is inviting and consonant with modern, secular life, this book presents an exposition of the Benedictine tradition that underlies most of the contemplative monastic orders.

Jean Leclerque.
The Love of Learning and
the Desire for God.
An enduringly useful study of the medieval monastic tradition that explores, among other things, the relationship between the intuitive, metaphorical, devotional monastic consciousness and the basis and nature of the monastic traditions of scholarly study.

Writings of the English Mystics

Richard Rolle, Walter Hilton, Julian of Norwich, and the anonymous author of *The Cloud of Unknowing*. Remember that the English monasteries were emptied and the monks turned out into the general population just about a century before the rise of Quakerism. These fourteenth-century, English representatives of the English mystical tradition range from the highly emotional, charismatic Rolle; through the thoroughly experienced and schooled Hilton; the visionary Julian who is especially valued today for the incarnational and gender-inclusive qualities of her visions of Jesus; and the author of *The Cloud of Unknowing* who anticipates much of the present-day development of centering prayer in his advice to a novice concerning contemplative prayer. There are several editions of the writings of these mystics. Paulist's series, Classics in Western Spirituality, and Penguin's editions are widely available.

Discernment in the Jesuit Tradition

Thomas H. Green, S.J. *Weeds Among the Wheat: Discernment, Where Prayer and Action Meet.* This book is a popular treatment of spiritual discernment in the Jesuit tradition, an older—and the only other— tradition to practice group discernment. The similarities and differences provide a basis for fruitful reflection on our own less articulate tradition.

David Lonsdale. *Listening to the Music of the Spirit: The Art of Discernment.* Examines the place of personal faith, images of God, our faith traditions and social conditions in our discernment of the Holy Spirit in our experiences, gifts, desires, feelings, ideas and ispirations.

The Reformation

Roland H. Bainton. *The Reformation of the Sixteenth Century.* This book ranges from Luther, through the Anabaptists, Calvin, and Anglicanism. It covers the struggle for religious liberty and for political, economic and domestic reform.

Rufus Jones. *Spiritual Reformers in the Sixteenth and Seventeenth Centuries.* This book by a beloved Quaker author traces continental and English reformers and mystics. Jones' hypothesis on their formative influence on Quakerism is widely challenged today. The book is worth reading for its highlighting of themes that later appeared in Quakerism.

Quakerism

A short course in Quakerism might follow a program in the history of Christian thought along the lines of the one in the previous section. In that case, the dimensions of Christian thought mentioned above may be examined either as they have influenced the formation of Quakerism, or as Quakerism has reacted against them.

We might examine the formative role for Quakerism of Biblical narratives, laws and prophets. We might look at several dimensions of mystical tradition particularly as it found expression in fourteenth century England. It formed monastic tradition there before the monks were turned out into the general population in the sixteenth century. We might look at the stew of ideas about church government and the social order that was seething in sixteenth and seventeenth century England. This was the matrix in which insights came together in the organic whole that is Quakerism, through the itinerant seeking after Truth of George Fox and other proto-Quakers in the mid-seventeenth century.

These dimensions might be examined historically by use of Cecil Sharman's *George Fox and the Quakers*, which is an historical companion to events in George Fox's *Journal*. Or you might use John Punshon's history of the sweep of Quakerism to the present day from a British perspective: *Portrait in Gray*.

You might also carry the study forward by means of modern selections from Britain Yearly Meeting's *Quaker faith and practice* and/or selections from *Quaker Classics in Brief*, Steere's *Quaker Spirituality* or West's *Quaker Reader*. John Punshon's *Encounter with Silence* is probably the best account of coming into modern Quakerism that combines both the perspective of expanding personal experience and that of understanding traditional Quaker forms and their possibilities. A more topical approach may be taken based on Howard Brinton's classic study, *Friends for 300 Years*, or Lloyd Lee Wilson's recent *Essays on the Quaker Vision of Gospel Order*.

Bruce Birchard's pamphlet, *The Burning One-ness Binding Everything*, is one of the few accounts of which I'm aware that relates both the salient points of his personal journey and his efforts to interpret it theologically. At all points along the way it is particularly important that a component of the program should be adequate opportunity for connection with the various dimensions of Quakerism on the level of personal spiritual experience rather than intellectual understanding alone.

The best vehicle is probably small worship sharing groups (see Volume I, chapter 7) in which people are encouraged to share with one another their personal, spiritual experience in the dimension under examination. This will not only encourage interpretation and articulation of the experience in terms of Quaker tradition, but will demonstrate to group members the range of personal experience of the Divine that may occur within the scaffolding of Quaker forms—experiences as various and unique as fingerprints.

Resources for an overview of Quakerism for the meeting library or more advanced study

Hugh Barbour and J. William Frost.
The Quakers.
A factual reference work for the history of Quakerism in America with a biographical dictionary of former Quaker leaders in America by two leading, contemporary, American Quaker scholars.

William Braithwaite.
Volume 1. *The Beginnings of Quakerism to 1660.*
Volume 2. *The Second Period of Quakerism.*
The second edition of an old, standard study of early Quaker history, in two volumes, that has withstood the tests of time very well.

John Punshon.
Portrait in Gray.
The current authoritative brief history of Quakerism from the viewpoint of an English scholar.

Resources for a short study program in Quakerism

British Yearly Meeting.
Quaker faith and practice.
Selections from the writings of Friends in all periods of Quakerism, topically arranged.

The Early Prophetic Openings of George Fox.
Excerpts of early spiritual insights from Fox's *Journal* that constitute the framework of Quakerism.

Bruce Birchard.
The Burning One-ness Binding Everything: A Spiritual Journey.
PHP #332.

Howard Brinton.
Friends for 300 Years.
The most popular introduction to Quakerism for nearly forty-five years.

Anna Cox Brinton, Eleanor Price Mather, and Robert J. Leach, eds.
Quaker Classics in Brief.
Abridged selections from Penn, Barclay and Penington.

Wilmer Cooper.
A Living Faith:
An Historical Study of
Quaker Beliefs.
The fruit of years of teaching
Quakerism at Earlham School
of Religion.

Sandra Cronk.
Gospel Order: A Quaker
Understanding of Faithful
Church Community.
PHP #297.

John Punshon.
Encounter with Silence.
A creative and skillful blending
of the development of personal
experience and understanding
of Quaker tradition.

Cecil Sharman.
George Fox and the
Quakers.
Integration of Fox's *Journal*
with the religious, political and
economic movements of his
time.

Douglas Steere, ed.
Quaker Spirituality:
Selected Writings.
Introduction and extremely
edited selections from the
writings of Fox, Penington,
Woolman, Stephen, Jones and
Kelly.

Joanne and Larry Spears.
Friendly Faith and Practice
Study Guide.

Elfrida Vipont.
George Fox and the Valiant
Sixty.
New edition of a classic
treatment of the early Quaker
movement as a series of stories.
Excellent annotated bibliography.

Jessamyn West, ed.
The Quaker Reader.
Essays illustrating various
dimensions of Quakerism from
a wide variety of authors and
historical periods.

Lloyd Lee Wilson.
Essays on the Quaker
Vision of Gospel Order.
Essays by a recorded minister
who understands deeply the
interior dimensions of our
traditional forms.

Summary and conclusions

I've offered above presentations and critiques of two major programs of Quaker spiritual formation available among us today. One emphasizes study of the Biblical, Christian and specifically Quaker dimensions of the tradition. The other emphasizes personal spiritual practice, supported by group sharing and listening, and some reading from a select but eclectic list.

Each of these modes of approaching spiritual formation and religious education can open out into the other. Study may acquaint us with aspects of the tradition that speak to our most profound interior spiritual experience and may beckon us more deeply onto that path. It can provide us with companions who have traveled the road before us, blazing trails, encouraging and empowering us to press further on our own.

On the other hand, support of regular spiritual practice may lead us into study in order to find frameworks for interpreting the resulting experience and, again, companions from the past to add to the companions in our groups or meetings.

In fact, there is no uninterpreted experience. Whatever we experience in our inner or outer lives is filtered through interpretative frameworks we have consciously or unconsciously developed or assimilated over our lifetimes. If we intentionally join or commit ourselves to a tradition, a major component of that commitment is adopting the interpretative framework of the tradition for our experience.

That is not to say that we stop the clock at any given point in the history of the tradition. Rather, we develop a sense of what it is that patterns the underlying gestalt of the core tradition as it has persisted through transmutations over time. We accept that the tradition will continue to adapt itself to changes in the surrounding culture, while remaining faithful to the underlying patterning of the gestalt—and, above all, remaining faithful to God. By becoming thoroughly acquainted with what Quakerism has been, we're prepared to enter, in faithfulness, into what it may become. Thus we dare to become co-creators in the ongoing unfolding of the Religious Society of Friends.

I believe the ideal spiritual formation and religious education programs would overtly seek to balance the dimensions of study and spiritual practice. Such a program would offer a clear plan of study of the tradition that supports, encourages, stretches and beckons forward personal spiritual practice. In optimum circumstances, these two aspects of spiritual formation are woven together in the tapestry of our individual faith. Whoever is present in the meeting, with whatever beliefs they have, constitute the meeting at that time. As individuals intentionally engage in deepening their spiritual practice, and integrating it with Quaker insights and traditions, the faith of the entire meeting may undergo a spiritual revitalization.

Pressure from those who wish to attend is generally for shorter programs with less reading and less commitment to attendance. A program that does justice to all these elements, however, would be more, rather than less, demanding of participants. It's possible to do something like Sandy Spring has done, as an entry level program. An essential element of spiritual formation, however, is commitment. Commitment involves a turning toward God that inevitably calls for discerning examination of the components of our lives, and of which components fall away as our lives become increasingly centered on God.

A thorough Quaker Formation Program would probably require at least two years, rather than one, to provide a sound background in all three of the areas of study discussed above, as well as in the strong prophetic, ethical thrust of Quakerism that I'll turn to in Volume III. There should be a program, of equivalent length with the others, acquainting people with various modes of prayer and meditation compatible with Quaker spirituality, and supporting them in whatever kind of meditation and prayer they are called to at any given time. It may be most convenient to offer this program prior to the study program to maintain the flow from one program of study to another, while spiritual practice underlies it all. Small support groups for spiritual practices would continue to meet throughout the entire program, whether one, two or three years in length.

It's a major commitment in anyone's life. Anytime I've offered an eight-week program several people have balked at the requirement of a commitment to attend all eight meetings. It's important to respect the limitations presented by the vicissitudes of human life; but ruling out prior or spur-of-the-moment commitments elsewhere is the essence of the commitment. Commitment is hard for busy, ironically over-committed, late-twentieth-century Friends. Yet I think it's an important first step in spiritual formation. A two-year commitment is a major step, as is a commitment to take all the components of the program, not omitting any, and to take them in the prescribed sequence for maximum coherence.

One possibility would be to divide the program into four semesters of ten to fifteen weeks in length. Meditation and prayer practices could come first. They would be supported by small spiritual discernment, accountability or friendship groups. The small groups would continue for the remaining three semesters, although the composition of some groups might need to be adjusted. There are virtues in being able to experience relationship with the widest possible number of people in the program. There is a different virtue in the depth of experience that can come of staying with the same few people through a prolonged period of their lives. The second semester would focus on Bible study, the third on the Christian experience and thought, and the fourth on Quakerism.

The final result of this process should be Friends who are able to go forward in their own study, given the resources with which they would have become acquainted. With Grace, their study of our roots as Quakers and how we met the questions of the past, should prepare them to meet questions facing us today. With Grace, this grounding will enable them to find a way forward, creatively and in faithfulness to the underlying, listening pattern of the tradition. With Grace, they may also be leavening for their meetings, providing restraint or encouragement of ministry as each is needed, grounding the activities of their meetings in discernment rather than consensus decision-making. Most of all, they should have grown in their own relationship with the Divine, increasingly giving over their own wills and egos, committed to listening for the movement of the Spirit in all things ... a pattern for all.

And this is ... a charge to you all in the presence of the living God, be patterns, be examples in all countries, places, islands, nations, wherever you come; that your carriage and life may preach among all sorts of people, and to them. Then you will come to walk cheerfully over the world, answering that of God in every one; whereby in them ye may be a blessing, and make the witness of God in them to bless you. Then to the Lord God you will be a sweet savour and a blessing.

Reference

George Fox.
Journal.
John Nickalls, ed. p. 263.

Appendices

Appendix A

Books and sources

Not all of the books in the following bibliography are written by Friends. However, they have all been selected for their underlying compatibility with the traditional spirituality·of unprogrammed Friends in the General Conference tradition as I understand and experience it. It is part of the spirituality of early Friends, carried forward in that tradition, to be respectful of spiritual truth wherever it is found—and to make the search for living experience of God of more importance than conformity to any orthodoxies or rejection of any sources.

Sources for books

Except in the case of obscurely published pamphlets or papers, I have not given—in the text—the full publication information that is in the following bibliography. As publishing houses swallow one another and their properties, quickly rendering out-of-print books that do not sell to the mass market, or republishing new editions for that market, publication information becomes less and less a reliable guide to finding a book.

These days, most book stores search first by author and title, either on computer or microfiche. Quaker book stores are usually aware of the range of Quaker publications by various groups through Quakers United in Publications (QUIP). They are also usually cognizant of a number of other publications with Quaker affinities.

For Quaker publications

AFSC Book Store (in Pasadena)
980 N. Fairoaks Ave., Pasadena, CA 91103
818/791-1978; Fax 818/791-2205; Email: afscpasa@igc.apc.org

Friends General Conference Book Store
1216 Arch St. #2B, Philadelphia, PA 19107
800/966-4556; Fax: 215/561-0759; Email: bookstore@FGC.Quaker.org

Pendle Hill Book Store
Plush Mill Rd., Wallingford, PA 19086
610/566-4514 (local) or 800/742-3150; Fax: 610/566-3679

Quaker Hill Book Store
101 Quaker Hill Dr., Richmond, IN 47374
800/537-8838; Fax: 765/966-1293; Email: books@xc.org

The Tract Association of Friends
1515 Cherry St., Philadelphia, PA 19102

The Quaker Book Shop
Friends House, 173-177 Euston Rd., London, UK NW1 2BJ
0171-387-3601; Fax: 0171-388-1977

For Servant Leadership School publications:

The Potter's House Book Store
1658 Columbia Rd., N.W., Washington, DC 20009
202/232-5483

For second-hand and out-of-print Quaker books:

Nancy Haines,
Vintage Books
181 Hayden Rowe St., Hopkinton, MA 01748
508/435-3499

For other out-of-print books, try:

Eureka!

800/563-1222

Periodicals

Cistercian Studies Quarterly.
Sister Sheryl Francis Chen OSCO
Santa Rita Abbey, HC1 Box 929, Sonoita AZ 85637-9705

The Conservative Friend.
1071 Greenwood Ave., Zanesville, OH 43701

Friendly Woman.
The editorship of this periodical shifts among Quaker women's groups. The current
address should be available through Quaker book stores or *Friends Journal.*

Friends Journal.
1216 Arch St., #2A, Philadelphia, PA 19107

Quaker Life.
101 Quaker Hill Dr., Richmond, IN 47374

Quaker Religious Thought.
Sponsored by the Quaker Theological Discussion Group.
Thomas Perkins, Business Manager
128 Tate St. Greensboro, NC 27403

Weavings. "Woven Together in Love":
A Journal of the Christian Spiritual Life.
The Upper Room, PO Box 189, Nashville, TN 37202

Appendix B

Projected contents of the third volume of *Listening Spirituality*.
Volume I was *Personal Spiritual Practices Among Friends*.

Volume III: Being Formed and Transformed in an Ethical Mysticism

Mystical Vision, Discernment and Ethics

Chapter 1
Listening for Truth in the Tension/Posture of Being in This World but Not of It

Chapter 2
Listening through Traditional Testimonies for the Spirit's Social Guidance

Tradition, Formation, Transformation and Continuing Revelation

Chapter 3
Spirituality, Listening and the Quaker Gestalt

Chapter 4
Grace, Practice and Tradition: Divine and Human Work in Transformation

Chapter 5
Encounter and Unity; Mutuality and Authority: The Roles of Solitude and Community in Personal and Corporate Spiritual and Ethical Formation and Transformation

Bibliography

For explanations of abbreviations, see list on p. xix in the front of this Volume.

Alphabetical listing by author's or editor's last name

Abrams, Irwin. "A Word About Listening". *FJ*, 6/1987, and in *DR*.

Bacon, Margaret Hope. *The Quaker Struggle for the Rights of Women*. Philadelphia: AFSC. Address delivered 9/7/1974.

_____, ed. *Wilt Thou Go on My Errand? Three 18th Century Journals of Quaker Women Ministers*. Wallingford, PA: Pendle Hill, 1994.

Bainton, Roland. *Christian Attitudes Toward War and Peace: A Historical Survey and Critical Evaluation.* Nashville: Abingdon, [©1990].

_____. *Early Christianity.* Princeton, NJ: Van Nostrand, [©1960].

_____. *The Reformation of the Sixteenth Century.* Boston: Beacon, [©1952, 1980, 1985].

Barbour, Hugh. *Margaret Fell Speaking.* PHP #206, [©1976].

_____. *The Quakers in Puritan England.* New Haven: Yale, 1964.

Barbour, Hugh and J. William Frost. *The Quakers.* Richmond, IN: FUP, [©1988].

Barclay, Robert. *Barclay's Apology in Modern English.* Dean Freiday, ed. Manasquan, NJ, [©1967].

Bauman, Richard. *Let Your Words Be Few: Symbolism of speaking and silence among seventeenth century Quakers.* Cambridge: University Press, 1983.

Benson, Lewis. *Catholic Quakerism.* Philadelphia: PYM, 1968.

Birchard, Bruce. *The Burning One-ness Binding Everything: A Spiritual Journey.* PHP #332, [©1997].

Bittle, William G. *James Nayler, 1618-1660, The Quaker Indicted by Parliament.* York, England: William Sessions, Ltd. with Richmond, IN: FUP, [©1986].

Bonhoeffer, Dietrich. *Life Together: a discussion of Christian fellowship.* NY: Harper, [©1954].

_____. *The Cost of Discipleship.* New York, NY: MacMillan, second edition, [©1959].

Borg, Marcus J. *Meeting Jesus Again for the First Time: The Historical Jesus & the Heart of Contemporary Faith.* San Francisco: Harper Perennial, [©1994].

Boulding, Elise. *Born Remembering.* PHP #200, [©1975].

_____. *Children and Solitude.* PHP #125, [©1962].

Bownas, Samuel. *A Description of the Qualifications Necessary to a Gospel Minister.*

Philadelphia: PH & Tract Assn., 1989.

Brain, W. Russell. *Man, Society and Religion.* London: QHS, Swarthmore Lecture, 1944.

Braithwaite, William C. *The Beginnings of Quakerism.* York, England: William Sessions, 2nd ed., 1981.

_____. *The Second Period of Quakerism.* York, England: William Sessions, 2nd ed., 1979.

_____. *Spiritual Guidance in the Experience of the Society of Friends.* London: QHS, 1909.

Brinton, Howard. *Friends for 300 Years.* Philadelphia: PH & PYM, 1965, [©1952].

_____. *Guide to Quaker Practice.* PHP #20, 1955, rev. 1997.

_____. *The Peace Testimony of the Society of Friends.* Philadelphia: AFSC, nd.

_____. *Prophetic Ministry.* PHP, #54, [©1950].

_____. *The Quaker Doctrine of Inward Peace.* PHP #44, [©1948].

_____. *Quaker Journals: Varieties of Religious Experience Among Friends.* Wallingford, PA: PH, [©1972].

_____. *The Religious Philosophy of Quakerism: The Beliefs of Fox, Barclay and Penn As Based on the Gospel of John.* Wallingford, PA: PH, [©1973].

_____. *Sources of the Quaker Peace Testimony.* PHP #27, nd.

Brinton, Anna Cox, Eleanor Price Mather and Robert J. Leach, eds. *Quaker Classics in Brief: William Penn's No Cross, No Crown, Barclay in Brief, The Inward Journey of Isaac Penington.* Wallingford, PA: PH, repr. 1978.

Britain Yearly Meeting. *Quaker faith and practice: The Book of Christian discipline of the Yearly Meeting of the Religious Society of Friends (Quakers) in Britain.* London: QHS, 1995.

Brown, Thomas S. "Freedom, Authority and Submission in the Context of Eldering". *CE.*

_____. "When Friends Attend to Business". Philadelphia, PA: PYM, nd.

Bruteau, Beatrice. "Trinitarian Personhood". *Cistercian Studies.* (1987) 3:199-212.

Cadoux, C. John. *The Early Christian Attitude Toward War: A Contribution to the History of Christian Ethics.* New York: Seabury, [©1982].

Caldwell, Samuel. "The Nurturing Aspects of Eldering". CE.

Calvi, John. "Released to Do Good Works". *FJ,* 11/1994, pp. 22-24.

Chambers, Sydney and Carolynne Myall. "Dear Helpful Hannah". *FJ,* 9/1991, quoted from "Speaking into the Silence", *Friendly Woman,* Vol. 9, No 8.

Chittister, Joan. *Wisdom Distilled from the Daily: Living the Rule of St. Benedict Today.* San Francisco: Harper, [©1990].

_____. *Wisdom Distilled from the Daily: Leaders' Guide.* San Francisco: Harpers, nd.

Claremont Friends Meeting. "A Meeting's Creative Experience". *FJ,* 7/1963.

_____. "Fellowship in Depth and Creative Renewal through Creative Listening. Suggestions for Leaders of Group Dialogues". (Claremont Dialogue, available through Ferner Nuhn, 420 W. 8th St. Claremont, CA 91711.)

Cooper, Wilmer A. *A Living Faith: An Historical Study of Quaker Beliefs.* Richmond, IN: FUP, 1990.

_____. *The Testimony of Integrity in the Religious Society of Friends.* PHP #296, [©1991].

Corbett, Jim. *The Sanctuary Church.* PHP #270, [©1986].

Cronk, Sandra. *Gospel Order: A Quaker Understanding of Faithful Church Community.* PHP #297, [©1991].

_____. *Peace Be With You: A Study of the Spiritual Basis of the Friends Peace Testimony.* Philadelphia: Tract Ass'n., nd.

Crouch, William. *Day by Day: Being a Compilation from the Writings of Ancient and Modern Friends.* Auburn, NY: Wm. H. Chase, Dennis Bros., 1869.

Curle, Adam. *The Basis of Quaker Work for Peace and Service.* London: Quaker Peace & Service, 1980.

_____. *Peace Making, Public and Private.* Philadelphia: Wider Quaker Fellowship, [©1978].

_____. *True Justice: Quaker Peace makers and Peace making.* London: QHS, [©1981].

Dass, Ram and Mirabai Bush. *Compassion in Action: Setting Out on the Path of Service.* New York: Crown, 1992.

Dass, Ram and Paul Gorman. *How Can I Help? Stories and Reflections on Service.* New York: Knopf, 1985.

DeAngeli, Marguerite. *Thee Hannah.* New York, NY: Doubleday, nd.

Dodson, Shirley. *Christian Thought: A Curriculum for Adult Friends.* Phila.: Religious Education Committee, Philadelphia YM, Fall 1987.

Dougherty, Rose Mary. *Group Spiritual Direction: Community for Discernment.* New York, NY: Paulist, [©1995].

Drake, Matthias. "Beyond Consensus: The Quaker search for God's Leading for the Group". *CD.* Also excerpted in *FJ,* 6/1986.

Duveneck, Josephine Whitney. *Life on Two Levels.* Palo Alto: Tioga, 1978; also in *DR.*

Edwards, Tilden. *Living With Apocalypse.* San Francisco: Harper, [©1984].

Esch, Keith. *A Quaker View of Ministry.* Richmond, IN: FUP, [nd].

Fager, Chuck, ed. *Reclaiming a Resource. Papers from the Friends Bible Conference.* Falls Church, VA: Kimo Press, 1990.

_____, ed. *The Bible, the Church, and the Future of Friends.* Wallingford, PA: PH, [©1996].

Fager, Chuck. *Without Apology: The Heroes, The Heritage and the Hope of Liberal Quakerism.* www.kimopress.com, [©1996].

_____. *A Respondent Spark.* www.kimopress.com., [©1984], rev. 1994.

Farnham, Suzanne, Joseph P. Gill, R. Taylor McLean, and Susan M. Ward. *Listening Hearts: Discerning Call in Community.* Harrisburg, PA: Morehouse Publishing, [©1991].

Fell, Margaret. "Womens' Speaking Justified", in Terry Wallace, ed., intro. *A Sincere and Constant Love.* Richmond IN: FUP, 1992.

Fingesten, Peter. "On Contemplation". *FJ,* 7/1/1985.

Fingesten, Peter and Carol. "Let the Silence Speak for Itself". *FJ,* 9/1/1987.

Finley, James. *Merton's Palace of Nowhere.* Notre Dame, IN: Ave Maria, [©1978].

Fiorenza, Elisabeth Schüssler. *In Memory of Her: A Feminist Theological Reconstruction of Christian Origins.* New York: Crossroad, [©1993].

Fitzgerald, Constance. "Impasse and Dark Night", in Tilden Edwards, ed. *Living with Apocalypse.* San Francisco: Harper, [©1984].

Foster, Richard. *The Freedom of Simplicity.* NY: Harper & Row [©1981].

Foulds, Elfrida Vipont. *Let Your Lives Speak.* PHP #71. 1953.

Fox, George. *Journal.* John Nickalls, ed. London: Religious Society of Friends, 1975. [©1952].

_____. *The Power of the Lord Is Over All: The Pastoral Letters of George Fox.* ed. and intro. by T. Canby Jones. Richmond, IN: FUP, [©1989].

_____. *No More But My Love. Letters of George Fox, Quaker.* Cecil W. Sharman, ed. London: QHS, 1980.

Freiday, Dean, ed. *Barclay's Apology in Modern English.* Manasquan, NJ, [©1967].

_____. "The Early Quakers and the Doctrine of Authority". *QRT.* Vol. 15, #1. Autumn 1973.

Freud, Sigmund. trans. by W. D. Robson-Scott. rev. and ed. by James Strachey. *The Future of an Illusion.* Garden City, N. Y.: Anchor Books, 1964.

Fuller, Georgia. "Johannine Lessons in Community", in Fager, ed., *The Bible, the Church and the Future of Friends.*

Garman, Mary, Judith Applegate, Margaret Benefiel and Dorothea Meredith, eds. *Hidden in Plain Sight: Quaker Women's Writings 1650-1700.* Wallingford, PA: PH, [©1996].

Gorman, George H. *The Amazing Fact of Quaker Worship.* London: QHS, Swarthmore Lecture 1973, rev. 1988.

Graves, Michael. "Mapping the Metaphors in George Fox's Sermons", in Michael Mullet, ed. *New Light on George Fox, 1624-1691, A Collection of Essays.* York, England: William Sessions, nd.

_____. "The Rhetoric of the Inward Light: An Examination of Extant Sermons Delivered by Early Quakers, 1671-1700". Unpublished Dissertation, University of Southern California, 1972.

Green, Thomas F. *Preparation for Worship.* London: QHS, Swarthmore Lecture, 1952.

Green, Thomas H. *Weeds Among the Wheat: Discernment, Where Prayer and Action Meet.* Notre Dame, IN: Ave Maria Press, [©1984].

Grundy, Marty. "Discerning Ministry and Gifts: the Meeting's Responsibility", Monday Night Lecture, Pendle Hill, 10/12/1998.

Gummere, Amelia Mott. *The Quaker: A Study in Costume.* New York: Benjamin Blom, 1968.

Gwyn, Douglas. *Apocalypse of the Word: The Life and Message of George Fox.* Richmond, IN: FUP, 1986.

_____. "John 15 and its Community". *QRT,* spring 1980.

_____. *The Covenant Crucified: Quakerism and the Rise of Capitalism.* Wallingford, PA: PH, [©1995].

Hall, Francis B., ed. *Quaker Worship in North America.* Richmond, IN: FUP, 1978.

Halliday, Robert. *Mind the Oneness: the foundation of good Quaker business method.* London: QHS, 1991.

Hart, Thomas N. *The Art of Christian Listening.* NY: Paulist, [©1980].

Heales, Brenda Clifft and Chris Cook. *Images and Silence.* London: QHS, Swarthmore Lecture, 1992.

Heron, Alastair. *Gifts and Ministries: a discussion paper on eldership.* London: QHS, [©1987].

_____. "Waiting Upon God". CD.

Herrman, John A. "A God Beyond Words". *FJ,* 11/1990.

Heschel, Abraham Joshua. *The Prophets.* New York, NY: Harper and Row, [©1962].

Hickey, Damon D. *Unforeseen Joy: Serving a Friends Meeting as Recording Clerk.* Greensboro, NC: NCYM, 1987.

Hill, Leslie. *Marriage: A Spiritual Leading for Lesbian, Gay, and Straight Couples.* PHP #308.

Hillman, James. *The Soul's Code: In Search of Character and Calling.* New York: Random House, [©1996].

Hinshaw, Cecil E. *Apology for Perfection.* PH #138, [©1964].

Hoffman, Jan. *Clearness Committees and their Use in Personal Discernment.* Philadelphia: FGC, nd.

Holden, David. *Friends Divided: Conflict and Division in the Society of Friends.* Richmond, IN: FUP, 1988.

_____. "Response to Panelists". *CE.*

Hubbard, Geoffrey. *Quaker by Convincement.* London: QHS, 1974.

Jones, Rufus. *Finding the Trail of Life.* NY: MacMillan, [©1926, repr. 1938, 1954]. Also in *DR.*

_____. "The Spiritual Message of the Religious Society of Friends". World Conference, 1937. LYM.

_____. "The Sense of the Meeting". *QR.*

_____. *Spiritual Reformers in the 16th and 17th Centuries.* Boston: Beacon, 1959.

Jones, T. Canby. "Friends Testimonies, Queries and Advices in Historical Perspective". *CTQA.*

_____, ed. *The Power of the Lord Is Over All: The Pastoral Letters of George Fox.* Richmond, IN: FUP, [©1989].

Kelly, Thomas R. *The Eternal Promise.* Richmond, IN: FUP, 1977.

_____. *The Gathered Meeting.* Philadelphia, PA: The Tract Ass'n, [nd]. Also reprinted in *The Eternal Promise.*

_____. *A Testament of Devotion.* NY: Harper & Row, 1941.

Knudsen-Hoffman, Gene. "Reflections on Speaking Truth to Power". *FJ,* 10/1/1981. Also in *DR.*

Kornfield, Jack. *A Path with Heart: A Guide through the Perils and Promises of Spiritual Life.* New York, NY: Bantam Books, [©1993].

Lacey, Paul A. *Leading and Being Led.* PH #264, [©1985].

_____. *Quakers and the Use of Power.* PHP #241 [©1982].

Lape, Herbert. "Friends Testimonies, Queries and Advices in Revising Faith and Practice". *CTQA.*

Leach, Robert J. *Women Ministers: A Quaker contribution.* PHP #227, [©1979].

_____, ed. *The Inward Journey of Isaac Penington.* PHP #29, [©1944].

Leclerque, Jean. *The Love of Learning and the Desire for God.* New York, NY: Mentor Omega Books, [©1961].

Levering, Sam. "What Future for the American Friends Service Committee?" *QS.*

Liveoak, Val. "Liberating Friends for Volunteer Service". *FJ,* 3/1993.

London Yearly Meeting. *Church government.* London: LYM, 1968.

_____. *Christian faith and practice in the experience of the Society of Friends.* London: LYM, [©1960].

Longacre, Doris Janzen. *More With Less Cookbook: Suggestions by Mennonites on how to eat better and consume less of the world's limited food resources.* Scottsdale, PA: Herald Press, [©1976].

Lonsdale, David. *Listening to the Music of the Spirit: The Art of Discernment.* Notre Dame, IN: Ave Maria Press.

Loring, Patricia. "Bill Stillwell's Legacy: A Retreat Based on Corporate Silence". *FJ*, 12/1986.

_____. *The Hidden Center and Outward Scaffolding of Quaker Spiritual Community.* Lecture. Gainesville, FL: SEYM, 1998.

_____. *Listening Spirituality: Volume I: Personal Spiritual Practices Among Friends.* Washington, DC: Openings Press, [©1997].

_____. *Spiritual Discernment: the context and goal of clearness committees.* PHP #305, [©1992].

_____. "Spiritual Responsibility in the Meeting for Business". Worcester, MA: New England Yearly Meeting, nd.

Maurer, Johann. "Response". *CD.*

Mayer, Milton. "The Idea of the American Friends Service Committee". *QS.*

McFague, Sally. *Metaphorical Theology: Models of God in Religious Language.* Philadelphia: Fortress Press, [©1982].

Mendl, Wolf. *Prophets and Reconcilers. Reflections on the Quaker Peace Testimony.* FHSC, Swarthmore Lecture, 1974.

Merton, Thomas. *The Wisdom of the Desert.* New York, NY: New Directions, 1970.

John Miller. "On Faith". *Quaker Religious Thought.* #86 (Dec. 1995).

Milligan, Edward H. "Membership and Pastoral Care". *Friends Quarterly.* vol. 5 (1951).

Morley, Barry. *Beyond Consensus: Salvaging Sense of the Meeting.* PHP #307, [©1992].

Morrison, Mary. *A Fresh Look at the Gospels.* PHP #219, [©1978].

_____. *Approaching the Gospels Together: A Leaders' Guide for Group Gospel Study.* Wallingford, PA: PH, nd.

Mullet, Michael, ed. *New Light on George Fox, 1624-1691: A Collection of Essays.* York, England: William Sessions, Ltd., [©1993].

Nesti, Donald S. "Early Quaker Ecclesiology". *Quaker Religious Thought.* vol. 18, #1 (Autumn 1978).

New England Yearly Meeting Ministry and Counsel. *Living with Oneself and Others; and Human Sexuality: Aspects and Issues; Living with Children.* Worcester, MA, 1993 [1985].

Newsom, Carol A. and Sharon H. Ringe, eds. *The Women's Bible Commentary.* Louisville, KY: Westminster/John Knox Press, [©1992].

Nuttall, Geoffrey. *The Holy Spirit and Ourselves.* Oxford: University Press, 1947.

O'Connor, Elizabeth. *The Eighth Day of Creation: Discovering and Using Your Gifts.* Washington, DC: The Servant Leadership School, [©1971].

_____. *The New Community.* New York, NY: Harper and Row, [©1976].

Olmstead, Sterling. *Motions of Love: Woolman as Mystic and Activist.* PHP #312, [©1993].

Palmer, Candida. "Friends Discipline in the 19th Century". *CE.*

Palmer, Parker. "The Clearness Committee: a Way of Discernment". *Weavings.* July/Aug. 1988, pp. 37-40.

Peck, M. Scott. *The Different Drum: Community Making and Peace.* NY: Simon & Schuster, [©1987].

Penington, Isaac. *The Light Within and Selected Writings.* Philadelphia: Tract Ass'n, nd.

Penn, William. *No Cross, No Crown.* York, England: William Sessions Book Trust, 1981.

_____. *A Collection of the Works of William Penn.* London, 1726.

_____. *The Rise and Progress of the People Called Quakers*. Richmond, IN: FUP, nd.

Philadelphia Yearly Meeting. *Rules of Discipline of the Yearly Meeting of Friends for Pennsylvania, New-Jersey, Delaware, and the Eastern Parts of Maryland; Revised and Adopted by the Said Meeting, Held in Philadelphia, ...* Phila.: Joseph Bradshaw, 1834.

Pitman, Ruth. *On the Vocal Ministry.* Tract Ass'n., [nd].

Prevallet, Elaine M. *Reflections on Simplicity*. PHP #244, [©1982].

Punshon, John. *Encounter With Silence: Reflections from the Quaker Tradition*. Richmond, IN: FUP, 1987.

_____. "The Peace Testimony". *Quaker Religious Thought*. Summer 1988.

_____. *Portrait in Gray: A Short History of the Quakers*. London: QHS, 1984.

_____. *Testimony & Tradition*. London: QHS, [©1990].

Radice, Betty, ed. *Early Christian Writings: The Apostolic Fathers*. New York: Penguin, [©1968].

Reichardt, Dorothy. *Finding Our Way in the Bible*. PYM, 1986, rev. 1991.

Religious Education Committee. *Opening Doors to Quaker Worship*. Philadelphia: FGC, 1994.

Renfer, Linda Hill, ed. *Daily Readings from Quaker Writings Both Ancient and Modern*. OR: Serenity Press, [©1988].

Roberts, Arthur O. "A Critique of Gunther Lewy's Peace and Revolution". *QS*.

Rothenberg, Donald and Sean Kelly, eds. *Ken Wilbur in Dialogue: Conversations with leading Transpersonal Thinkers.* Wheaton, IL.: Quest Books, [©1988].

Sands, David. as cited in William Crouch. *Day by Day: Being a Compilation from the Writings of Ancient and Modern Friends*. Auburn, NY: Wm. H. Chase, Dennis Bros., 1869. Also in *DR*.

Schmookler, Andrew Bard. *Sowing and Reaping: the cycling of good and evil in human systems.* Indianapolis, IN: Knowledge Systems, Inc., [©1989].

Scott, Janet. *What Canst Thou Say?* QHS: Swarthmore Lecture, 1980. Also in *DR*.

Seeger, Daniel A. "A Reflection on Gunther Lewy's Book". *QS*.

_____. *The Seed and the Tree: A Reflection on NonViolence*. PHP #269 [©1986].

Selleck, George. *Principles of the Quaker Business Meeting*. Richmond, IN: FUP, [©1986].

Selleck, Ronald. "The Early Quaker Norm for Freedom and Discipline". *CE*.

Sharman, Cecil. *George Fox and the Quakers*. London: QHS, 1991.

Sheeran, Michael J. *Beyond Majority Rule: Voteless Decision Making in the Society of Friends*. Philadelphia, PA: PYM, [©1983].

Smith, Allen. "The Renewal Movement: The Peace Testimony and Modern Quakerism", *Quaker History* 85:2 (Fall 1996) pp. 1-23.

Soderlund, Jean R. *Quakers & Slavery: A Divided Spirit*. Princeton: University Press, [©1985].

Soelle, Dorothee. *Suffering*. Philadelphia: Fortress, [©1975].

Spangler, David. *The Call*. New York: Riverhead Books, 1996.

Spears, Joanne and Larry. *Friendy Bible Study.* Phildadelphia: FGC, 1990.

_____. *Friendly Faith and Practice Study Guide*. Philadelphia: FGC, 1997.

Steere, Dorothy. *On Listening to God and to Each Other*. Philadelphia: FWCC, [©1984].

Steere, Douglas. *On Speaking Out of the Silence: Vocal Ministry in the Unprogrammed Meeting for worship*. PHP #182, [©1972].

_____. *Prayer in the Contemporary World*. PHP #291, [©1990].

_____. "Some Dimensions of the Quaker Decision-Making Process". *FJ*, 5/1982.

_____. *Where Words Come From.* London: QHS, 1955.

_____, ed. and intro. *Quaker Spirituality: Selected Writings.* New York: Paulist, 1984.

Stephen, Caroline Emilia. *Quaker Strongholds.* excerpted in PHP #59, [©1951].
Reprinted in entirety: Chula Vista: Wind and Rock Press, 1995.

Swift, Gladys H. "Our TLC Support Group". *FJ*, 5/1995.

Swift, Lloyd B. "On Discipline". *FJ*, 3/1989.

Sykes, John. *The Quakers: A New Look at Their Place in Society.* Philadelphia: J.B. Lippincott, 1959.

Taber, Frances. "Applying and Adapting the Tradition of Eldering for Today".
The Conservative Friend. Fall 1996.

Taber, William P., Jr. *Four Doors to Meeting for Worship.* PHP #306, [©1992].

_____. "The Friends Discernment Process: One View of Gospel Order". *CD.*

_____. "A Fruit of Gospel Order". *QL*, 4/89.

_____. "Introduction" to Samuel Bownas. *A Description of the Qualifications Necessary to a Gospel Minister.*

_____. "On Ministering to the Meeting for Business". Address to Worship and Ministry Retreat, PYM, 3/25/87. Printed in *FJ* (March 1988) pp. 12-13.

_____. "Worship in the Conservative Tradition". *QW.*

Thorne, Stephen J. "Oversight in Our Changing Society". Yearly Meeting 1959. QHS.

Tillich, Paul. *A History of Christian Thought From Its Judaic and Hellenistic Origins to Existentialism.* Carl E. Braaten, ed. New York, NY: Simon and Schuster, Touchstone, [©1967-68].

_____. *Systematic Theology. Three Volumes in One.* Chicago: University Press, Vol. 1 [©1951]; Vol.2 [© 1957]; Vol. 3 [©1963].

Tolles, Frederick B. *Meeting House and Counting House: The Quaker Merchants of Colonial Philadelphia 1682-1763.* Chapel Hill: Univ. of North Carolina Press, [©1948].

Turkle, Brinton. *Obadiah, the Bold.* New York, NY: Viking Press, [©1965].

_____. *The Adventures of Obadiah.* New York, NY: Puffin, [©1972].

_____. *Rachel and Obadiah.* New York, NY: Dutton, 1978.

_____. *Thy Friend, Obadiah.* New York, NY: Puffin, 1982.

Trevett, Christine, ed. *Womens' Speaking Justified and Other Seventeenth Century Writings About Women.* London: QHS, 1989.

Tucker, R. W. "Structural Incongruities in Quaker Service". *QS.*

Underhill, Evelyn. *Worship.* NY: Crossroad Publishing, [©1936].

Vanier, Jean. *Community and Growth: Our Pilgrimage Together.* New York, NY: Paulist Press [©1979].

_____. *From Brokenness to Community.* NY, and Mahway, NJ: Paulist Press, [©1992].

Vardey, Lucinda. *God in All Worlds: An Anthology of Contemporary Spiritual Writing.* New York: Pantheon, 1995.

Vipont, Elfrida. *George Fox and the Valiant Sixty.* Philadelphia: FGC, [©1975], North American edition, 1997.

Watson, Elizabeth. "Worship That Comes from Silence in the General Conference Tradition". *QW.*

Wallace, Terry S., ed. *A Sincere and Constant Love: an introduction to the work of Margaret Fell.* Richmond, IN: FUP, 1992.

West, Jessamyn, ed. *The Quaker Reader.* [©1962]; new edition: PH, 1992.

Wilson, Lloyd Lee. *Essays on the Quaker Vision of Gospel Order.* Burnsville, NC: Celo Valley Books, [©1993].

Wilson, Louise. *Inner Tenderings.* Richmond, IN: FUP, 1996.

Wilson, Roger C. *Authority, Leadership and Concern.* QHS: Swarthmore Lecture, 1949.

Wood, Jan. "Spiritual Discernment: the Personal Dimension". *CD.*

Woodrow, Peter. *Clearness: Processes for Supporting Individuals and Groups in Decision-Making.* Philadelphia: New Society, [©1976].

Woolman, John. *The Journal and Major Essays.* Phillips P. Moulton, ed. Richmond, IN: FUP and PYM, 1989.

Yarrow, Michael. *Quaker Experiences in International Conciliation.* New Haven: Yale University Press, 1978.

Yoder, John Howard. *The Politics of Jesus.* Grand Rapids, MI: William Eerdmans, [©1972].

Scholarly series for the meeting library

The Interpreters' Bible. NY: Abington-Cokesbury Press, [1951-57].

The Anchor Bible. Garden City, NY: Doubleday division of Bantam, Doubleday, Dell Publishing Group [1964-].

Pelikan, Jaroslav. *The Christian Tradition: A History of the Development of Doctrine.* Chicago: University of Chicago Press, [1971-]. A reference work in five volumes, it covers:
1) The Emergence of the Catholic Tradition (100-600);
2) The Spirit of Eastern Christendom (600-1700);
3) The Growth of Medieval Theology (600-1300);
4) Reformation Church and Dogma (1300-1700);
5) Christian Doctrine and Modern Culture (since 1700).

About the artist

Bob Schmitt is both a practicing sumi-e painter and a practicing Quaker. He lives in Minneapolis where he runs his own design business.

The discipline of being a brush artist in the Asian traditions parallels with the discipline of being a Friend.

Both require a stilling of the soul and an openness to being led.

About the author

Patricia Loring has been released by Bethesda (MD) Friends Meeting for nine years for "A Ministry in Nurture of the Spiritual Life". That ministry has included designing and leading adult religious education classes and workshops, retreat ministry, personal spiritual guidance and writing. Her work has been centered in Bethesda but reaches out to all parts of her yearly meeting and the country.

This book is the second of three volumes of *Listening Spirituality*, which gathers up the substance of her years of teaching. The first volume speaks of personal spiritual practice, formation and transformation among Friends. This second volume covers corporate practice and spiritual formation among Friends. The remaining volume will cover ethical practice and spiritual transformation in general among Friends.

Patricia has attended five terms at Pendle Hill, the Quaker Center for Study and Contemplation and two long-term programs in Spiritual Guidance and in Group Leadership at Shalem Institute for Spiritual Formation, as well as being a graduate of St. John's College in Annapolis and of the Hartford Seminary.

Friends General Conference Religious Education Committee Minute of Support Fourth Month 1998

Members of the Religious Education Committee of FGC have used *Listening Spirituality, Volume I: Personal Spiritual Practices Among Friends* for our own individual edification, and we have used it in groups. We have found it extremely helpful in Quaker spiritual formation. We expect this book will continue to be a much-needed tool to help us in our ministry, especially adult religious education, and of the ministry of Friends in general.

We look forward to Volume II: *Corporate Spiritual Practice Among Friends*, with its emphasis on listening to God as the basis of our Quaker faith and practice. We, as a Committee, continue to learn—and struggle with—how to listen for Divine guidance within the humanly-imposed constraints of time, finances, and energy. We need all the help we can get, especially from Friends like Patricia Loring who have prayed long, thought deeply, and gained wisdom through their own experience with the Inward Teacher.

Bethesda Friends Meeting Minute of Re-Release

Bethesda Friends Meeting reaffirms the release of our member Patricia Loring, in recognition of the authenticity of her leading to nurture the spiritual life among Friends and in celebration of its value to our Meeting and others.

Pat's teaching, which began in Bethesda in 1989 and for which she was released in 1991, has borne many fruits. By writing her book, *Listening Spirituality*, she is now gathering up the essence of that work and making it available to the wider world of Friends. We welcome the chance to experience her gifts in new ways and to help bring her spiritual nurture to more Friends and others beyond Bethesda.